THE POWER AND GRACE

— BETWEEN —

NASTY OR NICE

*Replacing Entitlement, Narcissism,
and Incivility with Knowledge, Caring,
and Genuine Self-Esteem*

JOHN C. FRIEL, PH.D., AND LINDA D. OLUND FRIEL, M.A.

Minnesota Licensed Psychologists

John Friel is also a Nevada Licensed Psychologist

[signature]

Health Communications, Inc.
Deerfield Beach, Florida

www.hcibooks.com

**Library of Congress Cataloging-in-Publication Data
is available through the Library of Congress.**

©2012 John C. Friel and Linda D. Olund Friel

ISBN-13: 978-0-7573-1586-2 (trade paper)
ISBN-10: 0-7573-1586-0 (trade paper)
ISBN-13: 978-0-7573-1608-1 (e-book)
ISBN-10: 0-7573-1608-5 (e-book)

Publisher: Health Communications, Inc.
            3201 S.W. 15th Street
            Deerfield Beach, FL 33442–8190

Cover design by Larissa Hise Henoch
Interior design and formatting by Lawna Patterson Oldfield

Sunlight gives us power
But moonlight gives us grace

Sue Rowe, Sue Rowe Studios
Stillwater, MN
http://www.suerowe.com

Donation

In the spirit of what we have written in Chapter 17, "Accountability, Integrity, Amends, and Reconciliation," we have decided to make the following donations based on sales of this book. Reconciliation needs to occur on many levels: within the person, between two people, within a family, within a community, within a nation, and between nations. These donations are occurring at the level of nation to nation, and also person to person.

Five percent of the authors' royalties will go to the Red Cloud School on the Pine Ridge Indian Reservation, founded in 1888 in South Dakota at the request of Chief Red Cloud, a leader of the Oglala Sioux Indians residing on the Pine Ridge Indian Reservation. A detailed description of their heartwarming successes, and their support by the Bill Gates Foundation, can be found at http://www.redcloudschool.org/. ABC Nightly News Anchor Diane Sawyer's powerful one-hour documentary "A Hidden America: Children of the Plains," aired on October 14, 2011, inspired us to donate here at home to another nation that has suffered immeasurable loss and heartache as a result of excesses of greed and power that ran amok so many years ago.

Five percent of the authors' royalties will also go to the Jhai Foundation, founded by our friend, American Vietnam veteran Lee Thorn, discussed in Chapter 17, as part of his incredible journey of healing and reconciliation with the people of Laos, who are still being maimed and killed by the more than 75 million unexploded U.S. cluster bombs that remain in Laos after an illegal, secret, nine-year U.S. bombing campaign that continued from 1964 to 1973.

This book is dedicated to James W. Maddock, Ph.D.

By Far the Finest Man We Have Ever Known

James W. Maddock

1942–2009

Without blaming them in the least for the errors that we have made in our professional work as psychotherapists, we can safely and with deep gratitude say that we owe the lion's share of what we do and how we think as psychotherapists to the mentoring and tutelage of St. Paul, Minnesota, psychologists James Maddock, Ph.D., and his wife, Noel Larson, Ph.D., coauthors of one of the seminal textbooks on ecological-systemic therapy for family systems, couples, and individuals affected by incest and domestic violence: *Incestuous Families: An Ecological Approach to Understanding and Treatment* (1995).

Upon his death in the summer of 2009, the obituary published in the *Minneapolis Star Tribune* described Jim as

Beloved husband, father, friend, mentor, "Grandpa Jim" and Professor Emeritus, University of Minnesota. Jim passed peacefully, with his loving family by his side. He faced seven years of cancer with courage, dignity, and generosity. Jim loved life: his family and friends, fishing, skiing in Colorado, and traveling—especially to Denmark. He enjoyed deep and thoughtful discussions about theory, philosophy—and over the last few years, politics, always providing his incisive perspective. During his thirty-six years at the university, he was an acclaimed author, writing dozens of articles and several books. He acquired a reputation for being a brilliant, generous teacher and collaborator. *Jim was a rare combination of a University of Chicago intellectual and a kind-hearted, sensitive human being.* He loved his work with students and consultees from all over the country, and was an innovative clinician and wise mentor. Jim was a founder of the University of

Minnesota Medical School Program in Human Sexuality, former president of the American Association of Sex Educators, Counselors and Therapists, and co-founder, with his wife [Noel Larson, Ph.D.], of Meta Resources Psychotherapy and Training Institute in St. Paul. (emphasis added)

At least in part because Jim was a "rare combination of a University of Chicago intellectual and a kind-hearted, sensitive human being," we were more profoundly touched at his memorial service at the University of Minnesota than perhaps any other funeral we had ever attended, including that of our parents.

One of the scenarios described by some people who are declared clinically dead and then revived is of finding themselves bathed in a loving, completely accepting light or presence, during which time the person was able to see and feel all of his transgressions, wrongdoings, and flaws, and hold himself accountable for those flaws, but in a spirit of growth and healing rather than paralyzing shame and self-hatred. Very often, Jim was like that being of light. He was tough, strong, and clear when presenting his version of reality or challenging another's distorted version, whether with therapist consultees or with his own clients. And yet he did it in a way that conveyed warmth, acceptance, and love, which is almost an impossible feat to accomplish, let alone time and again across such a variety of settings and with such a variety of people. His actions, then, weren't about the situations or the people necessarily, but about an exceptional combination of mature love and gracious power that resided comfortably inside of this rare man; all of us—clients, therapist consultees, and family members—were graced by his presence.

Jim Maddock was an exceptional psychotherapist, teacher, and mentor. Above all else, he was an exceptional man, for whose brief presence on this Earth we will be eternally grateful. To Noel, we send you our continued love and respect, and we honor your sorrow at the loss of the true love of your life.

CONTENTS

FOREWORD

"Life is an echo. What you send out comes back."

—*Chinese Proverb*

During a recent consulting trip to Greenland, I was told that some of the hunters were shooting their sled dogs because they could no longer feed them. For several years the sea ice has not frozen solidly enough for the hunters to be able to take the dog sleds out to catch the fish and seals necessary to feed their starving dogs. And recently two polar bears came in to Nuuk, Greenland's capital city of 16,500 people. The bears were looking for food in an area considerably distant from where they normally live. They were unable to walk to the areas with plentiful seals because the sea ice is melting, and unable to swim the great distances they would need to swim to find food. They, too, were shot. The changing fragile ecology is rapidly altering the Greenlandic Inuit culture that has persisted for well over a thousand years. The promising search for gas and oil in the frigid, iceberg-filled waters that surround the western edge of Greenland, coupled with the recent mining of precious gems like rubies and diamonds, guarantee even more rapid change. Can a people that have survived mainly by fishing and hunting adapt sufficiently and quickly enough to benefit from these changes, or will they suffer the wholesale destruction of their culture as many of our first peoples did?

The possibilities for "nasty" or "nice" in a rapidly changing ecology only escalate as the ecological balance is lost. Virginia Satir, noted family therapist and systemic thinker, frequently talked about her belief that we are biologically wired for "change" and biologically wired for "no change."

Affect dysregulation is now believed to be a fundamental mechanism of all psychiatric disorders. The etiology of affect dysregulation in adults is often linked to childhood abuse—emotional, physical, or sexual. "Nasty" at its worst. When a child's primary attachment object, his or her parent, is both the source of connection and the source of terror, the child's brain must rebalance itself to accommodate to loving a dangerous parent. It appears to do so in one of two ways: fight or flight. When a child experiences the terror associated with abuse, his or her brain very quickly moves into a hyper arousal mode, scanning for danger and organizing itself for offense or defense. As Louis Cozolino noted, the brain becomes poised for battle, and all of the hard-wired regulatory systems organize for survival. As the abuse stops and the threat recedes, the brain reorganizes itself for attachment, pleasure, compassion, etc. If the child experiences persistent threats to his or her survival over a number of years, the brain reorganizes itself to always be poised for battle. The brain is doing its primary job, namely insuring survival of the organism. The brain's "state of mind" has now become a "trait" of the child's personality structure as an accommodation to the child's context. The resulting patterns are typically "nasty" or "nice," perpetrator or victim: the child's brain is poised for battle, and all systems are organized for offense (perpetrator) or defense (victim): overpowered and undercontrolled (perpetrator) or overcontrolled and underpowered (victim). The same process happens when adults experience threats to their survival on a daily basis, as in war.

Writing for the *New York Times* on March 10, 2012, Erica Goode described the transformation that occurred within Christopher B. Epps, Mississippi's commissioner of corrections, and therefore the way that prisoners are now being treated at the state's super-maximum-security prison. Prior to Mr. Epps' changes, more than 1000 inmates were locked down in solitary confinement for as long as 23 hours each day: "allowed out only in shackles and escorted by guards, they were restless and angry—made more so by the excrement-smeared walls, the insects, the filthy food trays and the mentally ill inmates who screamed in the night. . . . Epps said he started out believing that difficult inmates should be locked down as tightly as possible, for as long as possible. By the end of the process, he saw things differently and ordered the changes. 'If you treat people like animals, that's exactly the way they'll behave,' he now says. Epps…likes to say prison officials started out isolating inmates they were scared of but ended up adding many they were simply 'mad at.'"

What happened next was counterintuitive and politically incorrect: "Instead of tightening restrictions further, prison officials loosened them. They allowed most inmates out of their cells for hours each day. They built a basketball court and a group dining area. They put rehabilitation programs in place and let prisoners work their way to greater privileges. In response, the inmates became better behaved. Violence went down. The number of prisoners in isolation dropped to about 300 from more than 1,000. So many inmates were moved into the general population of other prisons that Unit 32 was closed in 2010, saving the state more than $5 million."

Victimization, even of convicted perpetrators, breeds more perpetration. It is hard to imagine that many in the corrections industry still believe that brutally punishing inmates will "teach them a lesson" and cure them of their behavioral problems. It does teach them a lesson, but as Commissioner Epps discovered, the lesson is greater levels of perpetration built on their greater levels of victimization. It is interesting to note that prisons for Israeli citizens have as their primary mission to return inmates to their integrity.

My husband James Maddock and I have had the enormous pleasure of teaching "helpers"—psychologists, social workers, psychiatrists, pedagogues—and consulting with health care organizations—hospitals, clinics, private practice groups—in Denmark for the past thirty-two years. Over the decades our time there has totaled more than four full years, so we had the opportunity to learn about and experience the culture of the country and its people through our work and the decades-long friendships we have had the privilege to develop. There are good reasons why Denmark consistently polls as the happiest country on the planet. The platform for work groups is one of collaboration and cooperation rather than competition and conquest. People do not get ahead in their work environments by stepping on their fellow workers to get ahead, as is often the case here in the U.S. True, the Vikings were not a terribly civil group of marauders and conquerors, but the Danes of recent generations have become a model of compassion and generosity.

In her compelling book, *A Conspiracy of Decency*, Emmy Werner chronicles the stories of Danish Jews who were ferried to safety in Sweden during World War II: "The people of Denmark managed to save almost their country's entire Jewish population from extermination in a spontaneous act of humanity—one of the most compelling stories of moral courage in the history of World War II. [She] tells the story of the rescue of the Danish Jews from the vantage-point of living eyewitnesses—the last survivors of an extraordinary conspiracy of decency that triumphed in the midst of the horrors of the Holocaust." The Danes seem to have successfully moved beyond their Viking heritage. Our heritage is younger, so perhaps we, too, can move beyond the massacre of our first peoples, and our own holocaust of brutally kidnapping and enslaving men, women, and children.

John and Linda Friel powerfully challenge us to consider, within our own borders, the patterns of perpetration and victimization that exist at all levels of our society. They courageously invite us to develop and act on *our best self*, the self that is infused with integrity, compassion, and care. They counter-intuitively link *power* and *grace*, illuminating for us a path to being personally, interpersonally, and nationally powerful as a people and a country, and at the same time kind, compassionate, forgiving and accountable. In true ecological fashion, they examine our systems at all levels, moving from our neurobiological roots, to attachment and connection in couples, families, groups and communities, to cultural, religious and political patterns—all with a keen eye on how to understand and change our *nasty* and *nice* (perpetrator/victim) to patterns of *knowledge, caring, and genuine self-esteem*. In this season of devastating political incivility, they have written the book that offers us hope for our very future as a humane and civilized people.

—Noel R. Larson, Ph.D.,
Meta Resources, P.A. St. Paul, MN

PREFACE:

CHANGE AND BALANCE

> When we have found all the mysteries and lost all the meaning,
> we will be alone, on an empty shore.
>
> —*Tom Stoppard,* Arcadia

The only constant in the universe is *change*. The organizing principle is *balance*. In between, there is the dynamic tension called *life*.

The ecological-systemic approach to the study of human beings developed and advocated by Gregory Bateson (1972), Urie Bronfenbrenner (1979), James Maddock and Noel Larson (1995), and many others assumes that the universal organizing principle in any system is balance, so that while everything in the universe is in flux, it is always moving toward a stable state of balance that contains within it the seeds of future upheaval and change. Jonathan Swift wrote, "There is nothing in this world constant but inconsistency."

This dialectic describes how galaxies and solar systems organize, exist, and then cease to exist. It describes how empires rise, create an illusory sense of permanence, exert power over their realms, and then crumble. It describes how human beings are born, struggle to make sense of their lives, and then die.

Life is bigger than us. Those who learn to accept this fact with grace, while still choosing to assert themselves in the universe with thoughtful kindness, are the happiest, most peaceful, and most powerful, in the best sense of that word. To accept the disappointment that we will one day cease to exist, and yet to act in the world from our better selves despite our inevitable demise, is the essence of spirituality.

This book captures what we have observed in our clinical practices over the past thirty years as our clients have courageously struggled with the dilemma of finding power and effectiveness without being *victims* or *perpetrators*—a dilemma that faces every human being. In 1975 a major psychiatric textbook (Kaplan & Freedman, 1975) claimed that sexual abuse in families was a one in a million phenomenon, a preposterous conclusion that has since been unequivocally disproved. Therapeutic topics that had been mostly dismissed by professionals until 1979 began to be addressed. The physical, emotional, intellectual, spiritual, and sexual abuse of children came out in the open. The great cultural secrets of the past were no longer quite so secret. With the emergence of the Duluth Model of domestic violence treatment in 1981, perhaps the greatest secret of all throughout thousands of years of human history at last received serious attention.

Then a clinical dilemma slowly began to emerge. Do we help our clients who were the victims of childhood maltreatment become empowered, and if so, how? Should we help them identify and name the abuse that happened to them, and then encourage them to express their hurt, shame, loneliness, sadness, and outrage about it? Many clients hit many pillows with padded bats during these years while symbolically screaming at their families, "I am angry! I am angry! I am angry!" It seemed to help some people sometimes. But we wondered. We noticed that something was missing. Many people seemed to get stuck in the world of their painful childhoods, which adversely impacted their adult relationships.

As we continued with our work under regular case consultation with James W. Maddock and Noel Larson, it became clear that *the cure for being "too nice" was not to become "too nasty,"* and that *the cure for being "too nasty" was not to become "too nice."* We observed that clients got stuck seeing themselves one way or the other. We began to explore with our clients the untapped power they had, which could contribute to a strong life outcome. We looked at the way both nasty (perpetrator) and nice (victim)—thoughts, feelings, and behaviors—contributed to the problem.

At times we met our share of resistance from some who saw this approach as too hard on a victim, or as blaming the victim—and as too easy on a perpetrator, or babying the perpetrator. But we saw it as a more powerful and effective way to sort these things out. We learned to help our wounded clients heal their old wounds, not just as an end in itself, but as a stepping-stone to a sturdy and competent adulthood.

Then we wrote in *The Soul of Adulthood* (1995) what has become the centerpiece of all of the clinical work we do, paraphrased below:

> You know you are becoming a competent, healthy adult when you can choose what at times will be the exquisite pain and discomfort of fear, hurt, shame, loneliness, and sadness rather than hurt yourself, hurt others, or let others hurt you.

Our work has evolved from simply helping people identify issues of neglect and abuse to helping those same people become competent adults who have compassion, forgiveness, strength, power, integrity, emotional awareness, effectiveness, grace, and kindness, as well as the ability to express outrage and toughness in healthy ways when necessary.

A chapter in *The Soul of Adulthood*—"Love, Power, and Graciousness" —captured the essence of this challenge: we have included an edited version of it in this book. We stated that *graciousness without power was just being a victim*, that *power without graciousness was just being a perpetrator*, and that *combining grace and power* is what deep, genuine human love is about—and is what *defines a competent healthy adult*.

The "power and grace between nasty or nice" refers to the challenge facing each of us to find the balanced area that rests between being *too nasty* or too *nice*. The subtitle addresses a number of issues that we believe are underlying this struggle to find balance, and with which we see so many people, especially U.S. citizens, grapple every day.

Competence, Patience, Self-Restraint, and Genuine Self-Esteem

These chapters address the perplexing decline in U.S. (and other nations') children's proficiency in math, science, history, reading, and critical thinking when compared with children from other nations; the crisis in U.S. education and parenting; the negative effects of a self-esteem movement run amok; and the increasing polarization of our society around social, financial, and governance issues. These problems are partially the result of a lack of education and an exponential increase in misinformation over the Internet and on television.

Competence, patience, self-restraint, and genuine self-esteem address the fundamental root causes of a multitude of human problems, but in unique ways here in this country. The inability to delay gratification has become a pathology in the United States. The ability to wait patiently for what life has to offer, or for what we are truly hoping, separates the men and the women from the boys and the girls. *Self-restraint* is one of the most powerful human skills available to us, especially in a highly complex, rapidly shrinking world. To find happiness in spite of the many disappointments that life offers is truly what separates people who feel like abject failures from those who hit multiple roadblocks and then bounce back better and stronger than ever before. Genuine self-esteem, as opposed to "pseudo-self-esteem," can only be attained if a person possesses two things: (a) knowledge and competence, and (b) a network of support that includes people who see, hear, and understand him, "warts and all."

> *The inability to delay gratification has become a pathology in the United States.*

Care and Kindness

The idea of care binds up so many Americans because we have such a confused understanding of the way in which care functions to enhance our species' evolutionary and genetic survival. Many of us see care as a sign of weakness that comes from our own woundedness and ambivalence as children who were not cared for properly. Care is related to our natural and healthy dependence upon one another.

The notion of care implies connectedness—that we need each other's complementary skills, talents, and insights in order to survive. Even more, care is about the importance and biological necessity of knowing that others of our kind care about us and that they are willing to accept the fact that they need us to care about them.

This reciprocal need for care from each other, the exquisite ambivalence that it raises in each of us, and the ability to transcend that ambivalence are what separate dictators and despots from powerful, competent, gracious leaders; and megalomaniacs from leaders who are able to help us all create a society that is a *true* shining city on a hill rather than a sham of greed and cruelty. Paraphrasing Gregory Bateson's eloquent thoughts, a symmetrical, competitive relationship between the powerful and the weak will most likely result in the destruction of the species known as *Homo sapiens*.

Care is simple. It is kind. It is gracious. It is one human being seeing another human being and taking the time to acknowledge what one sees. It is taking the time to *listen without trying to fix, rescue, analyze, problem-solve, or therapize*. "I know I can't fix the pain you feel right now, but I want you to know that I am here, and that I can *see, hear, and understand you*." That's all that matters. As one of the authors (LDF) often says, "It is by connecting one heart to another, around seemingly small things, that love grows."

Grace and Power in Action

In Part 5 of the book, "Keep Your Balance, Keep Your Power," we offer some examples, stories, and hints to help the reader create one's own unique patterns of *neural networks*—also known as *cognitive templates*— to navigate with grace and power through our rapidly shrinking world.

Readers familiar with our work may notice that an occasional section in this book is adapted from one of our previous eight books. We deemed that material essential to the current book, and realized that we had written those few sections as well as we could and that they did not require changes. The majority of the chapter on rules (Chapter 4), for example, was taken from our parents, teens, and couples books.

To Be Seen, Heard, and Understood

Humans have continually found better and more effective ways to communicate with each other—from pictures carved onto stones, to words printed in books by a printing press, to the telegraph, radio, and television; and now via e-mail, text messages on handheld devices, the Internet, and social media.

Regardless of how we communicate, the *universal human need to be seen, heard, and understood* will always be there, because we will always be human, and we will always need each other, no matter how much we evolve. Our need to be connected to one another—to feel part of the human race, the tribe, the family, the community—is a universal, biological need of all human beings. That's what makes us uniquely human.

At some point, it all comes back to the willingness of human beings to take the leap of faith that is always required to be flexible enough to survive on a planet that is always changing, always evolving, and always trying to find a stable state of balance after the inevitable upheavals that are always part of the nature of systems in the universe.

> People destined to meet will do so, apparently by chance, at precisely the right moment.
>
> —*Ralph Waldo Emerson*

John C. Friel, Ph.D., and
Linda D. Olund Friel, M.A.
Minneapolis–St. Paul, Minnesota
June 1, 2012

Acknowledgments

First and foremost, we thank James Maddock and Noel Larson for guiding us as therapists, and as human beings, throughout the past twenty-nine years. The ways that they approached both love and work—as Freud so aptly summarized the two elements of life—have been constant neural maps for us of how to combine the two in our marriage and our professional work. To Jim and Noel, we will be forever grateful.

To Bill Doherty, professor of Family Social Science at the University of Minnesota, we thank you for your guidance and for your visionary work, both theoretical and practical, on the importance of family and community, and for community involvement and social action.

To Dave Schnarch and his wife, Ruth Morehouse, we thank you for your revolutionary ideas, including your Crucible® concept of marital and sexual therapy. The overlap between Jim's and Noel's ecological-systemic family therapy model and your approach has given us insights into couples therapy that have revolutionized our own work with our clients.

We thank Sandy Guminga in Minneapolis for being a dear friend and also an infinitely competent bookkeeper and office manager who kept our practice afloat in Minneapolis for more than a decade. Her skill and loyalty have been unparalleled.

We thank Ava Hahn in Reno, Nevada, for managing with competence and good humor the financial details of our practice since the mid-2000s.

From the academic world, we thank John D. Cone, JCF's doctoral advisor, for teaching John everything he knows about behaviorism, behavior modification, and cognitive behavioral therapy and John R. Nesselroade, Paul B. Baltes, and K. Warner Schaie for instilling in John a life-span perspective when approaching the human condition.

We thank Judy Phoenix and Frances Spikes in Reno, Nevada, for reading, commenting on, and engaging in spirited dialogue about the earliest drafts of this book while it was just beginning to take shape. What we batted around several years ago does not, on the surface, look at all like what we have now completed in this book—but without their early input, this book would never have made the several ninety-degree turns that it needed to make in order to become what it is now. We thank you for your dear friendship, and for your brilliant, wise, and well-informed input along the way.

To Mary Pietrini in St. Paul, Minnesota, our longtime colleague, co-therapist, and good friend, we owe you a mountain of thanks for your tireless, detailed, thoughtful, and incisive commentaries on the later versions of the manuscript. You worked above and beyond the call of duty, and your detailed reading of the manuscript, and pithy comments along the way, have been invaluable. We will always be grateful for your friendship.

We also want to thank our dear friends Dearbhla Molloy, Sean and Kate Murray, Peter Charad, John and Katrina Fenston, Deirdre Boyd, and Hilary Henriques for their ongoing support of our work from across the Atlantic. Our friends in England, Scotland, and Ireland feel as close to us as our neighbors next door.

We thank Peter Vegso, president of Health Communications, Inc., for standing by us since 1985 and supporting our ninth book with HCI.

We want to thank our editor, Allison Janse; Bob Land, coeditor, for your incisive and insightful edits of the later versions of the book; and to Cathy Slovensky for having the exacting eye of a peregrine falcon. We have known Kim Weiss in the marketing department of Health Communications, Inc., since our book, *The 7 Worst Things (Good) Parents Do* landed us on the *Oprah Winfrey Show* for an hour in 1999. Kim, you are the best. Thank you.

We especially thank the many clients with whom we have worked over the past three decades—individuals, couples, families, members of our men's and women's therapy groups, and the thousands of participants in our three-and-a-half-day ClearLife® Clinic therapy process. We are fortunate and grateful to be able to do work every day that we just plain love.

That would not be possible without all of you. Every human being has a story, and our work has taught us so well that every story is fascinating, heartwarming, painful, intriguing, and infinitely valuable, whether or not it appears mundane on the surface. There are no mundane life stories.

We thank our dear friends in Minnesota, Stan Pollock, Diane Naas, Ken and Tish Reddick, John Holtzermann and Karen Seaverson, and Mark and Cyn Stange; and our dear friends in Reno, Nevada, Roberta and Neal Ferguson, Judy Phoenix and Frances Spikes, Steve and Gretchen Graybar, Gwen O'Bryan, Traci Pitts, and Stephanie Dillon, for helping us stay afloat amidst innumerable sea changes that have occurred in our lives over the past ten to thirty years. And since 1995, the support of JCF's email "guy's list" has been immeasurable: Bill McIntyre, Bob Hurst, Steve Scanlin, Dave Friis, Larry Meyer, and Bob Parke. You all are the best.

We would never have been able to accomplish what we have done over the past thirty years without the support and encouragement of the therapists and program directors who believed in our Clearlife® Clinic work: Don Tripp, Lyndel Brennan, Stan Huff, Lynda Winter, Dan Burrows, Eileen and Steve Middleton, Joe and Julie Westerheide, Kyle McGraw, and Kermit and Mary Dahlen,

To Pat Love, Jon Carlson, Mel Pohl, Sharon Wegscheider-Cruse and Joe Cruse, and Ken Adams, we thank you for your interest in—and continued support of—our work locally as well as nationally and internationally.

As dyed in the wool Minnesotans, even though one of us was originally a San Franciscan, we thank Minnesota's own Garrison Keillor for decades of *A Prairie Home Companion* on Minnesota Public Radio, his writing, and most of all, for his bringing to the world his genuinely kind, poignant, and ironically funny portrayals of the people of Minnesota; who, over the years, have graced our lives with decency, honesty, sincerity, humor, kindness, warmth, and a deep sense of fairness.

We also thank Hawaiian slack key guitarists and vocalists Keola Beamer and Gabby Pahinui, whose enchanting music kept us focused and on task. And a special thanks to everyone involved in the writing, producing, directing, and acting in the *The Descendants*, a poetic and poignant film depicting a highly functional family caught in multiple, entangled crucibles that clearly demonstrate what this book is about—how human beings, acting from their best selves, despite white-hot pain and conflict, can come out the other side filled with love, understanding, and forgiveness.

We thank our brothers and sisters, Bill, Nancy, Richard, and Margo; and our children and grandchildren for who they are as individuals, for all that they have become, and for all that they mean to us. Wise parents know that the job is filled with unimaginable joys, disappointments and heartaches, incomprehensible magic, and unexpected moments of awe and wonder. There is nothing else in life that is as filled with as many paradoxes or with such warmth, such pride, and such love. Thank you to Kristin and Jeff, Rebecca and Scott, David and Lolly, and to the next generation—Connor, Madeline, Carter, Marin, and Blaise. You are the lights of our lives.

And last, we thank our nieces and nephews and "the grand ones," Brian and his daughter Scarlett; Carrie, her husband Holger, and children Dylan and Quinn; Mark, his wife Linh, and their children Liem and Tai; John Michael; and Mary Joanna (in Hebrew, "God is gracious") Friel.

In Mary Joanna's memory, we offer a special thanks to you for all of the joy and love and spirituality that you brought into the world and that you shared with so many people. You left this world too soon. Or maybe you left just when you were supposed to.

We send all our love to all of you,
in the only language that says it all for us—Aloha!

Part One:

THE POIGNANCY OF BEING HUMAN

Long before science existed, sharp-eyed men and women told each other stories about how people are, stories that have never lost their power to enchant and instruct. The purpose of using science to investigate human nature is not to replace those stories but to augment and deepen them. Robert Frost once wrote that too many poets delude themselves by thinking the mind is dangerous and must be left out. That principle is mirrored in the study of the brain, where too many experts, out of plain fear, avoid mentioning love.

—*Thomas Lewis, Fari Amini, and Richard Lannon,*
A General Theory of Love *(2000, p. 15)*

CHAPTER 1

THE FATE OF THE SURPRISINGLY SMART NEANDERTHALS

The nonalcoholic world has many lessons which it might
learn from the epistemology of systems theory and the ways of AA.
If we continue to operate in terms of a Cartesian dualism of mind
versus matter, we shall probably also continue to see the world
in terms of God versus man; elite versus people; chosen race versus
others; nation versus nation; and man versus environment.
It is doubtful whether a species having *both* an advanced technology
and this strange way of looking at its world can endure.

—*Gregory Bateson, "The Cybernetics of 'Self':
A Theory of Alcoholism" (1971, p. 337)*

The extraordinary success of *Homo sapiens* is a result
of four things: intelligence, language, an ability to manipulate objects
dexterously in order to make tools, and co-operation. . . .
At the moment, co-operation is the most fashionable subject of
investigation. In particular, why are humans so willing to collaborate
with unrelated strangers, even to the point of risking being cheated
by people whose characters they cannot possibly know?

—The Economist *(2011, July 30)*

This book is about the place of power and grace in human systems. Every system is part of a larger system, and has smaller subsystems within it. So this book is about the place of power and grace within a single person, between partners in a marriage, among members of a family, a community, a state, a nation, and the world. The principles of human systems apply the same way regardless of which level you choose to examine.

We chose to begin this book with the genetic-evolutionary-survival level of being human because it is the least visible in our day-to-day lives, yet is ultimately the most powerful in directing the overall course of human beings' existence on this planet. It may just be the level of understanding that allows *Homo sapiens* to actually survive on Earth the longest. At some point in the therapy process, we ask our clients to trust that we have their best interests at heart. In that same way, we ask the reader to trust that there is "a method to our madness," and to trust our conviction that this information will help the reader pull together everything else in the book by the time he is done reading it.

Homo neanderthalensis

For many decades, Neanderthals were believed to be stupid and crude, so much so that their name became a pejorative term applied to certain brutish, apelike, "knuckle-dragging" men in contemporary society. But according to the most recent anthropological evidence reported in a three-part *Nova* documentary on PBS titled "Becoming Human: Last Human Standing," Neanderthals actually had bigger brains than ours, but were more limited in cognition, memory, spatial abilities, and language. They managed to exist on Earth for 400,000 years, roughly twice as long as we have thus far. While much of the Earth was covered by glacial ice, Neanderthals courageously exercised their fiercely focused ability to hunt large animals using large spears at very close range—a most dangerous undertaking that gave them an average life span of a mere thirty years.

They completely vanished from the fossil record approximately 28,000 years ago.

Homo sapiens—modern humans—emerged in the Great Rift Valley roughly 200,000 years ago during a period of massive climate upheaval, which included one of the longest, coldest ice ages in history, as well as massive droughts in Africa. The modern human population dwindled to 600 breeding individuals, which anthropologists have called a genetic "bottleneck," causing a severe crimp in genetic diversity. Approximately 140,000 years ago Africa became essentially uninhabitable, and the few remaining modern humans headed for caves on the South African coast, where they used their more flexible brainpower not just to hunt for animals but also to gather fruits and berries. They developed more sophisticated tools. They discovered the relationship between the phases of the moon and the tides so that they could head to the shore at low tide and gather shellfish. Approximately 25,000 years ago, they began to use red ochre to create symbols and art, painted their bodies, and wore ornaments—that is, they began to store information outside of their own brains. Their culture became more complex and, as a result, easier to pass on to the next generation.

As the climate began to improve 60,000 years ago, *Homo sapiens* was ready to take over the world, which we did, spreading out in every direction around the planet from that long, hunkered-down existence in South Africa. One wave of humans went up through the Middle East and into Europe, where they must have encountered *Homo neanderthalensis*. Authors of the *Nova* documentary noted that *Homo sapiens* had a tendency to "squeeze out everything from the environment," causing extinctions of large animals all over the planet. In Australia, most animals over 100 pounds vanished within 1,000 years of our arrival there.

Ultimately, it was (1) the survival strategy of Neanderthals—to consume 5,000 calories per day by hunting only large animals, (2) the severe climate swings that challenged their slightly less flexible brains and less adaptive bodies, and (3) the overwhelmingly superior adaptive flexibility of *Homo sapiens* that left Neanderthals unable to endure. The fossil record at the end of their existence is dramatic and poignant. It shows *Homo neanderthalensis* gradually dying off as they moved west across Europe until roughly 28,000 years ago, with the last remaining evidence of their existence found on the Rock of Gibraltar. There was simply nowhere else to flee.

Homo sapiens

In this same *Nova* documentary, the narrator reported,

> Culture is the storehouse of our complex ways of thinking and perceiving, and we pass it on to our children as surely as we pass on our genes. The ways in which cultural evolution and genetic evolution interact will be at the forefront of the research of tomorrow, because one thing is for sure: evolution is not stopping.

Just as those early human beings living in South African caves 25,000 years ago began to develop more complex and task-specific tools to aid their survival, our continued invention of increasingly sophisticated tools allows us to better understand ourselves and our survival on this planet. Few tools are more helpful in our understanding of ourselves than those emerging from the field of genetics.

Genes, Caring, and Our Ultimate Survival or Our Ultimate Extinction

Recent research has suggested an intriguing connection between our genes and how much we contribute to charitable causes, whether we are liberal or conservative, how much risk we are willing to take, how good we feel when we work at a soup kitchen, and how tolerant we are of others' differences (Reuter, Frenzel, Walter, Markett, & Montag, 2010; Brinn, 2005; Settle, Dawes, Christakis, & Fowler, 2010; Cohen, 2008).

One of the genetic theories that may have the strongest bearing on our current political climate as well as on modern humans' ability to survive has to do with the controversial notion of the "selfless gene," first proposed by British anthropologist William Donald Hamilton (1964a, 1964b, 1966). He called it "altruism," and he began his studies by wondering why and how some creatures could sacrifice their own well-being, even their own lives, in the service of helping others of the same species. How could this trait increase the survival of one's gene pool, when from a logical perspective, it would seem to mean that one's genes would *not* be passed on as a result of caring for others? The reader can find a more detailed discussion and compelling support for Hamilton's theory in Olivia Judson's article titled "The Selfless Gene" in the October 2007 edition of *The Atlantic*. One part of that theory that is especially pertinent to the current book is this:

> Many social animals thus live in huge flocks or herds, and not in family groups—or even if the nexus of social life is the family, the family group is itself part of a larger community. In species such as these, social behavior must extend beyond a simple "Be friendly and helpful to your family and hostile to everybody else" approach to the world. At the least, the evolution of social living requires limiting aggression so that neighbors can tolerate each other. And often, the evolution of larger social groupings is accompanied by an increase in the subtlety and complexity of the ways animals get along together. (emphasis added)

Between 100,000 years ago and 10,000 years ago, the human population barely grew, due in part to extreme climactic volatility, but also because as much as 15 percent of the human population may have destroyed each other in wars. In the same article, Judson cited the work of Sam Bowles of the Santa Fe Institute in New Mexico and the University of Siena in Italy:

> Groups of supercooperative, altruistic humans could indeed have wiped out groups of less-unified folk. However, his argument works only if the cooperative groups also had practices—such as monogamy and the sharing of food with other group members—that reduced the ability of their selfish members to out-reproduce their more generous members. . . . Conversely, people who fit in—sharing the food they found, joining in hunting, helping to defend the group, and so on—would have given their group a collective advantage, and thus themselves an individual evolutionary advantage.

Judson concluded the article as follows:

One of the most important, and least remarked upon, consequences of social living is that individual behavior must be highly flexible and tailored to circumstance: An individual who does not know whom to be aggressive toward, or whom to help, is unlikely to survive for long within the group . . . Indeed, the ability to adjust our behavior to fit a given social environment is one of our most important adaptive characteristics, yet it's so instinctive we don't even notice it, let alone consider it worthy of remark. But its implications are profound—and hopeful. It suggests that we can, in principle, organize society so *as to bring out the best facets of our complex, evolved natures.* (emphasis added)

Based on the work of our mentors, James Maddock and Noel Larson, and our colleagues David Schnarch, Ruth Morehouse, and William Doherty, among many others, and the model of marriage and family therapy that we endorse, one of the central principles of marital intimacy, happiness, and depth, and of family and societal health, is the extent to which *each individual* in an ecological social system *can act from his best self, regardless of the behaviors of those around him.*

Indeed, in its purest form as described in the New Testament, and as demonstrated by the parables that Jesus employed to try to teach people, without encouraging the shallow and empty rule-following that pervaded the religious practices of his time, Christianity boiled down to two simple rules: (1) love God, and (2) love your neighbor as yourself.

To the people of Jesus' time, Samaritans were the lowest of the low—regarded as negatively then, by the average citizen, as perhaps some Muslims are regarded by a small and very anxious group of citizens in the contemporary United States. The parable was clearly designed to confront the hypocrisy of calling oneself a loving person while ignoring a wounded person along the side of the road. It was only the Samaritan, despised by all, who proved himself to be more holy and righteous than the many who were already calling themselves *the most* holy and righteous. Jesus' parable was a kind, empathic scolding of those who would let their prejudices define them and make them *act from their worst selves*, and a praising of the hated Samaritan, who—by his compassion and care for a fellow human being—proved that he was what Christianity was really all about: *acting from one's best self, even under the most challenging of circumstances.*

The Evolutionary Drama Continues

We *Homo sapiens* are truly unique. But we have only been here for a very short time, relative to our ancestors. Our ability to invent and create and discover increasingly sophisticated tools and cultures and systems of thought have enabled us to take over much of the world with great intensity and focus. But *if* William Donald Hamilton is correct (and maybe he isn't),

> *We are, after all, pack animals who experience loneliness when we are separated from our own kind.*

we will ultimately survive on Earth only if we also maintain our *genetically directed care and concern for one another. We are, after all, pack animals who experience loneliness when we are separated from our own kind.*

In the June 11, 2011, edition of *The Economist*, in an article titled "Who Needs Leaders? The aftermath of the March 11th disasters shows that Japan's strengths lie outside Tokyo, in its regions," the author noted:

The earthquake, tsunami and nuclear accident that struck Japan three months ago have revealed something important about the country: a seam of strength and composure in the bedrock of society that has surprised even the Japanese themselves. Not only has this resilience helped the hundreds of thousands suffering from the loss of families, homes and livelihoods to cope with their suffering, despite the self-absorbed dithering of their national politicians in Tokyo. By reminding Japan of the hidden depths of its local communities, especially compared with the shallowness of central government, it has also provided a sense of how Japan could emerge stronger from the crisis, ending years of economic drift.

One of the most heroic examples of community spirit was 24-year-old Miki Endo, who used the loudspeaker system in Minamisanriku, a fishing port close to the focus of the 9.0 earthquake, to urge residents to do what they could to escape the incoming tsunami. She drowned at her post. Television footage shows the rising sea approaching, with her haunting voice echoing over the waves. More than 1,000 of the town's 18,000 residents died.

Ecological-Systemic Imbalance and Challenge in the United States

It's all about change and balance. The health of a marriage depends on the balance of power and control *within* both partners, and *between* both partners (Maddock & Larson, 1995). If I don't control my impulses enough, I will overpower you. If you don't exert your power enough, you will disappear. A large portion of effective marital therapy involves the rebalancing of power and control within and between partners.

This kind of rebalancing in *any* system always creates temporary upheaval. No marriage can grow without this upheaval. The dramatic power imbalance in South Africa could not have moved toward balance without the upheaval that came with the end of apartheid. The power imbalance between African Americans and Caucasians that existed in the United States prior to the Civil Rights Movement could not have rebalanced without this upheaval. We are now faced with a rebalancing challenge on a global scale, and the upheavals accompanying it are certainly being felt globally, as well as in the United States.

The evolutionary-genetic drama that will be unfolding as long as *Homo sapiens* still exist on Earth is simply shifting to a more global phase. More and more people are connecting with, and falling in love with, more and more people from different races and cultures. For this kind of systemic rebalancing, the "melting pot" that is the United States has always been the model of success for the rest of the world. And it still is today. But rebalancing—change—can never occur without upheaval; that is, without a lot of anxiety. In our opinion, much of the political and sociocultural distress experienced in the twenty-first-century United States is actually the evolutionary survival distress of certain groups fearing for their very future existence.

As for Neanderthals, DNA evidence suggests that approximately 4 percent of the DNA of Europeans and Asians is shared with ancient

Neanderthal DNA, which is a very good thing for some of us. According to Stanford University microbiologist Peter Parham, some of those genes give those of us who have them a distinct edge in fighting off germs and viruses (Perlman, 2011).

If we stubbornly refuse to honor the altruistic part of ourselves that allows a better chance for our genes to survive, then Gregory Bateson's warning will be of utmost importance for our evolutionary survival on this planet. Genetic diversity has thus far been the most powerful mechanism for our global genetic survival. If just 4 percent of Neanderthal DNA gives its bearers a distinct immune system advantage, imagine the enormous genetic survival advantages attained by the merging of various races and cultures around the planet.

According to an August 14, 2008, Bloomberg report written by Thomas Penny, "The white majority in the U.S. will be outnumbered by Americans of other races by 2042, eight years sooner than previously projected by the Census Bureau." By 2042 the United States will be a country of minorities.

> WASHINGTON (AP)—For the first time, minorities make up a majority of babies in the U.S., part of a sweeping race change and growing age divide between mostly white, older Americans and predominantly minority youths that could reshape government policies. (CBS News Online, June 23, 2011)

Joel Achenbach (2011), writing for Slate.com, noted,

> This will be the century of disasters. In the same way that the 20th century was the century of world wars, genocide, and grinding ideological conflict, the 21st will be the century of natural disasters and technological crises and unholy combinations of the two. There are several reasons for this. We have chosen to engineer the planet. We have built vast networks of technology. We have created systems that, in general, work very well, but are still vulnerable to catastrophic failures. It is harder and harder for any one person, institution, or agency to perceive all the interconnected elements of the technological society. Failures can cascade. There are unseen weak points in the network. Small failures can have broad consequences.

Achenbach's predictions have nothing to do with race or culture. They have to do with natural disasters like the earthquake and tsunami that hit Japan and caused a massive technological failure at the same time. They have to do with the reality of a vast technological system that by its very vastness will be subject to the normal failures in a system that has become too complex and interconnected. All complex systems are subject to errors and degradation sooner or later that have nothing to do with race or religion or culture. *They just happen, because that's how systems work.*

Every system in the universe is constantly changing, constantly attempting to achieve balance at the same time. When a system is subjected to enough pressure or stress, the changes become more dramatic and less predictable. When a child lives in a family that is very limited in its ability to connect emotionally with each other, she may finally "act out that family shortage." It might be in the form of using drugs, getting pregnant at age fifteen, or by being a superhero at school who eventually attempts suicide because she is so emotionally alone and misunderstood by a family that at one level is so loving, but at the crucial right-brained level is very shut down, thereby making her feel "crazy." When any system is stressed beyond the normal limits of its competencies, skills, abilities, or purely physical limitations, such as in the case of rivers or planets or star systems or the like, then all hell breaks loose. What happens to a family if they are pushed beyond their limitations? What will happen if our planet becomes more stressed than at any time in modern recorded history? How will each of us respond? From our better selves, like Good Samaritans? From our genetic directives that say we need to watch each other's backs?

During the Republican Party primary debates of fall 2011, the majority of American viewers were shocked by the Conservative Republican audience reactions—enthusiastic cheers at the number of prisoners executed in Texas despite the common knowledge that many death row inmates are often innocent; shouts of "Let him die" at the dilemma of an ailing human being lacking health insurance; the mocking of an honorable gay Iraq War veteran who had risked life and limb and brain and sight for our country, and who had simply asked about gays in the military; and the cheers at candidate Herman Cain's puzzlingly confident statement that the unemployed in this country were at fault for their own unemployment, implying that they were lazy and unmotivated, while ignoring the mind-boggling irony of the billions of dollars of *corporate welfare* bailouts that have already been given to Wall Street, despite the fact that there is compelling evidence to pin the economic collapse in the U.S. on unregulated Wall Street excesses, as documented so clearly in Charles Ferguson's (2010) *Inside Job*.

Matt Taibbi wrote on his Rollingstone.com blog:

> You get busted for drugs in this country, and it turns out you can make yourself ineligible to receive food stamps. . . . But you can be a serial fraud offender like Citigroup, which has repeatedly been dragged into court for the same offenses and has repeatedly ignored court injunctions to abstain from fraud, and this does not make you ineligible to receive $45 billion in bailouts and other forms of federal assistance. . . . A normal person, once he gets a felony conviction, immediately begins to lose his rights as a citizen. . . . But white-collar criminals of the type we've seen in recent years on Wall Street— both the individuals and the corporate "citizens"—do not suffer these ramifications. They commit crimes without real consequence, allowing them to retain access to the full smorgasbord of subsidies and financial welfare programs that, let's face it, are the source of most of their profits.

A letter to President Barack Obama, Senator Harry Reid, and Representative John Boehner, asking that tax rates be increased for incomes over $1 million, and posted on the website Patriotic Millionaires for Fiscal Strength, had been endorsed by more than 135 millionaires in the United States as of November 11, 2011. Bill Gates, Warren Buffett, and Ted Turner are just a few of the extremely wealthy Americans who have donated the majority of their billions to various humanitarian causes throughout the world. At the same time, over the past forty years the line between those who are on the opposite sides of this issue seems to have hardened as if set in cement. These divisions have run so passionately, so deeply, and for so long that we began to wonder whether it was less a cultural divide and more of a biological-genetic divide.

Are some people just cold, self-serving, cruel, unfeeling, and uncaring? Or are we witnessing a much deeper systemic divide that is controlled by the two genetic survival strategies postulated by Hamilton? As each year passes, we find ourselves leaning more and more toward the latter explanation. The focused but tragically and inflexibly limited survival strategy of Neanderthals kept them on Earth for 400,000 years, but in the end, they ceased to exist—except for that 4 percent of their genes that remains in some of us. The ultimate question for humanity as we know it is as follows: Can we supposedly wise *Homo sapiens* rely on our ever more sophisticated *tools* to help us survive, while also listening to the subtle directives of our *genes* that are telling us that tools are not enough, and that *we will never be able to make it on this complex planet unless we work together*?

Gregory Bateson, one of the most brilliant men of the last century, wrote more than forty years ago, "It is doubtful whether a species having *both* an advanced technology *and* this strange way of looking at its world can endure" (Bateson, 1971, p. 337; emphasis in original). It is our belief that the rigid, overly simplistic, black-and-white thinking—the mind-body split and all of its corollaries—of which Bateson wrote, are, indeed, the root of much of the pain, heartache, war, and trauma that exists in people, marriages, families, communities, states, nations, and in the world. And in this book, we hope to cast some light on one aspect of this paralyzing and simplistic duality.

CHAPTER 2

WHEN SIMPLE IS COMPLICATED AND COMPLICATED IS SIMPLE

> If you work on your mind with your mind, how can
> you avoid an immense confusion?
>
> —*Seng-Ts'an*

Everything that a human being does makes sense, whether it is self-destructive, hurts others, or is infinitely kind and spirituality uplifting. Everything we do, we do for a reason, even if our reasoning is flawed. For that reason, human beings will always be the most interesting creatures on the planet.

One of the most important challenges encountered by our clients during their process of healing and growing is the paradox that in so many cases, the more one tries to simplify life by ignoring its underlying complexity, the more confused and destructive one becomes. And the more one allows life to be as messy and complex as it truly is, the clearer and healthier and more peaceful one becomes. That is what we will try to convey in this chapter. To illustrate this critical paradox, we will examine the famous case of Dan and Betty Broderick (Kingston, 2004).

Betty Broderick's husband, Dan, was, by her account, a dirty rat. She had given birth to five children in the early years of their marriage, and he had gone to medical school. When he went to Harvard Law School to eventually become an MD/JD, she worked various jobs to support him. They moved to La Jolla, California, where he became a successful medical malpractice attorney, and they were part of the upper-crust social scene in the San Diego area. After founding his law practice, he began an affair with former flight attendant Linda Kolkena; he eventually divorced Betty and married Linda.

Betty accused him of using his extensive connections in the San Diego legal and social communities to help extract an unfair divorce settlement. After months of acts of infantile rage, driven by bitterness and feelings of revenge typical of someone with borderline personality disorder (BPD), she stole a key to Dan and Linda's new house from her elder daughter's purse, went to their home, and murdered them in their bed. After a second trial, Betty was sentenced to two consecutive terms of fifteen years to life.

It was just another sad high-profile murder case involving betrayal and intrigue, and two marital partners who were emotionally very little. By "little" we mean a person in an adult body who is still operating at an emotional level of one who is five or ten, or perhaps twelve, at the most, as is the case with some very powerful, successful adults who were pushed to achieve quickly and competitively rather than growing up from the inside out, at the slow pace that is required to do so.

But there were some important defining considerations in this case: Many women hailed Betty Broderick as a feminist hero. Her story was a huge ratings hit on *The Oprah Winfrey Show*. Two widely watched made-for-television dramas were devoted to her story. A number of behavioral experts labeled her as having BPD. In our thirty years of private practice with couples, and with adults who grew up in painful or neglectful families, we have yet to see a couple in which both partners were not equally healthy and equally dysfunctional, regardless of how preposterous that might seem on the surface. To frame the story simply as one about a "dirty rat" or simply about an unstable, "borderline" woman makes for successful television drama, but it reflects little of the reality of their painfully destructive relationship. Finally, regardless of any of the above circumstances, Betty Broderick is a murderer. To call Betty Broderick a feminist hero clearly demonstrates how confused many Americans are about what constitutes a *victim*, what constitutes a *perpetrator*, and what constitutes a *healthy, competent adult*. As we explain in more detail later in this book, every human being has a victim part, a perpetrator part, and, in most cases, at least a small part that is grown up and healthy. Many experts agree that someone with BPD flips back and forth rather quickly between a highly developed victim part and a highly developed perpetrator part (Larson, 2009, 2011; Maddock & Larson, 2004). Few analysts dispute that, in addition to genetic causes, anyone who grows up with an especially large perpetrator part was likely the victim of a good deal of childhood abuse and neglect.

Trying to see Betty Broderick as a feminist hero or as evil incarnate, or to see Dan Broderick as a dirty rat or as a hapless victim, is a perfect example of how attempts to make life simple and black-and-white result in rendering it confusing and complicated, which just doesn't make sense.

To clarify our thoughts about this case and the larger principles we are trying to explicate and explore, consider these two very different summaries of the Broderick case:

1. Betty Broderick was a feminist hero who supported her husband through law school, bore and raised his children, and was then betrayed and scorned by him when he, like "most" men, decided that he was ready for a younger, prettier wife now that he was settled in a lucrative career in an upwardly mobile social community. He dumped her for a younger woman just like most men do. He was, indeed, a dirty rat.

2. Betty Broderick and Dan Broderick followed the rules of mating and pairing—that we always pair up with a partner who is equally as dysfunctional *and* healthy as ourselves. They were probably "not old enough to date," as we often say—meaning that developmentally they were functioning inside of their adult bodies from the position of elementary schoolchildren, at best.

They entered into an unspoken agreement about how a marriage should unfold based on hollow stereotypes they had stored in their own cognitive templates, which they had acquired while growing up in their respective families of origin. And as long as the bargain they struck was not subject to any extreme outside influences or unusual stressors, they could sail along looking like the perfect couple, all the while rarely connecting emotionally in the ways that deeply intimate, grown-up, truly passionate, erotic couples do. Things changed. And when things change in a fragile system that looks great on the surface but has little of substance underneath, the system rapidly collapses.

If one of the two partners also tends toward BPD, then even more dramatic consequences often ensue. It's a sad tale of two little kids who tried to play at being adults, and when things got out of hand, the situation quickly became quite painful and messy.

A simplistic explanation is briefer and easier to understand, and has some kind of primitive, visceral "truth" to it that isn't truth at all. It's the kind of "*truth*" that would cause a band of townspeople to label a woman a "witch," and then burn her at the stake because she was a little odd, made us uncomfortable because we didn't understand her "oddness," and frightened us for those reasons. Then, to manage our fear, we would concoct a myth that became a simple, comforting explanation that would justify our removing her from our presence to reduce our anxiety. This myth would also allow us to generate anger, which would help us deny real feelings like guilt and shame, while making us feel righteous and grand in saving our town from an evil foe. In this scenario, everybody comes out a winner . . . except for the woman who was illegally, immorally, unmercifully, and cruelly burned at the stake while her community of fellow human beings taunted her, laughed at her, called her crude names, and damned her to hell as she shouted blood-curdling screams of pain while she was slowly devoured by piercingly hot flames. What many people think is simple—she's an evil witch—can turn out to be so complicated and distorted as to be unbearably inhuman, at the very least.

An elegant, gracious response to this odd woman—one with integrity, decency, compassion, kindness, grace, and the best of what humanity has to offer rather than the worst—might have been for the anxious, emotionally distant, fear-driven townspeople to sit down and talk to her. Get to know her story. Hear how she had lost her entire family in a famine or freeze the year before, and how her mother beat her when she was a little girl so that she fears getting close to others, and . . . and . . .

> *Life can be so complicated and convoluted when we try to make it artificially simple. It can be so simple when we allow life to be just as complicated as it really is.*

Life can be so complicated and convoluted when we try to make it artificially simple. It can be so simple when we allow life to be just as complicated as it really is. Of course, for these townspeople to have been able to choose the cleaner, more elegant plan, they would have to have been able to soothe their own primitive anxieties enough to allow their innate care and kindness toward their fellow human being override their primitive, animalistic fears.

Our colleague Mary Pietrini pointed out in a 2011 personal communication that

> The Malleus Maleficarum (1496) was written as a "Handbook for Inquisitors" and insisted that witches were "primarily women" (often elderly spinsters or widows) who lived without the protection of husbands or sons (males). Women alone were viewed as rebellious, possibly even demonic, threats to the social order—while single men were not. These women were often herbalists, midwives, and healers of various kinds viewed then (and now?) as dangerous rivals to certain clergy.

Gregory Bateson, the brilliant British anthropologist, social scientist, philosopher, and cyberneticist who first brought systems theory to the study of human behavior while studying schizophrenia with colleagues Donald Jackson, Jay Haley, and John Weakland in the 1950s—together they were known as the Palo Alto Group—said it most elegantly: "The major problems in the world are the result of the difference between how nature works and the way people think."[1]

---

[1] From *An Ecology of Mind*, a documentary about the life and work of Gregory Bateson, produced and directed by Nora Bateson, Gregory Bateson's daughter (www.anecologyofmind.com).

CHAPTER 3

THE GRACE AND POWER BETWEEN NASTY AND NICE

The significant problems we face
cannot be solved at the same level of
thinking we were at when
we created them.

—*Albert Einstein*

Too Nasty: Murder in Beverly Hills

Lyle and Erik Menendez brutally murdered their parents, Jose and Kitty, with multiple shotgun wounds in the den of the family's Beverly Hills, California, home. During the first trial, their attorney, Leslie Abramson, presented extensive evidence of physical and sexual abuse of the boys at the hands of their father, Jose, which resulted in a hung jury. In the second trial, introduction of that evidence was severely restricted, and the boys were convicted and sentenced to life imprisonment without the possibility of parole.

A lingering question remained: Why would their history of child abuse—if they were not under immediate threat of being abused or killed at the moment of the murders—result in a hung jury?

The Media Rep

"I kicked their ass!" gloated Sandra Hart in April 1995. A renowned public relations executive, she had been picked up by the Minneapolis police, who thought they had run across a "slumper"—a drunk driver who had pulled over in her car and fallen asleep or passed out. When her case came up before Judge Myron Greenberg, he regretfully dismissed it because of technicalities. Hart had a long history of alcohol-related driving arrests and convictions, but claimed that they had all occurred in the 1970s. The record showed otherwise. She had actually been arrested for drunk driving in 1981, 1983, 1984, 1988, 1990 (twice), and again in 1993.

When she commented on the judge's reluctant decision, she crowed, "I kicked their ass! I was never afraid or fearful. I had two things on my side: God and the justice system." It is an interesting comment in light of the fact that *people who tend more toward the perpetrator stance (1) deny ever being ashamed or afraid, and (2) tend to believe that they are always right, always justified—and if they claim to believe in God—always have God on their side.*

> *People who tend more toward the perpetrator stance (1) deny ever being ashamed or afraid, and (2) tend to believe that they are always right, always justified—and if they claim to believe in God—always have God on their side.*

A strange thing about human beings is that some of us have a strong tendency to actually pity and protect people who do cruel, hurtful things. At some level we detect how damaged a person must be to treat others that way, so the compassionate part of us tries to take over from the wiser part of us that would still have compassion, *but without pitying or excusing.*

When we recount the details of the Sandra Hart incident to audiences of professionals attending a training seminar on working with victim-perpetrator dynamics, their immediate reaction is shock or disgust. As we interact more with the audience, asking questions and probing a bit beneath the surface, what some participants discover is that their inner reaction to things is not always the same as their surface reaction.

For example, people who are angry at the law or bureaucrats or their parents or the government may find themselves secretly applauding this woman's actions. People who are alcoholic or drug-addicted may feel unconsciously protective of this woman because they share an addiction. People who were intimidated and hurt by abusive or neglectful parents may find themselves either wanting her crucified or wanting to protect her out of misdirected pity, or because of an unconscious and irrational fear of somehow getting hurt again if they don't protect her.

Too Nice—Codependency: It Looks like Love, But Isn't

When someone is frightened or hurt, especially if he is a vulnerable child, there are certain predictable ways that he instinctively and unconsciously tries to protect himself. One is to fight back. A child who fights back in order to save himself might beat up his little brother or sexually abuse his little sister. He might fail in school despite having a high IQ, setting himself up to be a very bright and very troubled young man. He might get addicted to alcohol, especially if he has the six or seven genes discovered in the Human Genome Project that seem to be correlated with alcoholism. The thinking is, *If you scare me and hurt me, I'll lash out and fight back. I will not let you get to me.* The survival sentiment is noble and admirable, even if it backfires later.

Many successful people have grown up chanting this mantra to themselves from the time they were five or six years old. Despite the millions of dollars they have earned in successful business ventures, the problem resurfaces when they try to have an intimate relationship with another person, as in a marriage, or when they encounter the legal system as a result of acting out. Then they may find themselves divorced or in prison.

Then there are those children who, for whatever reason—genes, birth order, the parent to whom they were most bonded—found a path to self-soothing and self-protection that was the opposite: *If I can be the very best child imaginable, if I can go to church more often than anyone else in the family, if I can soothe Mom's pain or divert Dad's anger away from beating up my brother again, then maybe everything will eventually be okay in my family.* As Maddock and Larson (1995) suggested, these children tend to latch on to the *victim role*, seeing life as painful and unyielding, withholding, and filled with deprivation and desperation.

This child lives with inner mantras that include *I can't, because,* and *If only,* and *I must simply wait until my parents or guardians give me what I want and need; there's no mechanism in the family system for me to ask for what I need, and to be taken seriously—or at least, to not be punished or criticized for asking.*

So, while one child in the family is saying to himself, *To hell with it. If I wait for what I want and need, I'll never get it, so I'm just going to take it, no matter whose feelings I step on in the process,* the more compassionate or sensitive child is saying, *There's way too much pain in this family already. I'm going to do whatever I can to reduce the tension and pain.*

As we initially defined this loosely associated set of symptoms and behaviors back in the early 1980s, the *classic codependent* person (Friel & Friel, 1988) embraced a fascinating and contradictory set of traits and behaviors as a logical way to survive childhood. The overhead transparencies that we once used in the early 1980s—now PowerPoint slides—listed the primary indicators of what was called "codependency" back then:

Martyrdom

The "Owe/Pay" Syndrome—I'll do all these nice things for you and then be
    mad at you when you don't do nice things for me.

Controlling as a way to soothe anxiety

A power disorder

A problem of will

Inability to surrender

Inability to be used, mentored, guided

Sometimes the perpetrator role disguised in a victim's cloak

An identity disorder

An intimacy disorder

Inability to tolerate separations

Moral superiority

Difficulty embracing paradoxes

Perfectionism

Rigidity and being stuck in attitudes and behaviors

Difficulty adjusting to change

Feeling overly responsible for others' feelings or behavior

Difficulty identifying feelings

Difficulty expressing feelings

Difficulty containing feelings

Problems in maintaining and forming close relationships

Constant need for others' approval

Difficulty making decisions

General feelings of powerlessness

Basic sense of shame and low self-esteem

Disordered intrapsychic, interpersonal, and intergenerational boundaries

In other words, in our attempts to adapt and survive, *some of us act out our pain by hurting others*, while others *act out our pain by depriving ourselves of our needs and wants, trying to control others, and inadvertently victimizing ourselves.* For those who mistakenly think that this behavior was something new to the late twentieth century, we often refer to this passage from the 1604 (or 1605) play by William Shakespeare, *All's Well That Ends Well*:

Demetrius:
Do I entice you? Do I speak you fair?
Or, rather, do I not in plainest truth
Tell you, I do not, nor I cannot love you?

Helena:
And even for that do I love you the more.
I am your spaniel; and, Demetrius,
The more you beat me, I will fawn on you:
Use me but as your spaniel, spurn me, strike me,
Neglect me, lose me; only give me leave,

UNWORTHY AS I AM, TO FOLLOW YOU.
WHAT WORSER PLACE CAN I BEG IN YOUR LOVE,
AND YET A PLACE OF HIGH RESPECT WITH ME,
THAN TO BE USED AS YOU USE YOUR DOG?

Demetrius:
TEMPT NOT TOO MUCH THE HATRED OF MY SPIRIT;
FOR I AM SICK WHEN I DO LOOK ON THEE.

Helena:
AND I AM SICK WHEN I LOOK NOT ON YOU.

Being too nice can be just as manipulative as being too mean and nasty. In reality, they can be equally destructive, each in their own way. If we were simply left with these two either/or options for how to operate, the world would be an impossible place to live. No one could ever be happy or content, let alone spiritual.

But fortunately, on a regular basis, there comes a person by whose actions and life choices we are shocked out of our blindness, complacency, fear or selfishness, and by whose actions we are challenged to examine how we frame our conflicted stance about life having to be either nasty or nice. Then we are graced with an entirely different view of how we can survive in this world—despite all of its painful, inexplicable contradictions.

A Competent, Powerful Adult: Grace in South-Central Los Angeles

In 1990 Myrtle Faye Rumph's son was killed in a drive-by shooting. Within hours, friends and relatives had gathered to plan revenge. They watched and waited, put the neighborhood under surveillance, and planned to murder his killers. But Myrtle Faye intervened, stating quietly that she didn't want to avenge her son's death, but rather she wanted to memorialize his life. With no money and no government assistance, she set up the beginnings of a storefront teen center in his name. It was to be a safe and supportive place for teens to congregate, away from the violence and death they experienced regularly.

When she ran out of money, she sold her house and kept the center going. Five years later, her center had a yearly budget of $200,000, and had 125 teenagers gathering there on a daily basis. She summed it up when she said, "I didn't want to wait around for the city, the county or the state to give me the money to do it. It's up to black people to change our own destiny. That's what I'm trying to do."

As journalist Miles Corwin (1995) pointed out, Rumph "had an unlikely manner and scholastic background" for someone who accomplished this. She had to drop out of high school in her junior year to help support her family and later came to Los Angeles as a single mother with five dollars to her name.

Fifteen years later, Corin Ramos (2010) reported,

> In April 2010, Ms. Rumph received the Spirit of Peace Award from the Stop the Violence Increase the Peace Foundation, a 501(c) nonprofit community prevention and intervention organization. The award honors extraordinary individuals and organizations who have been dedicated to the work of ending the cycle of violence in urban communities, as well as provide support for a regional collaboration of 120 agencies who provide prevention and intervention services to women and children living in poverty.

Moreover, on August 4, 2010, she was awarded the 2010 Presidential Citizens Medal, the nation's second-highest civilian honor, with the following description on the White House website:

> For decades, Myrtle Faye Rumph has lent her talent and compassion to impacting the lives of at-risk youth. Her commitment to reducing gun and gang violence in her community has steered countless young men and women away from dangerous habits, and altered the course of their futures. Rumph receives the Citizens Medal for her tireless efforts to replace violence and despair in her community with a beacon of hope and humanity.

Myrtle Faye Rumph is one of the clearest examples of the pairing of power and grace that we have ever encountered in the contemporary press.

What Does It All Mean?

While speaking to professional audiences or the general public on the topic of victim-perpetrator dynamics, one of the authors (JCF) often takes out his wallet, opens it up, and looks through it while saying,

> I grew up in an alcoholic family, and it has taken me a number of years of therapy to unravel the more destructive templates for living that I acquired as a child. But no matter how hard and how long I search inside of my wallet, for the life of me I've never been able to find a *license* that says I have the right to hurt myself or others because of that pain I experienced when I was little.

Over the course of nearly thirty years in clinical practice in Minneapolis –St. Paul, and now also in Reno, Nevada, we have witnessed thousands of examples of the unraveling of painful, highly conflicted marriages and other long-term family relationships that have run the gamut from deeply respectful—albeit sad and painful—to incomprehensibly sadistic and cruel. We have seen families who rally at the eleventh hour to "bring their best selves forward" (Maddock, 1999, personal communication; Schnarch, 1991, 1997, 2009) despite the pain, ambivalence, and uncertainty that each family member is feeling. We also see families whose members are so emotionally primitive that the best they can muster are raw, shame- and terror-based reactions that do nothing but tear the family apart, in many cases for decades—and in some, forever.

Why is that? Why can some people behave fairly honorably under duress, while others rapidly disintegrate into the most primitive versions of humanity known to humanity? We attempt to answer this question later in this book. But even after we have presented all the complicated explanations, what remains clear is that the answer isn't very complicated. People only make it complicated because of *the difference between how nature works and the way people think* (from Nora Bateson's documentary about her father, Gregory, 2010).

Part Two:

RULES OF THE ROAD AND THE FUEL THAT DRIVES US

When we believe that the rules don't apply to us, all hell breaks loose, whether it's a nuclear reactor melting down, or a family descending into the depths of emotional despair.

—*John and Linda Friel*

CHAPTER 4

The Rules

A safe but sometimes chilly way of recalling the past
is to force open a crammed drawer. If you are searching for
anything in particular, you don't find it, but something falls
out at the back that is often more interesting.

—J. M. Barrie, from the dedication to his first edition of Peter Pan

Before we proceed to the next chapters in this book, we believe it will be helpful to explain a number of basic principles of human interactional systems, especially marital and family systems, because they have such a direct bearing on victim-perpetrator interaction patterns. [*Author's note*: The majority of this chapter is adapted or condensed from our books *The 7 Worst Things (Good) Parents Do*, *The 7 Best Things (Smart) Teens Do*, and *The 7 Best Things (Happy) Couples Do*.]

Extremes Often Equal Dysfunction

When a couple is fighting about laxness versus strictness in their child-rearing styles, the first thing we do is let each present his or her side of the story for sixty to ninety seconds. The one who is too lax yells, "Of course I cut deals with the kids behind your back. If I didn't go around you at times, they wouldn't be able to breathe or test themselves out or have any fun!" The one who is too strict yells, "Of course I'm too strict with the kids. If they didn't have some boundaries, they'd all end up in prison someday!"

We stop them, pause, and then solemnly look them both in the eyes and say, "Well, you can both be 100 percent assured that your partner is wrong."

An interesting silence ensues, followed in most cases by warm smiles of acknowledgment. When we approach it this way, with no time for them to back up into the overthinking and defensiveness that have been the primary ways they have been relating to each other and protecting their respective positions, we accomplish the ultimate systemic goal of disrupting the stuck system, allowing each of them to see that it isn't about all-or-none, right-or-wrong, win-or-lose. They realize in that nanosecond of insight that, indeed, they *are* both wrong, *because they are both polarized*—operating from the extremes—which usually means that their position is neither helpful nor useful.

Small Changes Yield Big Results

One change instituted consistently for six to twelve months can turn an entire system around. Think about one of our space probes just leaving Earth's orbit on its way to Jupiter. Imagine it being off course by a fraction of a degree. Imagine Mission Control officials being unable to make this tiny midcourse correction due to a malfunction in the probe's thrusters. Imagine where the probe will be, years later, when it is supposed to be entering Jupiter's atmosphere. That's right. It will be millions of miles off course by then. *Small changes yield big results.*

Sometimes people enter therapy looking for high drama and quick fixes. Sometimes people are seeking the magic bullet that will change their entire life overnight. In so doing, people miss the fact that one small change, maintained consistently and with integrity, can indeed change an entire system. Another metaphor we have found helpful is to visualize a dial with a 360-degree scale on it and with a strong spring inside that tries to keep the dial at zero degrees. Imagine yourself cranking that dial clockwise 270 degrees and then letting it go. We all know what happens shortly after this change. The dial quickly snaps back to business as usual.

Now imagine turning that dial seven degrees and holding it there for twelve months despite the strong spring inside the dial that is trying to pull it back to zero degrees. After twelve months of working diligently to keep it at seven degrees, you let go of the dial and find that it stays at seven degrees; the spring inside has adjusted to the new setting. Furthermore, you discover that many other aspects of your life have changed in important ways because of the internal growth that took place as you chose to acquire the patience to achieve this success instead of going for the quick fix.

We Pair Up with People Whose Emotional Cups Are Filled to the Same Level as Our Own; They Are as Grown-Up or Not Grown-Up as Ourselves

Part of victim-perpetrator dynamics is the strong tendency to blame the other person, while taking little or no responsibility for one's part in the systemic problems in the family. Many people get themselves stuck in the inevitable quagmire of believing that their long-term relationship partner is significantly "healthier" or "more dysfunctional" than they are. Notice that we emphasize "long-term relationship partner." Part of the process of dating as opposed to mating is that in dating it is assumed that you go out with people of many different emotional health levels. But as you get into the

> *Part of victim-perpetrator dynamics is the strong tendency to blame the other person, while taking little or no responsibility for one's part in the systemic problems in the family.*

mate selection phase, this variable balances out between the two partners. We have been presenting this information for years, and it still amazes a lot of people. Audience reactions range from nervous giggles of recognition to angry silence.

Think about it this way: it is fairly common for someone who grew up with a childhood history of abuse to marry someone who by all appearances had one of those "perfect" *Father Knows Best* or *Leave It to Beaver* childhoods. Many people ask how this could be, because their childhoods were so different. Part of it has to do with the distinction between *overt dysfunction*, which is easy to see, versus *covert dysfunction*, which is hidden from view. The "perfect" family may have many shortages that our

> *Painful events don't just go away, until people are able to share them openly and grieve together.*

blinders prevent us from seeing easily. Dad and Mom could be overly protective, too lax, or too strict. Everything could be in order *except* that painful events aren't dealt with. Perhaps the family tries to ignore painful or confusing aspects of life in the hopes that they will just go away. But painful events don't just go away, *until* people are able to share them openly and grieve together.

Someone who is overly dependent is just as dysfunctional as one who is overly independent. The confusion often comes because on some other measure, like financial health, the people may not be equal. An overly independent person may make more money or manage his money better than an overly dependent one.

Paradoxically, It Isn't 50/50

Our discussion above refers to an overall measure of emotional maturity and emotional health. If you and your partner are both three-fourths full, then you're in good shape. But no matter how much we grow and how healthy we get, we're still human, and therefore we still have limitations. So when there is a "problem" in the relationship—something that is causing distress and conflict and struggle—is it always a 50/50 proposition? No.

If I have a problem with my back, it is my problem. It certainly affects you at times, but all in all, it's an 80/20 proposition. It's my back, and therefore it's my problem. What might your 20 percent be? Maybe you hover over me too much instead of letting me handle it myself. Or maybe you're too insensitive about it. Maybe you nag me to go see the doctor after I just got back from the doctor and there's nothing more anyone can do for the time being. So, there are things you could do to help reduce the distress or conflict in our household related to my back problem, but the majority of responsibility and effort at managing the problem is mine.

If you are physically abusive, the majority of the problem is yours, because there simply is no excuse for physical abuse. My part may be that I keep staying in the relationship, naively hoping that "this time will be the last time that you hit me." Or my part could be that I have so little genuine emotional support outside of our relationship that just the thought of leaving to protect my own safety produces paralyzing fear—and therefore keeps me stuck in the victim role.

We Pick Partners Who Have Some of the More Painful Parts of Our Families of Origin for a Very Positive Reason

There is a fundamental difference between intimate relationships like a marriage and all other relationships. Because of this difference, the potential for volatility is so much greater in a romantic-sexual type of connection. The notion that we unconsciously pick romantic/sexual partners based on our childhood wounds is one of the cornerstones of Harville Hendrix's Imago therapy (1988). While partner choice is a very complex process, we do pick partners based partially on the characteristics of the people we grew up with and who therefore were our first love experiences. When someone says, "You're just like my mother or father!" there will be some truth to it. So why would we do something so counterintuitive as to pick the very person we vowed we would never pick? Hendrix suggests that we do so because it then affords us the unique opportunity to grow and to heal old wounds, without the impossible feat of going back and reliving our childhoods.

Reenactment Is a Given

People sometimes become frustrated, angry, and disappointed, and then act from their worst selves when they realize that they are breaking one of the vows they made as children. We replay the major functional as well as painful aspects of our childhoods, at least in our twenties and thirties—and very often well beyond—no matter how strongly we believe or vow otherwise. Each person typically does this in such a way that she is almost completely oblivious to it; she will be convinced that she has moved beyond early painful patterns because her nature is to do it this way.

We vow not to do certain things in *our* marriages that happened in our parents' marriages, and then years into our marriages we realize that we are doing the very same things, but with subtle, nuanced differences that allow us to be fooled into thinking that we aren't like our parents at all. But who *are* we going to be like when we grow up? The mailman? Only if it turns out that he is secretly our biological father.

Emotions Need to Be Expressed and Contained

People who believe that their emotions should always be expressed and *routinely acted upon* are at very high risk for doing great harm to their partners and ruining their romantic relationships. Emotions need to be expressed. There can be no emotional connection between people without that. But *emotions also need to be contained* at times. The belief that "if I feel it, I should act on it" is a dangerous one unless it is also tempered by a parallel belief that "I must evaluate which feelings to express, how to appropriately express them, and which ones to contain." Otherwise, we are nothing more than wild animals acting out our primitive impulses.

Human nature is to hurt the people closest to us; as the song goes, "You always hurt the ones you love." The obvious reason for this is that the only relationship a human has that taps directly back into primitive, right-brained, family-of-origin patterns is a romantic-sexual relationship. Our business relationships, tennis or golf buddies, and work mates all operate according to a much less stringent set of rules and expectations that are further helped by the less intimate nature of the relationship. Our greatest investments and our greatest potential for losses are with those with whom we are closest. But the people who are unable to rise above this aspect of human nature continue to have troubled or broken relationships until they change this pattern. In other words, we are responsible for our emotions and how we choose to act on them. Just because we *believe* that what we say or do isn't hurting anyone does not mean that it is true.

It is quite common to hurt people and think we're "just kidding," when in fact we're just hurting the person.

Struggle Is Good

More and more people in the United States are getting angrier and angrier or sadder and sadder because they have a tragically immature belief about the value of struggle. *Struggle is good.* Without it, we would not be alive. We would have no reason to exist. We would have no sense of accomplishment. The only time in our brief lives when we don't have to struggle is when we are in utero, or presumably, after we have died. When parents try to remove all the roadblocks from their children's paths, they simply create a fantasy world and an emotional prison for their children. If home is the only place on Earth where I don't have to struggle and I never learned how to appreciate struggle in the first place, then guess what? I can't leave home. Even if I leave home physically I'll never grow up and leave emotionally. Given these circumstances, why should I?

You Can't Change What You Aren't Willing to Admit, and What You Don't Admit Tends to Run the Show

If your home is in chaos, your children are out of control, you secretly resent your spouse for siding with the kids all the time, and you fantasize about running away to a remote tropical island with your next-door neighbor, but you aren't willing to admit any of these feelings to anyone, including yourself, then you surely aren't likely to change any of these things.

What's more, it is quite possible that you *will* run off with your next-door neighbor eventually. If you won't admit that there's a problem, how can you possibly fix it? And if you won't get the feelings out in the open, *whatever isn't discussed and talked out tends to get acted out.* Saying that you feel like running away isn't the end of the world. Waiting until you do run away may be the end of the world for you.

There Are Always Reasons and Payoffs for Our Unhealthy Behaviors; Otherwise We Wouldn't Engage in Them— Be Honest About What Those Reasons Are

This is a corollary to "You can't change what you aren't willing to admit." All human behavior is motivated by something. Human beings do not do things without a reason. Why would someone drink herself to death? Because the pain of dying from alcoholism does not seem as awful as the pain of living sober. Why would someone let his kids stay up until all hours of the night rather than enforcing a consistent bedtime? Because he wants to be liked, to be seen as the "good guy," or because the guilt he would feel if he did enforce a bedtime seems more painful than the consequences of letting them stay up.

Why would someone share her marital problems with her children rather than with her husband or other adults? Because children are vulnerable, accepting, need parents, and are a captive audience, and because talking with other adults is scarier than sharing that information with children, even though, at some level, we know that sharing these personal problems with children has no place in healthy parenting or family life. If we stated more bluntly what this strategy actually means for all involved, it would sound something like this: *I am too little to engage in constructive conflict with my partner, so I will be "open and honest with my children" about what is going on. But being hurt and little, I will say things like "Mommy fell out of love with Daddy, and it's her choice to leave, and Daddy doesn't want it to happen and is heartbroken."* That message is both awful and confusing for children.

Life Is Not a Test; It's an Experiment, So Give New Things a Try

There are no perfect planets, continents, nations, states, counties, communities, families, marriages, parents, or children. If people leave you with the impression that they have created perfect families, either they or you are deluded. No one is going to grade you on your life skills. No one is keeping score. You don't have to do it perfectly. You *can't* do it perfectly. You make mistakes. Some of these lead to temporary heartaches, but heartache is a necessary and deepening part of life. Nobody gets through life without some pain. Accept this truth and you will find the true joy that exists in life, side by side, with the moments of great sorrow that are experienced by *everybody*—not just you.

> OUR PLENTEOUS JOYS,
> WANTON IN FULLNESS,
> SEEK TO HIDE THEMSELVES IN DROPS OF SORROW.
> —William Shakespeare, *Macbeth*

CHAPTER 5

FEELINGS

The momentousness of emotions in human lives
stands in befuddling contrast to their impossible brevity.
Emotions are mental mayflies, rapidly spawned and dying almost
as quickly as they arose. . . . Like the ghost of Hamlet's father,
an emotion appears suddenly in the drama of our lives to nudge the
players in the proper direction, and then dissolves into
nothingness, leaving behind a vague impression
of its former presence.

—*Thomas Lewis, Fari Amini, and Richard Lannon,*
A General Theory of Love *(2000, p. 43)*

Understanding why human beings get caught in victim-perpetrator patterns of interacting is not possible without first understanding some of the basics about feelings. For the purposes of this book, we use the words "feelings" and "emotions" interchangeably.

Feelings are the fuel that drives all of our actions. They are the gasoline, the diesel, the nuclear energy, the solar radiation, the wind, and the ocean waves that give us life—the ability to function in the world and to make things happen. People who act as if they have no feelings are not deluding themselves, nor are they necessarily being defensive. They simply aren't aware of what makes a human being *act*. They still do things. They just don't know why.

A family can be nearly perfect in all other ways, but if that family isn't comfortable with feelings—if they stay up in their heads and intellectualize things like love and death and sex and conflict—then they probably struggle just as hard to have truly intimate relationships as the family that is troubled with more obvious problems. For many of our clients, coming to grips with this fact is the most daunting challenge that they face in therapy.

We in the United States are admired for our inventiveness, practicality, and fierce independence; we are also, however, viewed by many others in the world as uncaring, excessively entitled, naive, and violent. Ask the average American if he knows whether his neighbor is depressed, anxious, suicidal, or on the verge of divorce, and be prepared to get a nervous, blank stare. In Gallup's Well-Being World Polls conducted in 2010, Americans were listed twelfth on the list (Ray, 2011). We have more wealth than most people, but it doesn't seem to make us feel as good about ourselves as we would like to think.

The Subtlety and Nuance of Emotional Communication

Feelings are the same as emotions, and yet millions of people believe that they can have an *emotionally intimate* relationship with another person just by *talking about* feelings, which is quite a bind. How can one be emotionally connected by *not expressing* emotions? Talking about feelings isn't the same as expressing them. Feelings are not conveyed very clearly by intellectualizing them, yet millions of people intellectualize their feelings because it *seems* like a much safer and more adult way to communicate.

> *Talking about feelings isn't the same as expressing them.*

On the one hand, I can tell you in a calm, intellectual way, with flat affect and no change in facial expression, that I feel lonely and disconnected from you, but that statement is unlikely to reach your *heart*. On the other hand, I can get it across to you flawlessly in a few seconds if I actually *express and show that feeling*, as follows: With tears welling up in my eyes, with my lip quivering, with an ache in my heart, and an emptiness in my soul, I say to you, "I am *so* lonely, and I so *long* for what we used to have. I *miss* you so much. It feels like my heart is aching."

Granted, that would be a big risk. I'd be transparent and vulnerable, and I would have no guarantee that you would respond the way that I would like. I'd be out there all by myself, open and exposed. And there is always the danger that if you are really hurt and angry and unable to act from the better part of yourself, you might see it as the perfect opening to hurt me. "Yeah," you might say, sarcastically, "you *really* miss me. What a joke!"

Feeling the Feelings

Various texts have slightly different lists or combinations of what are considered the "primary feelings" that people experience. In the discussion below we first present a primary feeling or feeling cluster, followed by some of the words that express varying degrees of that feeling, and then those are followed in bold type by the evolutionary survival function of each feeling. In other words, several words fall under the category of *safety, warmth, comfort, and dependency*, and then the survival function of those feelings is *trust and hope*.

To understand what we mean by "evolutionary survival function," consider the fact that pack animals feel *loneliness* because it is necessary for pack animals to feel uncomfortable when they are separated from each other. The discomfort pushes them back into groups, which increases their chances of survival. Because they are not pack animals, snakes don't feel loneliness. Dogs, wolves, porpoises, chimpanzees, and *Homo sapiens* do feel loneliness.

At the end of each section, we describe the *extremes* on each feeling continuum, implying that between those extremes lies the healthy, functional, grown-up expression of that particular feeling cluster.

- **Safety, warmth, comfort, and dependency**/*okay/good/peaceful/ relaxed/calm/fine/trusting/free from anxiety*—**Trust and hope**

This cluster of emotions is the very base—the foundation—of a healthy family system. If, when you walk through the door of your home at the end of the day, you can't let your hair down, be yourself, and feel like everything in the world is okay no matter how bad your day has been, then your family system has a problem. When we are physically or emotionally in danger, this feeling of safety quickly diminishes. The *dependency* part of this feeling cluster refers to the fact that human beings are social animals who depend upon one another for our survival. In the hyperindependent United States, we need to learn to acknowledge our reliance on one another and to embrace the fact that only the *extremes of dependency* indicate a problem—that is, being *needy and clingy* or being *overly independent and need-less.*

Families can be *too safe*—with overprotective "helicopter parents" who do not let kids fall down and skin their knees either physically or emotionally. Or families can *always* meet their child's needs, leaving the child with doubts about her ability to meet her needs on her own. Or families can *lack adequate safety*—with emotional or physical abuse or neglect, expecting kids to grow up too soon, or inadequate boundaries and structure. Either extreme can cause problems.

• **Pain**/*hurt/damaged/wounded*—**Avoid or recognize damage**

Pain is essential for an organism's survival. Pain tells you when you should stop walking on a broken ankle, when you should avoid touching a hot stove, and when you should avoid someone who just gave you a black eye. Pain warns us when we have been damaged or when we are about to sustain damage, so this is crucial for emotional and physical health. In families in which pain is ignored, denied, minimized, or belittled, children lose critical survival information. If you minimize how painful an abusive relationship is, and make excuses for horrible treatment from another person, your life may be in danger. If you grow up in what we call a *pain denial family system*, you may have a difficult time realizing how and why you keep getting into really painful situations, and you won't have the crucial feedback you need in order to extricate yourself from the pain. Part of the survival mechanism of a domestic violence victim is to ignore emotional and physical pain, which paradoxically is part of what keeps that person stuck in the relationship. Pain is good. It helps us avoid further damage.

As for extremes, people can either *deny* their pain too often, or they can be *physical or emotional hypochondriacs*—focusing on every little ache and pain, or every little emotional injury, as if each were life-threatening.

- **Sadness**/*sad/melancholy/depressed/down/blue*—**Heal loss, grieve**

Sadness is the emotional world's immune system; it is the "healing feeling." As such, it doesn't require rescuing, fixing, analyzing, or "futurizing and cheerleading" (this is a nonintimate response that seems like a nice thing to say, as in, "I just know everything is going to be okay for you—you have it all together, trust me"). When we are sad, we just need to be seen, heard, understood, and witnessed. One of the most intimate interactions between two human beings is when one sheds tears with his eyes open, looking into the eyes of the other person, while both realize that neither needs to be fixed or rescued, and nobody needs to run out of the room, get angry, or rescue because of discomfort.

The extremes of sadness are either clinical depression or being constantly "happy" and upbeat in a Pollyannaish and shallow way, rather than in a realistic way.

- **Anger**/*mad/angry/irritated/annoyed "frustrated"/ticked-off/pissed/ furious/enraged*—**Set boundaries, create energy to make change**

Anger is there to set boundaries and to create the energy to make change. "No! For the last time! I don't want you to hug me right now!"

When a drunk driver killed Candy Lightner's daughter, Candy's anger—her outrage—gave her the energy and determination to fight on against near-hopeless odds to eventually get the drunk driving laws changed in the United States. She founded Mothers Against Drunk Driving (MADD).

We do not believe that anger ever occurs by itself, without first being *triggered* by fear/anxiety, hurt/pain, shame/embarrassment/feeling defective, or some combination of those feelings. For example, when we work with a person convicted of road rage, we ask him what his first feeling was when a car sped past him traveling at eighty-five miles per hour; a typical response is a boastful "I was pissed!" But of course, when someone endangers your safety that way, your first reaction is a *startle*, and being startled is just another word for being scared or frightened. The unconscious dialogue in the man's mind is, *You S.O.B.! You scared me! Nobody scares me! I'm going to get you for scaring me! I'm going to catch up with you and teach you a lesson!*

The extremes of anger lead to two common outcomes:

1. To express it too often and with too much intensity—that is, *overt rage.*
2. To hold it in so that it comes out sideways or indirectly, as in *passive-aggressive rage*—being "sweet and nice"; intellectualizing everything and thereby being extremely controlling while completely denying any anger or coercion (which often makes the other person feel agitated, "crazy," and very appropriately angry); digging one's heels in and passively refusing to cooperate; pouting; or being too easily hurt and punishing with silence (Evans, 1992).

We caution people that volume by itself does not indicate rage. One can whisper while grinding one's teeth or glaring in a menacing way and be rageful (just watch a few episodes of *The Sopranos*), and one can yell at the top of her lungs and *not* be rageful, as in this interchange: "I love you. I will always love you, but right now I am so angry at you that I can't figure out why I married you! You are SO frustrating at times!" The nonverbal spin that accompanies the emotion determines whether it is rage.

Because setting boundaries is important, people who do not express anger well are not able to attain very deep levels of intimacy.

- **Pleasure and joy**/*happy/ecstatic/enthralled/delighted/joyful/pleased*— **"Wants" and identity**

Pleasure and joy define our identities. We are defined by what we want and don't want, what we like and don't like, what stirs our souls and our passions and what doesn't, and what drives us to do the things we do and what doesn't. One person takes great joy in designing a house, another in solving a mathematical mystery, and another in teaching young children. Our wants and desires describe who we are. They are what distinguish each of us from the rest. Families or marriages that deny one's desires also deny that person's *self*. "I want a blue car" says something about who I am. "I want to put flowers on the table." "I want to listen to Beethoven's

Fifth Symphony." "I want to major in chemistry." If the reaction to such statements of yours is typically, "What do you want to do *that* for? That's stupid," then your "self"—your spirit, your soul, your identity—is being ignored, belittled, or crushed.

If you are thwarted in your developmental challenge to acquire your own true self, you won't experience or accomplish much of value in your life until you activate your *True Self*. An elegant and profound way of describing the maturation process from childhood into adulthood is to look at whether you have a *True Self*—a *Real Self*—or if who you are simply reflects a self that is an adaptation to what you were told to be or expected to be when you were growing up, without ever questioning that and discovering for yourself, on your own, if that is who you truly want to be.

The extremes of pleasure and joy are found in people who rarely do things that they find pleasing, or those who spend inordinate amounts of time and energy pleasing themselves to the detriment of their own growth, their relationships, or their livelihoods.

- **Shame**/*shameful/embarrassed/ashamed/broken/dirty/bad/unlovable/ defective/no good/worth less than others/better than others/superior/ inferior/stupid/ugly/unworthy*—**Accountability and spirituality**

Shame lets us be accountable, accountability lets us have humility, humility helps us to be spiritual, and spirituality allows us to have healthy power. One definition of a perpetrator is someone who is shameless. Having high self-esteem does not mean that we have no shame. It means we have *appropriate* shame. Shame is the feeling that we are flawed—that we have defects—and all human beings have defects. So all human beings feel some shame from time to time. When we can be embarrassed about those defects, we can change them.

"I keep making sarcastic comments to people, thinking that it's cute or funny. But Joe Smith called me on it in front of everyone the other day, and I was really embarrassed. It hurt, too. At first I was really angry at Joe and wanted to lash out and get even, but now that I've thought about it for a while, I think it's me who needs to change, not him. He was right." That is healthy shame in action.

Psychologist Gershen Kaufman (1980) noted that shame comes from the denial of our right to depend on others. When we feel cut off or alienated from the rest of the group or tribe, we feel shame. Shame can thus come in the form of feeling "less than" everyone else, but also from feeling "better than" everyone else, which is why the distorted sense of entitlement showing up in so many young adults nowadays is difficult to treat. If you're constantly told that you're better than everyone else, you'll probably become arrogant, snooty, spoiled, and narcissistic, which is the antithesis of humility and true power.

Kaufman wrote of the strong connection between shame and the defensive reaction of rage. *One of the most powerful ways to shame someone is to ignore him.* That is why people often react so violently and so deeply when someone ignores them, and is why being passive-aggressive is so destructive. When you reach out to a friend, hoping for a response, and you get no response at all, you have expressed your need for connection, which is an admission of your vulnerability, yet your need was ignored. It may even feel as if you have fallen into a dark, bottomless pit, and that something about you is "bad" or "wrong." Then you may feel like retaliating, and therein lies the rage.

What complicates the above example is that expecting others to always respond to our requests for attention isn't reasonable. People who are being narcissistic expect everyone to drop whatever they are doing and respond right away. For people who are on this extreme end of the shame continuum, sometimes the best thing that can happen to them is to be ignored.

As painful as shame is, one of the most holy, spiritual, and healing acts any human being can do is to openly acknowledge a defect: "Hi, my name is Phil, and I am an alcoholic," or "Hi, my name is Mary, and I hit my four-year-old daughter." One of the equally holy and spiritual acts one can do is to acknowledge and thank the other person for admitting her defect, and thereby honoring her and you. Some of the more complex paradoxes in human relationships are tied in with this very powerful emotion.

At one extreme are people who are so *shame-filled* that they feel worthless and broken; at the other extreme are people who appear to be *shame-*

less. While shame is present in all human beings, for some the shame is so well defended against that a person is not aware of it at all: "I don't have any shame. I'm great! I have high self-esteem! You're the one with the problem. You're suffering from low self-esteem!" Actually, one of the best ways to describe and define a bully—one who is mired in the perpetrator role—is one who appears to be shameless. "Uh, hmm, uh, I know I've made some mistakes in my life and that I have some defects, but right now I just can't think of any."

- **Guilt**/*guilty/conscience hurts/remorseful/did something wrong*
  —**Conscience drives us to correct our mistakes**

Guilt represents our conscience and is there to propel us in the direction of correcting our mistakes and making amends. Shame and guilt often occur at the same moment, but it is said that with shame, you feel like you *are* a mistake (core self has defects), whereas with guilt, you feel like you *made* a mistake (behavior needs to be corrected). It is easier to repair guilt than shame.

One extreme on the guilt continuum is for a person to have an *overactive conscience*, so the person is constantly paralyzed and tortured by pangs of guilt. In the 1970s and 1980s, millions of women who decided to go back to school and work were plagued by guilty feelings that their partners' reactions often magnified. "Who is going to cook me dinner every night after my long day at work if you're taking classes three nights a week?" "You'll be so tired that we won't have time for sex anymore."

For women especially, trying to balance work with the needs of family has prompted a number of researchers to conclude that the most stressful career of all is not air traffic controller or firefighter or police officer; it's being a working mother, for what should be obvious reasons. Caring for aging parents has also become one of the most stressful and guilt-inducing responsibilities for contemporary adults. Trying to balance the needs of others and one's own needs always induces some guilt.

The other extreme on the guilt continuum is to have an *underdeveloped conscience* or *no conscience at all*. The latter would be a sociopath. The former would be the child or adult who is so narcissistic that she finds it very difficult to empathize with others, especially the effects of her own behavior on others. We described a perpetrator as being *shameless*. She would also be someone with an underactive conscience and a limited ability to empathize with others. The result would be a person who doesn't apologize for having stepped on your toes because she isn't aware that she did, or because when you say "Ouch!" she fires back, "Why did you yell 'Ouch!' to me? I didn't do anything to you. *You* stuck your toes under *my* foot!"

In Erik Erikson's (1963) third stage of human development, *initiative vs. guilt*, which first appears from ages three to six, the challenge for the child is to begin *making things happen*, and the parents' job is to create enough structure for that child so that he does not harm himself or others. If parents have too many rules and restrictions, such as those that might be in play in a home that is not at all childproofed, then the child will start to feel like everything he does is *wrong*. If there are *no* limits and boundaries, then eventually that child learns from people outside of his limitless home that much of what he does is unacceptable to others, thereby inducing guilt. "I can jump on the couch and spill food all over the carpet in *my* house. Why can't I do it in *your* house?"

- **Fear**/*scared/afraid/terrified/petrified/worried/anxious/tense/nervous*
  —**Wisdom**

Fear gives us *wisdom*. Being fearless means doing foolish things. Being courageous means doing scary things because they must be done, but knowing how scared we are when we do them. Watch the opening minutes of the film *Saving Private Ryan*, depicting the Allied troops storming the beaches at Normandy during World War II, and this will be terrifyingly apparent. If you pretend you have no fear because whenever it occurred in your family, it was shamed and belittled—or because no one in your family acknowledged fear in front of you—then you will continue to burn your hand on the same stove or get hurt in the same kind of relationship over and over again.

If we never learned that expressing fear was acceptable and healthy, and because fear is such a vulnerable emotion, then when we feel it, we also feel very exposed. When we feel exposed—when the potential for harm increases enough—we protect ourselves with anger. If we are *very* threatened by something, and are equally defended against expressing fear, then we will likely go to the extreme of anger, which is *rage*.

One fear extreme is being fearless. If, while hiking, you thrust your hand under a rock and barely avoid being bitten by a timber rattlesnake, your fear will serve you well in the future—unless you pride yourself in being *fearless*. In that case, be sure to carry a snakebite kit and a vial of antivenom serum with you at all times. The other extreme is to be so paralyzed and constrained by fear that you won't even leave home, let alone go out onto the dance floor when someone asks you to dance.

- **Loneliness**/*lonely/disconnected/alienated/separated/longing for relationship*—**Embrace self, propel us into groups**

Loneliness is a very uncomfortable feeling, which causes many people to ask how it could be a positive emotion. Loneliness is positive because we have been able to survive on the planet longer, as social creatures, than if we were roaming the planet alone, foraging for food, isolated from one another. The discomfort of loneliness propels us into groups, and we are then more likely to survive. Recent research shows that people with a good support system also live longer and fight serious disease much better than people who are emotionally isolated from others. If you're interested, read cardiologist Dean Ornish's *Love and Survival* (1998). In it he cites most of the major studies that show the powerful effect of relationships on our physical health, including the conclusion that *the lack of truly intimate social support is more of a public health risk than smoking cigarettes.*

If we lack the unconscious rules that would make having complex relationships possible, then we eventually create a shell around ourselves so that we won't keep getting hurt. Unfortunately the shell we create is the very thing that prevents further relationships, so we become even more lonely and isolated. A negative spiral begins, and we get stuck. To get out of this trap we need to admit how lonely we are and then recognize that the loneliness is actually more harmful and painful than would be the hurt that comes from trying to make our relationships work.

The Neurotic Paradox first proposed by the neo-Freudians in the 1940s and 1950s stated that the very thing we need to do in order to get better and heal and become less neurotic is the same thing we fear the most, which places us in an endless loop. One of the authors (JCF) knew that to grow up, he needed to join a therapy group, but he avoided joining a therapy group for seven years because he was too frightened to do it.

The extremes of loneliness are either to be *isolated from people*, or to be so *constantly in need of connection* with others that we are debilitated by depression, anxiety, and loneliness when not always with someone—that is, a paralyzing fear of abandonment.

Working with These Feelings

In the next chapter, we try to help the reader understand how these feelings function in typical interpersonal interactions, how we can make sense of them and learn to express them well, and how we can learn to both *express them and contain them at the same time*, which is no small feat. As for learning what these feelings are and learning how to identify when we are experiencing them, we have had thousands of clients over the years who have printed these feelings words on index cards or the like. Then they placed their "feelings lists" in strategic locations (refrigerator, car dashboard, desk) so that they could begin to train their brains to connect them with their own internal states, as well as with external events that might be triggering these feelings.

Becoming adept at this activity can take a year or two of practice, which may seem like a long time, until you realize that once you become comfortable with them, and facile at identifying them fairly quickly, the quality of your life and your close relationships will be transformed. Our clients have shown us over and over, across the span of many years, that gaining this seemingly simple and trivial skill—which, once achieved, no longer seems trivial—transforms them and the way they interact in their most important relationships.

CHAPTER 6

FEELINGS IN ACTION

Anger sharply increases blood pressure on a short-term basis,
for instance, but it may well be the recurrent stewing over provocative
events that causes sustained hypertension in touchy people like Type A
executives. The limbic brain, unable to distinguish between incoming
sensory experience and neocortical imaginings, revisits emotions upon
a body that was not designed to withstand such a procession.

— *Thomas Lewis, Fari Amini, and Richard Lannon,*
A General Theory of Love *(2000, pp. 45–46)*

In the next section we focus in more detail on the roles of fear, hurt,
and shame—and, to some extent, loneliness and sadness—in triggering
anger in family and societal relationships, keeping in mind that while we
believe that *anger is a primary emotion, we don't believe that it ever occurs
by itself. Anger is always preceded by one or some combination of the following: fear, hurt, or shame. It can also serve as a cover for loneliness or sadness.*
[*Author's note*: A large portion of this chapter is adapted from our book,
The 7 Best Things (Happy) Couples Do.]

Shame and Hurt in the Front Yard

You are outside shoveling the snow off the stone walkway leading up to
your home. Your husband has just opened the garage door and is rolling
the trashcan out to the curb for the weekly pickup. As he turns and walks

back toward the house he sees you there, and suddenly he feels a wave of anxiety sweep over him. He approaches you hurriedly and says with a mix of a bark and whine, "Why don't you toss the snow over there?" as he points a commanding finger at a spot between the low-growing evergreens and the sugar maple you planted five years ago. "If you pile it where you're piling it now, you're gonna smother those evergreens!"

As if someone shot a syringe of pure adrenaline directly into your aorta, your blood pressure skyrockets, your heart races, your breathing quickens, and you feel a rage in your belly the likes of which you've never felt. You wheel around and face him with fire in your eyes and shout, "Why don't you shut the f— up!" *I never swear*, you tell yourself, horrified. You glare at him as he shrinks before your very eyes and then sheepishly skulks back into the house.

Fear and Loneliness in the Dining Room

You and your wife are having dinner together on a quiet Thursday evening. The week is almost over; it's been a long one, and tougher than usual. Neither one of you is in top form, yet you're enjoying being with each other without major distractions for the first time all week. You're peacefully discussing plans for the weekend. Suddenly you remember that you promised one of your good friends that you and your wife would go to the opening of the play he is in at the local community theater. The opening is tomorrow night. You genuinely forgot, and you're hoping beyond hope that your wife will look up, smile excitedly, and say, "Oh, great! I'm so glad we get to go! I'm so excited for him!" But she's not likely to say that. You know her better than that.

"You *what*?" she began, angrily. "What the hell were you *thinking*? I am *exhausted*!" She stood up from the table, whirled around, and as she stormed out of the dining room she yelled back, "You are *so* inconsiderate! I can't believe you!" You become engulfed by anxiety as you hear the bedroom door slam. Because you're tired, you can't soothe yourself. The fear gets bigger. It feels like the marriage is suddenly over. The gulf between the two of you is unbearable. Instead of settling yourself down, which would give her some room to do the same, you head upstairs to the bedroom. The door is locked. Your fear gets bigger. You're flooded.

You pound on the door and in desperation try to reason with her in a voice you hope is loud enough to pass through the door. She yells, "Stop yelling! Just go away! I just need some space!" Well, to a person who is on the verge of emotionally flooding, the phrase "I just need some space" is code for "I am locked in here because I am about to pick up the phone and call my associate from work who is divorced and who talks all the time about how much fun she's having dating and having sex with all these exciting new men she's found." You finally slip across the boundary between upset and flooded.

"Open this door *right now!* I *mean it! OPEN IT!*" You pound harder and harder until the doorjamb starts to split.

"That's it! I'm out of here!" she screams.

The Feelings Beneath the Rage

Scenes like the two scenes above are played out across the country in the homes of doctors, lawyers, plumbers, bricklayers, drug dealers, prostitutes, schoolteachers, psychologists, and everyone in between. They demonstrate two critical facts:

1. Violence and rage occur as a reaction to our own fear, hurt, and shame, and indirectly to our loneliness, sadness, or some combination of them all.
2. The violence and rage that we perpetrate on others happens, not because of something the other person does, but because of something we do not do—that is, control ourselves.

Fear, hurt, and *shame*—and, peripherally, *loneliness* and *sadness*—are pivotal emotions because they are involved in the *deepest connections* between people, as well as the *most damaging wounds* that people inflict on each other. When we say that "the deepest experience of intimacy takes place at the level of our weakness," we qualify it by adding, "but only if we stay 'big' and grown-up when we are being vulnerable."

Being Vulnerable Versus Being Out of Control

In order to have truly deep intimacy at the level of one's weakness, a person must be very strong. Healthy strength, of course, is the ability to experience emotions while keeping them relatively well contained, so that they do not spill over and flood everyone around us. Thus we note the profound difference between being with someone who is shedding tears profusely, sobbing with gut-wrenching grief and depth—but who we know is able to contain herself—versus being with someone who cries uncontrollably but leaves us with the fear that at any moment she will go off the deep end. The problem in trying to explain this, especially in a sound bite, is that on the surface the two instances look exactly alike, especially to someone who lacks emotional intelligence.

Consider the following reflection:

> When she'd come up and sit by me, I felt myself recoiling inside. I just assumed it was because I was a guy—you know, guys aren't supposed to be comfortable with feelings—but it wasn't because I was a guy. It was because she had no boundaries inside of herself. It was like her intestines were spilling out into my lap and onto the floor, and I was supposed to sit there calmly and take it all in, or be accused of lacking the ability to be intimate! I am so glad I talked to a therapist about this. It *was* me, but not in the way I first thought. It was me doubting my own perceptions.

The more at ease we become with the beauty of the complex parts of ourselves, the more distinct the line is between what this man just described and what this next man described

> We were having breakfast one Saturday morning and I started reading an article to her from the newspaper. It was an emotional story, and my lip started to quiver as I took a breath and looked up at her for a second. Her eyes had begun to well up with tears. I stopped. She started to speak, and her voice cracked as the tears trickled down her cheeks. "My father was so cruel," she began. "I don't know what was wrong with him. And my mother to this day has never acknowledged it. When I was a little girl he made nasty, snide

remarks to me for no reason. I was a sweet little girl trying to be good all the time. He said, 'You think you're so smart. Well, *I* know better.' I looked up into my mother's eyes hoping for something, anything, some acknowledgment that what he said was wrong, and she just looked down at the potatoes she was peeling and said, 'Come over here and help me. I always have too much work to do.'"

This man continued. "One of the things that I admire and appreciate so much about her is how she can do that. In all our years together, I have never felt smothered or engulfed by her feelings, and yet she is remarkably open without being out of control. She can be vulnerable without being needy. I have learned so much from her. She is such a gift."

The Difference Between "Falling Apart" and "Falling Together"

To understand what we are trying to get across here, you must realize that quite a few people would describe the women in both stories above as "having a breakdown." If it weren't so confusing for him, it would almost be comical to hear a man say, "I almost had a breakdown during our sales meeting when the CEO singled me out and started blaming me for the company's poor third-quarter performance. The two VPs and the entire sales force were at that meeting. Despite the fact that my sales exceeded everyone else's, I felt two inches tall!"

"You almost had a breakdown?" we asked.

"Yes. I could feel my lip start to quiver, and it was all I could do to keep my emotions in check."

"What happened next?"

"I composed myself and then I said, 'My sales figures are the best of the entire team. I think we can recover our performance if we look at what's really going on in the marketplace.'"

We said, "What a great way to handle it." Then we asked, genuinely puzzled, "So, where was the near breakdown?"

"You know. I almost cried."

One of us (LDF) helps clients distinguish between *falling apart* and *falling together*. As mentioned earlier, fear, hurt, and shame, and, peripherally, loneliness and sadness, are normal, healthy emotions. They are also very powerful emotions. When they are *not contained*, or when they aren't identified and acknowledged, they can lead to rage and violence or to extreme manipulation and smothering. When they *are integrated and contained*, they lead to the deepest levels of intimacy imaginable. People who get confused by this distinction . . .

- Have a hard time separating their own reactions from the reactions of others.
- Tend to clump all emotional reactions into one category and get flooded by their own or others' healthy emotions, or are not able to distinguish between emotions that are over the top and emotions that are expressed with integrity and grace.

Important "Feelings Facts"

When looking at the examples that opened this chapter, Daniel Goleman (1995) might say that these people's brains were being *emotionally hijacked*. John Gottman (1994) would probably call them instances of *emotional flooding*. Redford Williams and Virginia Williams of Duke University, authors of *Anger Kills* (1998), might be concerned that these people's elevated cortisol levels could create lesions inside their coronary arteries. James Masterson (1998) might say that they were not demonstrating the healthy *capacities of the real self*. David Schnarch (1997, 2009) might say that they were not self-soothing, were not acting with emotional integrity, were not well-differentiated psychologically, and were not displaying *grounded responding*. Whatever you call it, this inability to manage one's emotions isn't good for you, and it isn't good for the relationship.

In years of research with couples, John Gottman has shown that any interchange that occurs after you're flooded is going to damage the relationship. Really great couples have ways to *soothe* themselves and, indirectly, each other, so that the frequency and intensity of these incidents are minimized. But some people don't even know what is happening to them before, during, or even after such scenes.

Biology and psychology students learn that the most primitive defensive reactions are centered in what is referred to as the *reptilian brain*, because it's as complex as a reptile's brain: designed only to react quickly to the environment. That's pretty much it: *fight or flight*. These reactions are more complex in the case of mammals who have developed a *limbic system* in their brains. For a very well-written, comprehensive explanation of how this all works, see Daniel Goleman's *Emotional Intelligence* (1995), or Lewis, Amini, and Lannon's *A General Theory of Love* (2000), and study the sections on the brain and emotions. It is fascinating.

In a nutshell, a stimulus event happens—seeing a rattlesnake coiled up and ready to strike five feet in front of you, having your husband criticize the hard work you are doing, or believing that your wife is about to leave you—and then a rapid-fire sequence follows. Information hurtles back to the visual or auditory cortex of the brain so that you can see or hear what is happening. It then radiates back and down to the limbic system where you "feel" something about the information—fear, hurt, or shame, for example. Then the information radiates up into the cerebral cortex, the higher part of the brain that allows you to think, unlike a snake. We think, and then hopefully we temper our reaction to better fit the situation. Goleman pointed out one intriguing additional element in the sequence: in some cases a small portion of the stimulus event goes *directly* to the limbic system—where the more sophisticated emotions reside—via the thalamus, which is the gatekeeper of sensory experiences. In other words, we react to the rattlesnake—to use Goleman's example—a split-second before we actually "see" it. The upshot of all this activity is as follows:

- We respond very quickly to what is going on around us and inside of us.
- We're going to feel what we feel whether we *think* we will or not.
- In most cases, once we feel the feelings, *Homo sapiens* have the great good fortune to be able to *choose* how we further respond because we have a neocortex.
- People can get into trouble because they aren't aware of their feelings, or because they are *too* aware of them.

- Feelings are expressed nonverbally, so the words are almost irrelevant.
- While they are registered in the brain, feelings are *felt in the body*.
- *All* feelings are going on *all the time*. From the time you awaken in the morning until you fall asleep at night, you will have experienced all of these primary emotions numerous times, When you say, "I'm not feeling anything right now," we know that you must mean you aren't *aware* of what you're feeling right now.

Soothing Yourself

In *The Search for the Real Self: Unmasking the Personality Disorders of Our Age* (1998), psychiatrist James Masterson created a universal and timeless list he called "The Capacities of the Real Self." These capacities are what distinguish a mature, intact, integrated person from a less fully developed, perhaps wounded person. The capacities include the "ability to experience a wide range of feelings deeply," the "ability to be alone," and the "*ability to soothe painful feelings.*" The lack of this ability to soothe one's feelings is implicated in a wide range of mental health problems, but nowhere is its presence as obvious as in addictions and disorders of impulse control, especially rage problems.

When a wife goes into a rage and hurls a crystal goblet at her husband, the reason is her inability to soothe herself. When a husband gets so hurt by his wife's criticism of him that he stubbornly refuses to interact with her for days, and when his hurt is just as "big" three days later as it was when she first made the critical remark, it is often a self-soothing problem. Increasing the ability to self-soothe is one of the integral parts of David Schnarch's Crucible approach to couples therapy (1991, 1997, 2009). The ability to soothe oneself has biological as well as behavioral roots. In psychology graduate programs during the 1970s, the newly emerging field of newborn infant physiology was taking shape (e.g., Porges, Arnold, & Forbes, 1973). We learned that there are often vast individual differences in infants' reactivity to stimulation—that some infants remain calm and unflappable while others startle and cry when presented with the identical stimulus. Some seem to soothe themselves automatically, and others require a great deal of help from their parents.

By the time a person is an adult, it is hard to determine how much of this "soothing capacity" is learned and how much is physiological. We know that if you were traumatized repeatedly as a child, or if you suffered a massive single trauma, you *might* develop post-traumatic stress disorder (PTSD), the symptoms of which are now familiar to many people: over-reactivity to stimuli that parallel the original trauma, emotional numbing, powerful flashbacks, depression, and a generalized increase in emotional arousal. We now know that traumas like these can actually "turn on or turn off" certain genes and alter the neurochemistry of the brain, so that the change becomes *relatively* persistent. That is why beta-blockers such as propranolol have been shown to help with PTSD, especially if administered right after the traumatic event occurs (Vaiva, Ducrocq, Jezequel, Brunet, & Marmar, 2003).

Clinical depression can act as a magnifying glass for uncomfortable feelings such as anxiety, sadness, shame, hurt, and loneliness, and treating depression can often help a great deal. But make no mistake about it: a man who beats up his girlfriend, a woman who tries to scratch out her husband's eyes, or someone who runs another car off the road in a fit of rage is not necessarily suffering from PTSD or clinical depression. In fact, we suspect that a large number of these are not. You could just as easily raise a person who fails to soothe her feelings and therefore rages by babying and spoiling her as she grows up, exposing her to role models who display little impulse control, or constantly violating her age-appropriate boundaries as she is growing up, to name just a few.

Soothing Strategies

Physical Health

By far, the most common emotions involved in victim-perpetrator interactions are hurt, shame, and fear of abandonment, as demonstrated in the first two examples in this chapter. We are most likely to lose control when we feel under psychological attack or when we fear the loss of an important relationship. What can be done?

If you are having problems calming yourself or managing your feelings, look first at your physical health, which includes your neurophysiology and your diet. People can be irritable because of a shortage of serotonin, hormonal imbalances, dietary deficiencies, metabolic disorders such as hyperthyroidism, and what appears to be depression but may actually be hypothyroidism. You may have trouble soothing yourself if you drink too much coffee or if you have high blood pressure. Certain herbal supplements can cause all sorts of problems, including fatigue and memory difficulties. Ginseng can cause high blood pressure and nervousness in some people. We mention these first because they are often the last thing that anyone looks at in diagnosing emotional problems, and it would save a lot of pain and heartache if they were among the first.

How You Think

In *An Adult Child's Guide to What's "Normal"* (Friel & Friel, 1990), we included a chapter titled "You Are What You Think (Sometimes)." Therapists who help their clients by using cognitive behavior therapy (CBT) methods, and the researchers who developed these techniques (e.g., Beck, 1967; Ellis, 1975; Padesky, 1995), know that the general way in which we view the world has a tremendous impact on how we handle our feelings. It has recently been demonstrated that doing cognitive behavioral training with people who have severe obsessive compulsive disorder (OCD) can not only help them begin to manage their obsessing and repetitive behaviors by managing how they think, but when they do, their brain activity changes just like it would if they were being treated for the problem with medication. In other words, our brain chemistry affects how we think, but in some cases, how we think can also alter our brain chemistry.

Martin Seligman, past president of the American Psychological Association and author of the bestselling *Learned Optimism* (1991) is one of many experts who have made cognitive behavioral therapy available to the general public in a very user-friendly form. He shows his readers how to correct the kinds of negative thinking that keep many people stuck in the victim role. For some people, adversity is quickly framed as a challenge to be faced and eventually overcome, even if overcoming the adversity means accepting tragic loss and moving on to a new life. For others, adversity is quickly interpreted as further proof that "life's a bitch and then you die."

Many clients over the years have told us that events they are able to handle quite well in the present would have thrown them into an irreversible tailspin a few years earlier. They attribute much of the difference to changes in the way they think about the world. "Life's a bitch and then you die" is one way to look at an imperfect world in which painful and unfair things happen to everybody, and if you're wearing just the right pair of lenses, the world fits it perfectly. Of course, what we see is often what we get. A person might have an attitude that results in the following: "My lenses actually help me create the kind of miserable life with which I am so unhappy. If every twist or turn in the road is met by my whines of misery, then of course, the only people who will tolerate being around me are either other victims like myself, or perpetrators. Either way, they'll make my life even more miserable."

But with a different set of lenses, voilà! "Life's a bitch and then you die" becomes "Life is a wondrous mystery filled with routine annoyances, frustrations, tragedy, unbearable misery, rapturous joy, and the endless excitement that comes with getting up each day, meeting the people we meet, loving those we love—and getting angry at them—and continuing to grow and deepen right up until the day we die." It's the difference between having and not having trust and hope in the face of seemingly hopeless situations, which leads to the next source of soothing.

Connections with Others

Because human beings are the ultimate social animals, disconnections from each other are prime sources of intense distress. By the same token, *healthy connections with others are the primary source of trust and hope.* In summarizing a large-scale study of adults who experienced significant trauma in childhood, distinguished developmental psychologist Urie Bronfenbrenner of Cornell University found that only one thing separated those who eventually "made it" psychologically from those who didn't: having at least one person in your life when you were a child who was "just plain crazy about you." As we have mentioned before, having truly intimate relationships increases our resistance to all sorts of problems, including physical illnesses. Dean Ornish noted that there is a new field called "psychoneuroimmunology"—the study of the effects of social factors on the immune system of animals. In discussing what psychologists call the theory of "object relations," he noted:

> People often develop patterns of relating as adults that are not so different from how they learned to relate as children. If you grew up in a family in which love, nurturing, and intimacy are in short supply, then you are more likely to view your current relationships with mistrust and suspicion. (1998, p. 39).

Of course, the reverse is also true. If you grew up with healthy love from your family, then you are more likely to be "open and trusting in your ongoing relationships" (Ornish, 1998, p. 39). The bottom line is that one of the most important soothing agents a human being can employ is the support and friendship of other human beings. For men, it is especially important that a good chunk of this support come from nonsexual, nonromantic relationships, because putting all of one's needs for intimacy into a romantic type of relationship can be risky and additionally stressful.

Before we close this chapter, remember that most people in the United States die of diseases of lifestyle—lack of exercise, poor diet, smoking, alcohol and drugs, stress, and above all, lack of true emotional support. All these risk factors increase stress. Learning to reduce these risk factors not only increases your life span but it also soothes you, and soothing yourself in healthy ways means that you will be less likely to slip into victim-perpetrator interaction patterns in your daily life.

Part Three:

Painful Patterns and Their Intriguing Causes

When pain has been intertwined with love and closeness, it's very difficult to believe that love and closeness can be experienced without pain.

—*Gloria Steinem,* Revolution from Within:
A Book of Self-Esteem

CHAPTER 7

PARALYZING POLARITIES: VICTIM-PERPETRATOR INTERACTION PATTERNS

> You know you are becoming a *competent, healthy adult* when
> you can choose the discomfort of *fear, hurt, shame,* or *loneliness* rather
> than *hurt yourself, hurt others,* or *let others hurt you.*
>
> —*John and Linda Friel*

Tit for Tat

Everyone has a *perpetrator* ("too mean") part, a *victim* ("too nice") part, and hopefully, a *grown-up—psychologically differentiated—* part (Larson, 1999, 2009, 2010a, 2011; Maddock & Larson, 1994, 1995; Friel & Friel, 1995; Schnarch, 1991, 1997, 2009). Within a given individual, these parts come in different sizes.

Someone who tends to be overpowering and domineering may be 60 percent perpetrator, 20 percent victim, and 20 percent grown-up. One who lets oneself be taken advantage of most of the time may be 75 percent victim, 10 percent perpetrator, and 15 percent grown-up. In many marriages that contain mild to moderate incidences of domestic violence (pushing, shoving, blocking, screaming, nasty name-calling), both partners may be

45 percent perpetrator, 45 percent victim, and 10 percent grown-up. In relationships that can be described as dangerously violent and abusive, the person who repeatedly beats one's partner is often 80 percent perpetrator, 15 percent victim, and 5 percent grown-up; the other partner in this relationship may be 80 percent victim, 10 percent perpetrator, and 10 percent grown-up. These numbers can vary quite a bit from one relationship or family to another.

While very informative and useful, static percentages like these are like taking a snapshot of a marriage or a family. The snapshot contains a lot of information—who is standing next to whom, who is smiling, who looks scared or sad or joyful—but a snapshot lacks the massive amounts of information that are contained in a moving picture of the same people. In a film or video we have the opportunity to see the *interaction patterns* among all of the people involved.

We might see the little brother being silly while everyone focuses on him in order to distract themselves from the underlying tensions in the family. We might see Mom try to be affectionate toward Dad, while Dad acts annoyed that she is trying to get close to him. We might see the older sister anxiously trying to get everyone arranged "properly" for the photo shoot. We might see Dad snap at Mom, and Mom putting her tail between her legs as if she actually did something wrong, even if she didn't. We might see the older brother resisting the whole process, trying to get away from the family because he "has something better to do," but in fact he's trying to get away because he believes that there is no way for him to be seen and heard and understood, and he's actually hurt and angry. These are *interactional patterns*.

In ecological-systemic therapy (Maddock & Larson, 1995; Larson, 2010b; Maddock, Friel, & Friel, 2009), the primary focus of treatment is not each of the individuals in the system. The primary focus is on the *victim-perpetrator interaction patterns* between family members, or between partners in a marriage. This is a unique and powerful way of looking at human problems, and because it is a more complex way of looking at things, not all therapists are comfortable with it. But remember, when one lets life become as complicated as it really is, it often becomes much simpler to comprehend.

When the grown-up part of both partners is smaller than the combined total of the victim and perpetrator parts—for example, 20 percent grown-up, 40 percent perpetrator, 40 percent victim—the chances increase dramatically that people will engage in what our colleagues, psychologists David Schnarch and his wife, Ruth Morehouse, have so aptly termed *normal marital sadism* (Schnarch, 2009). These are the commonly occurring, cruel things that people do to one another when they have been frightened, feel ashamed, or hurt and wounded by their partner, but are not grown-up enough to contain their own emotions; they are unable to act from their best selves. She gets hurt, scared, and ashamed. Then she slices back with an equally painful emotional paper cut that nicks and wounds. He responds in kind. An eye for an eye. Tit for tat. "I'll stop doing it if you do, but don't expect me to be the first to stop, because I'm not grown-up enough to handle it if I stop and then you don't."

The example above is a systemic blueprint for a never-ending, circular series of mutual emotional torture sessions. On and on it goes—an *interactional pattern* of mutual victimization/perpetration that can continue for days and days, punctuated by fitful sleep in a bed where you are miles apart from your partner; pouty avoidance around the breakfast table; cold, lonely, empty Sunday afternoons; and tiptoeing around each other in front of the children at the Sunday dinner table, so that by the end of the weekend the kids have stomachaches and the adults are numb.

She makes a nasty comment about how she believes that he doesn't provide for his family as well as George next door. Her nonverbal messages may even be more powerful than her words. She may have a pronounced tone of disappointment in her voice and a powerful facial expression that says, "I am *so* disgusted with you as a husband right now."

He immediately floods (Gottman, 1994) with shame—he has a shame attack—followed instantly by rage, the emotion that typically bursts forth from the depths of a shame attack (Kaufman, 1980). "You are such a spoiled brat!" he shouts. "You are such an ingrate! A princess! You are a

worthless load! You do *nothing* to contribute to this family aside from getting your hair and nails done and playing golf with your deadbeat friends
who suck blood from their husbands!"

His cruise missile scores a direct hit. She is hurt, wounded, humiliated,
devalued, and then . . . enraged even more. "You worthless piece of ——!
How *dare* you! You've been a loser since the day we met. You were living
off your parents' money and acting like you were the king of the world.
You were so entitled and spoiled! It was pathetic!"

"And you were a controlling, know-it-all b——! I supported you
through your last year of medical school and you never once thanked me
for it. You looked down on my financial services career despite the fact
that I have earned double your physician's income every single year since
we got married! You think I'm a loser? You're pathetic! Worthless!"

When couples are *gridlocked* (Schnarch, 1991, 1997, 2009) like this,
there are only three possible outcomes. They remain gridlocked and torture each other for decades; one or both individually decide to grow up
regardless of whether their partner does; or they head for divorce court.

The Power/Control Dialectic

Some people are bullies. Other people are unconsciously attracted to
bullies and are more subject to being bullied. Yet in our thirty years of
clinical experience, we have encountered thousands of people who are
also capable of altering those destructive tendencies so that the victim-
perpetrator interaction pattern subsides enough for them to have deeply
intimate, loving relationships.

In any system, change cannot happen until the system becomes unstable. When a man or woman feels the anxiety that comes with disequilib-
rium in the marital and family system, and then chooses to capitalize on
that small window of opportunity by making a few small, positive changes
before the old system pulls everything back into its original balanced state,
miracles can happen; we see them every day.

People who have learned to *combine grace and power* spend the majority of their time engaging in neither of these painful patterns of behavior.

They find ways to meet their needs and the needs of their families while remaining socially appropriate, respectful, and kind; while having personal integrity and decency; and yet the individuals involved remain powerful, competent, and effective. Some of this is pure luck of the draw. If you were born into a relatively healthy family, you would have learned how to be this way by unconsciously absorbing the behaviors that were around you all the time, without even thinking about it. If you weren't so fortunate, then you learned these patterns of interacting the hard way—through life experience and perhaps even extended psychotherapy.

No matter how you learned them, a fact of nature is that *power* and *control* are essential components of everyday human existence, whether you choose to believe that they are or not. As Maddock and Larson have stated so eloquently and clearly,

> Both power and control are necessary and legitimate components of human experience, particularly in the context of close, ongoing relationships. If not kept in balance, however, they can become distorted and create negative interaction patterns, including within the family (Cartwright, 1959; Cromwell & Olson, 1975; Gray-Little & Burks, 1983; Haley, 1976; Stock, 1985).
>
> In its simplest dictionary definition, power is the *capacity to influence*. Power is the energy of life, literally and figuratively moving out and taking up space in the world. Control can be defined most simply as a reciprocal to power, that is, as the *capacity to restrain or regulate influence*. Control is the boundedness of life, recognized in the inevitable limitations on everything that exists. In our view, power and control are interactive concepts that can be understood best in relation to each other. Defined in this way, a deeper meaning arises out of the tension between them, and the terms can be combined into a single dialectical construct: *power/control*.
>
> The human experience of power/control is the experience of living as a self interacting with a world. . . . If control becomes excessive in a relationship, the opportunity for individual self-expression or self-actualization is reduced; when power dominates, the stage is set for competition and conflict. In human interactions that are positive and effective, a balance of

power/control is achieved. The result is an experience of *mutuality*, in which the characteristics of each party to the interaction are influential in the outcome, and regulation is a shared endeavor (Erikson, 1959, 1968; Wynne, 1988). In the experience of mutuality, each individual can retain a sense of self-identity and worth while simultaneously feeling connected and even intimate with others as part of a larger relationship system (Stierlin, 1969; Wynne, 1988). Put another way, in a relationship characterized by balanced power/control, or mutuality, participants are both *a part* of the relationship and *apart* from the relationship as individuals. Although there are numerous family dynamics influencing the evolution of violence or abuse, probably most important are the distortions in power/control which arise within the family's two major dyadic structures—male-female and parent-child relationships. (1995, pp. 54ff.)

Understanding Power and Control in Everyday Life: Power, the Capacity to Influence

Imagine that you are in a seminar with twenty-four other participants. The room is full. A man carrying an oversized satchel bursts through the door, thrusts himself in front of the podium, and grandly announces, "I have $26 million in this satchel, and I will give each one of you $1 million, including the seminar leader, if one of you stands on his or her head in the corner of the room continuously for a half hour. You can figure out how to do it in any way you'd like. You can take turns holding the person up by their ankles, or whatever else you think would allow you to earn the $1 million." Would you do it? We would. We'd all be millionaires!

Imagine that you are in the same seminar room, and crashing through the back door of the conference room come four men brandishing fully loaded AK-47s. They surround the room while the leader bolts to the podium and fires several rounds into the right knee of the conference presenter, who falls to the floor, screaming, writhing in pain, with blood splattered all over the front of the room. The leader shouts, "One of you needs to stand on his or her head in the corner of the room continuously for thirty minutes. I don't care how you accomplish this. You can help each other in any way you see fit. But if you do not accomplish this in the next thirty minutes, we will systematically kill every one of you." Would you do it? We would. We'd all remain alive.

Imagine that during the middle of a seminar, the door off to the side of the front of the room opens very slowly and quietly. A small man pokes his goofy but intriguing head into the room and looks around, and then the rest of him follows, just as slowly and carefully. He is an interesting-looking fellow. He walks up to the podium with a disarming, calm, gentle confidence, then nods to the presenter as if to ask, "May I?" The presenter steps aside as if he had been expecting the man to take over the lecture right at that moment, even though he hadn't. The man turns toward the group and looks everyone in the eyes as he speaks in a warm, loving, accepting voice. Everyone is drawn right into his gaze, already in a light trance.

He talks about how lonely people are nowadays, and how much they long for love and connection. He praises them for being here, together, today, and he talks about the power of the Holy Spirit, and how he can feel the Holy Spirit in the room more and more as they listen to him and open their hearts to the love emanating from the people sitting next to them. He offers that God doesn't expect much from us, except for a small sign now and then that we believe in him. He smiles softly and warmly, suggesting that even a gesture like one of the group members standing in the corner on his or her head continuously for thirty minutes might just be all that God was looking for, and that he could feel the Holy Spirit hovering in the room now, and he could feel the Spirit choosing someone to stand on his or her head, and suddenly one of the participants stands up and shouts, "It's me! The Spirit has chosen me!" Sighs of surprise and affirmation fill the air, and quickly everyone is standing up, moving toward the corner of the room, so that they can help that person accomplish the Lord's task. When they are all done, they feel warm and connected and intimate and at peace, and then the man asks them to open their wallets and purses and contribute to the glory and love of the Spirit in the land, which they quickly and joyfully do. Would you do it? Millions of people around the world would.

Imagine that you are attending a team-building seminar paid for by the corporation for which you work. The seminar leader presents a group of twenty-five participants with a challenge: "Is there any way that one of you—a former high school gymnast or compulsive exerciser—could stand on his or her head in the corner continuously for thirty minutes?" It is a challenge to the group, and immediately the group springs into action, asking clarifying questions and discussing among themselves solutions to the problem that would ensure success. "Can we help the one who chooses to do it?" they ask. "Yes," the leader answers. "Can we trade off who helps at any given time?" they ask. "Yes," the leader answers. They then proceed to pick who they all agree would be the most fit person to try standing on her head for thirty minutes, and then they decide who will hold her up by her ankles for the first five minutes, the second five minutes, and so on. Then they do it. At the end of the exercise, the team-building leader praises them for a job well done. If you were in this situation, would you do it? Of course you would.

Power is neither good nor bad. It is without judgment. It is an essential part of the proper functioning of the universe. It isn't either/or; it just is. It's what we *do* with it that creates a tale. As Maddock and Larson (1995) wrote, "In its simplest dictionary definition, power is the *capacity to influence*. Power is the energy of life, literally and figuratively moving out and taking up space in the world."

Control: The Capacity to Restrain or Regulate Influence

If you think about it for a moment, *control* is what we do when we feel *afraid*. A few of the words in the English language that capture nuances of this primary emotion include "fear," "scared," "afraid," "anxious," "worried," "tense," "terrified," "petrified," and "concerned." We try to control the temperature in our homes because we are afraid that we will either freeze to death or die of heatstroke—or that, at the very least, we will be physically uncomfortable.

When a dear friend tells us, in a state of heightened distress, that her boyfriend hit her again and broke one of her teeth, our biological human response as a social animal is to feel *anxious*. We are anxious because we see a fellow human being in pain. A reptile would not feel that anxiety, which requires at the very least some rudimentary empathy regarding a fellow creature's distress. In order to reduce *our own feelings of distress*, we try to reduce our friend's distress with attempts to control her. "You need to file a police report." "You need to go stay with someone else so that he can't find you and do it again." "You need to get an attorney and have a restraining order put in place so that he has legal consequences if he ever does it again." The *paradox*, of course, is that the more distressed and helpless she becomes, the more we try to control her behavior to get her to do what we are logically certain she must do in order to solve the problem. But the more controlling *we* become, the more we enter into the *same victim-perpetrator interaction pattern* with her that is already at the root of her problem. In our attempts to be helpful, *we become perpetrators*, until we get so frustrated with her paralysis—that is, scared that she won't be safe—that we let her see our frustration. We get mad at her, and then we bully her. "I've told you a dozen times to get counseling and legal help! Why won't you do what I'm telling you?" Now she feels embarrassed, ashamed, and then angry—at us! It's the same dead-end, circular pattern of interaction that was there in her life all along, and we have simply been drawn into it as (unconsciously) willing participants.

Control is about trying to manage one's own fear. For those of us who live on the Mississippi River, the locks and dams constructed by the Army Corps of Engineers are part of the lifeblood of our communities. They ensure the stability of our economies, the safety of our homes and neighborhoods, and the quality of our recreational experiences. But from time to time, the Mighty Mississippi decides to take charge and overflow its banks, while members of the Army Corps of Engineers are left to scratch their heads and admit that they simply can't control everything on Earth.

Exerting control over those for whom we have solemn responsibility is of paramount importance. If you are a teenager and you say that you want to join your friends for a weekend at someone's parent's cabin at Lake Tahoe or "Up North" in northern Minnesota, your parents' job is to determine the proper amount of control to exert. If you are fourteen, your parents might be very hesitant. They might ask you how many adults will be supervising, who will be driving the several cars that will be traveling the 200 miles on curvy roads to get to the cabin, and they might want to speak directly to the parents and size them up before they make the final decision as to whether you can go. When you say that your friend's parents will actually be in Washington, D.C., on business, and that the chaperone for the whole weekend will be your friend's eighteen-year-old brother, your parents will probably exert extreme control and flatly deny the request— and if they are healthy parents, they will be able to tolerate your initial anger and then lead you into some weekend activities that you will enjoy more than if you'd gone to the cabin . . . where, as it turns out, three kids used cocaine, one drove his car into a tree while drunk, and four spent the night in jail. Saying "no" is an appropriate use of control and an appropriate creation of a systemic boundary. There are limits as to how much freedom a fourteen-year-old should have, and kids need to have parents who can set appropriate limits.

Say that you are the husband of a severely alcoholic wife. She is an award-winning cardiologist who has tried very hard to get and stay sober by attending three twenty-eight-day inpatient treatment programs for alcoholism during the past seven years at Hazelden's Residential Treatment Program in Center City, Minnesota, and she is still struggling with her alcoholism. You may be faced with some dicey control dilemmas. Do you comb the house every day, searching for that very last bottle of whiskey that she actually stashed in a secret removable cinder block in the southwest corner of the foundation of your house that you never suspected had been turned into a place to stash booze? And if you were to find it after many hours of angst and toil, would it make any difference? If someone is under the spell of a full-blown alcohol addiction, could *anyone*, let alone a smart nuclear physicist like you, *really* stop her from drinking if she wanted to? Addictions are bigger than all of us put together. *Life* is bigger than all of us put together. So what do you do? Do you finally surrender and admit that *your* addiction to *her* addiction has gotten *out of control*,

READER/CUSTOMER CARE SURVEY

HEFG

We care about your opinions! Please take a moment to fill out our online Reader Survey at **http://survey.hcibooks.com**.
As a **"THANK YOU"** you will receive a **VALUABLE INSTANT COUPON** towards future book purchases
as well as a **SPECIAL GIFT** available only online! Or, you may mail this card back to us.

(PLEASE PRINT IN ALL CAPS)

First Name _____ MI. ___ Last Name _____

Address _____ City _____

State _____ Zip _____ Email _____

1. Gender
☐ Female ☐ Male

2. Age
☐ 8 or younger
☐ 9-12 ☐ 13-16
☐ 17-20 ☐ 21-30
☐ 31+

3. Did you receive this book as a gift?
☐ Yes ☐ No

4. Annual Household Income
☐ under $25,000
☐ $25,000 - $34,999
☐ $35,000 - $49,999
☐ $50,000 - $74,999
☐ over $75,000

5. What are the ages of the children living in your house?
☐ 0 - 14 ☐ 15+

6. Marital Status
☐ Single
☐ Married
☐ Divorced
☐ Widowed

7. How did you find out about the book?
(please choose one)
☐ Recommendation
☐ Store Display
☐ Online
☐ Catalog/Mailing
☐ Interview/Review

8. Where do you usually buy books?
(please choose one)
☐ Bookstore
☐ Online
☐ Book Club/Mail Order
☐ Price Club (Sam's Club, Costco's, etc.)
☐ Retail Store (Target, Wal-Mart, etc.)

9. What subject do you enjoy reading about the most?
(please choose one)
☐ Parenting/Family
☐ Relationships
☐ Recovery/Addictions
☐ Health/Nutrition
☐ Christianity
☐ Spirituality/Inspiration
☐ Business Self-help
☐ Women's Issues
☐ Sports

10. What attracts you most to a book?
(please choose one)
☐ Title
☐ Cover Design
☐ Author
☐ Content

TAPE IN MIDDLE; DO NOT STAPLE

BUSINESS REPLY MAIL
FIRST-CLASS MAIL PERMIT NO 45 DEERFIELD BEACH, FL

POSTAGE WILL BE PAID BY ADDRESSEE

Health Communications, Inc.
3201 SW 15th Street
Deerfield Beach FL 33442-9875

FOLD HERE

Comments

that *you* therefore have a problem that is systemically just as large as hers, and that whether or not she goes to Alcoholics Anonymous, you should be going to Al-Anon meetings to help you learn how to (a) stay connected to the woman you dearly love while (b) remaining disconnected from and uninvolved with her battle with her own addiction? Remember what Maddock and Larson wrote: "Put another way, in a relationship character-ized by balanced power/control, or mutuality, participants are both *a part* of the relationship and *apart* from the relationship as individuals"(1995, p. 56). The well-known Alcoholics Anonymous "Paradox of Surrender" suggests that this would be your wisest strategy—the paradox being that when you are finally able to stop being so *willful* (controlling), and are able to *become willing* to surrender to the fact that all of your attempts to control have been to no avail, the chances that things may improve almost immediately increase.

In the Preface to our first book, *Adult Children: The Secrets of Dys-functional Families* (Friel & Friel, 1988), we described codependency as the "chase-your-spouse-around-the-house-with-the-self-help-book-syndrome" (p. viii). This power/control interaction dynamic isn't just a feature of alcoholic families. It's not just about frightened, desperate wives or husbands trying to do battle with their spouse's alcoholism by attempting to micromanage an addictive behavior over which neither they nor their spouse have any control.

In close, ongoing relationships, people frequently try to control others' behaviors because they are frightened. In domestic violence relationships, the person in the victim role tries to control all kinds of things. She tries to make sure that the children are quiet and studiously doing their home-work when Dad gets home from work. She tries to ensure that the house is picked up and that a perfect meal is on the table when he gets home from work, and when he is two hours late from work, she tries to make the best of it rather than getting upset. She tries to make sure that the children stay out of his way after he gets home, and that no demands are placed on him in the evening that might trigger one of his tantrums. She tiptoes around her daily existence while the imbalance of power/control between them gradually erodes what little remains of the foundation beneath their relationship. As this imbalance gradually erodes her own foundation, she awakens one day to realize that she no longer knows who she is, what she wants, what she likes, or what she wants to do next with her life. By being so out of balance she has lost herself in the service of trying to prop him up and support his "littleness." This kind of systemic imbalance can only be corrected by a *disturbance in the system* that will make the whole family uncomfortable before it eventually allows the emergence of a healthier interaction pattern based on mutual respect and functional boundaries. As Maddock and Larson stated, "Control is the boundedness of life, recognized in the inevitable limitations on everything that exists" (1995, p. 55). When we are able to admit that life is bigger than all of us, and that the gracious acceptance of these limits—the most profound of which is our own death—is what separates the men and the women from the wounded boys and girls, then we find that we can truly appreciate and find joy in the fact that life at times is messy and incomprehensible.

CHAPTER 8

NASTY-NICE IN A NUTSHELL

God, grant me the serenity to accept the people
I cannot change, the courage to change the person I can,
and the wisdom to know it's me.

—*Author unknown,*
with a nod to Reinhold Niebuhr

In Chapter 3 we presented some real-life illustrations of the differences between being too mean, being too nice, and demonstrating authentic grace and power. The elements in the following table are more explicit examples of the characteristics that separate those three ways of handling one's life anxieties.

Early in the process of self-discovery, many people have difficulty discerning the difference between *victim* and *perpetrator*, between *nasty* and *nice*, or between having *competent power* and being a *bully*. We feel that it might be helpful to give the reader a view of these differences *from many different angles*, because we realize that understanding any system often requires building a three-dimensional, "holographic" image of the many interrelated parts of the system, until at some point they all converge into a single, simple, coherent picture.

When our clients begin their therapy process, or when participants begin our three-and-a-half-day ClearLife® Clinic, we tell them that they will absorb a certain amount of what occurs during the process, and that they needn't worry about absorbing it all. As they absorb and digest one part of the system from which they came, or in which they are now embedded, they will eventually find themselves able to absorb the next part, and then the next.

In that spirit we present the following table.

GROWN UP
Psychologically Differentiated

TOO NASTY	HEALTHY RANGE	TOO NICE
Too much power—not enough self-control	Thoughtful use of power—balance of power and control	Too much self-control—not enough healthy power
Too nasty	Kind/assertive	Too nice
Perpetrator	Grown-up, differentiated	Victim
Rigid boundaries	Clear, flexible boundaries	Weak boundaries
Invulnerable	Appropriately vulnerable	Too vulnerable
Domineering, over-powering with words and body language	Staying put, engaging, not being frightened, and therefore working to push for resolution via dialogue	Yielding, shrinking, feeling paralyzed and speechless; just wanting the tension to abate
Overtly aggressive	Assertive	Passively aggressive
Temper/sarcastic/dismissive/name-calling/cynical/argumentative/combative/tactless/rude/bully/too hard/condescending	Not easily bullied or intimidated/Not bullying or intimidating/Force and power derived from being centered and calm and determined to move through conflict/Not willing to lose self in the process	Appeasement/being "little"/overly solicitous/never saying anything harsh or "mean"/being "oh so nice"
Cruel	Respectful	Overly solicitous/enabling
Mean	Loving	Groveling

GROWN UP Psychologically Differentiated *(continued)*

TOO NASTY	HEALTHY RANGE	TOO NICE
Often expresses contempt for religion as a cover to avoid acknowledging one's healthy vulnerability	Does not confuse religious belief with the need to assert one's personal power in relationships	Hides behind religious platitudes as a cover to avoid standing up for self
Never defers	Thoughtfully defers	Always defers
Blames others	Integrity/accountability	Blames others
Only "I" count	We "both" count	Only "you" count
Uses anger too much/ intimidates/bullies	Uses anger well/balances anger with kindness and empathy	Avoids anger/stores anger/ then rages from time to time
Never compromises	Compromises with concern for both people	Always compromises
Unwilling to surrender	Grasps the paradox and value of thoughtful surrender	Always surrenders
Insensitive	Sensitive	Too sensitive
Cynical/skeptical	Realistic	Too trusting/naive/ Pollyannaish
Cavalier	Both reverent and playful	Too serious
Too sincere	Both reverent and playful	Too sincere
Acts from woundedness	Acts from healed self and continually healing self	Acts from woundedness
Grandiose	Self-possessed	Feels worth-less-than
Not emotionally trans-parent/emotionally and personally guarded	Appropriately emotionally transparent in intimate relationships/appropri-ate boundaries in other relationships	Too transparent/ boundary-less/shares too much, too often, with too many people

GROWN UP Psychologically Differentiated *(continued)*

TOO NASTY	HEALTHY RANGE	TOO NICE
The normal need to depend on others is frightening, resulting in keeping everyone at arm's length with abrasiveness and hostility	Acknowledges healthy dependency on others without giving up identity and self in the process	The normal need to depend on others is frightening, resulting in the inability to admit own needs and the appearance of being need-less and "strong" without actually being strong inside
To manage life's anxieties and uncertainties, breaks rules beyond what most would consider reasonable; cites and rigidly follows specific rules in order to justify abusive behavior; morally superior	Follows rules, but with reason, balance, and care	To manage life's anxieties and uncertainties, rigidly follows rules; knows what is "right" for everyone else; morally superior
Withdraws and pouts when wounded	Can "stay connected" and tolerate the anxiety of unresolved conflicts without overreacting; trusts that the other person is not fragile	Works too hard to fix things when own or others' feelings are hurt, or withdraws and pouts when wounded
Attacks directly when wounded in order to cover up hurt, shame, and fear—makes it all about the other person's flaws	Stays connected with partner and with self, and tries to resolve uncomfortable, painful feelings that both are experiencing	Believes that partner is "too little" to tolerate adult conflict, and so immediately tries to repair when partner is wounded, even if it means loss of self
Overreactive	Active problem-solving that includes empathy for both self and others	Overreactive

GROWN UP Psychologically Differentiated *(continued)*

TOO NASTY	HEALTHY RANGE	TOO NICE
Hotheaded, or too rational and "reasonable"— acting as if being calm is superior to being angry—which only creates rage in the other person, because being calm and rational when you are actually angry is emotionally dishonest— in other words, intellectually or emotionally passive-aggressive	Strong, firm, clear, healthy, life-affirming anger	Too restrained and reticent, or too rational and "reasonable"—acting as if being calm is superior to being angry—which only creates rage in the other person, because being calm and rational when you are actually angry is emotionally dishonest— in other words, intellectually or emotionally passive-aggressive
Invulnerable	Vulnerable	Too vulnerable
Indifferent	Caring, tempered with the thoughtful awareness of the limits of the other person's ability to be in a grown-up relationship	Too invested, given the lack of investment on the part of the other person
Scary Intimidating Offender Perpetrator	Being reverent and yet tough/commanding respect by the force of one's moral presence and one's inherent decency	Too "safe," not challenging in relationships, not willing to stand up for oneself, easily frightened and intimidated, folds or collapses in the face of others' bullying
Thinks only of self because to think of others might open up parts of the self that could be too painful or frightening to address—the narcissistic wound	Is able to think of both self and others because paralyzing narcissistic wounds were never there—or have been healed—and are not a part of the interpersonal transaction	Thinks only of self (by paradoxically focusing on others as a way to reduce self-anxiety) because to think of others (in an authentic way) might open up parts of the self that could be too painful or frightening to address— the narcissistic wound

GROWN UP Psychologically Differentiated (*continued*)

TOO NASTY	HEALTHY RANGE	TOO NICE
Can't get close	Can get close without losing self because interpersonal anxiety is no longer paralyzing	Can only get close in entangled and enmeshed ways
Doesn't want others to get close for fear of revealing vulnerable parts of self, which are seen as weak and therefore potentially dangerous to the self	Wants to get close to others. Desires the kind of intimacy that includes sharing one's deepest flaws and foibles, as well as one's deepest love and need for others	Acts as if wants to get close to others, but this is only a facade to defend against the fear of truly getting close and revealing the "real self" to others. Therefore, the same fear exists about revealing vulnerable parts of the self, which are seen as weak and therefore potentially dangerous to the self
Doesn't manage self well	Manages self well	Tries to manage everyone else except oneself, and so neglects self—but talks a lot about how much self-care she/he is engaged in, such as yoga, exercise, therapy, twelve-step groups
Shares too much of the shallow things, and too little of the intimate things	Shares oneself in appropriate ways in appropriate settings	Shares too much of the vulnerable, painful things, and not enough of what makes one's life interesting and valuable
Lives in a world of excess	Lives in a world of "enough" and gratitude	Lives in a world of deprivation and desperation
Overpowering	Effective	Overcontrolling
Too free with one's own anger	Uses anger with discretion and forethought	Afraid of one's own anger
Needs to appear "tough" much of the time	Understands that power and grace have little to do with being "tough" and "nice"	Needs to appear "nice" much of the time

GROWN UP Psychologically Differentiated *(continued)*

TOO NASTY	HEALTHY RANGE	TOO NICE
Too easily hurt	Doesn't take rejection and hurt too personally	Too easily hurt
Need-less, overly independent, strong to the point of self-destruction	Interdependent, gaining strength and depth from reliance on others in a non-needy way	Helpless, too needy, clingy
Too abrasive, dangerous, reckless, and scary; too uncomfortable to be around	Challenging, trustworthy, ethical, kind, supportive, fun, spontaneous	Too soothing, too safe, too comforting, stuck, unwilling to take life-enhancing risks
Believes that he is "out there" and open with who he is, but hides true self beneath bravado, bluff, and bluster	True self is apparent whether with powerful, influential people or with regular folks	Feels as if she/he is an open book, and yet also feels like no one really knows the real her/him
Proud of intimidating others, frames it as "commanding respect"	Respected and respectful	"S&N": sweet and nice
Sees children as needing to be "toughened up," not encouraged to be babies	Sees children as needing to be guided, taught, and provided healthy structure and limits	Sees children as needing to be overly protected from life's difficulties
Too hard	Strong, flexible	Too soft
"I always have choices— too bad for you if you don't like them."	"I always have choices, but I consider the consequences."	"I don't believe I have choices"
Overly powerful	"I make things happen, but with regard for how my actions affect others."	Powerless
"I take what I want and need when I want and need it, regardless of the consequences."	"I will, I can"	"I can't, because . . ."; "If only . . ."
Scoffs at concept of hopefulness	Hopeful	Hopeless
It's never enough	Grateful	It's never enough

CHAPTER 9

BIOLOGY IS SOMETIMES DESTINY, EXCEPT WHEN IT ISN'T

*Many of us like to believe that all adults
possess the same capacity to make sound choices.
It's a charitable idea, but demonstrably wrong.
People's brains are vastly different.*

—David Eagleman, *author and neuroscientist at*
Baylor College of Medicine (2011, p. 115)

A Cautionary Note About the Difference Between Understanding and Consequences

As we have said before, the bottom line for us as clinical psychologists in the trenches with clients every day is best summarized in variations of the quote we've used since the inception of our ClearLife Clinic process in 1985: *"You know you are becoming a healthy adult when you can choose the pain of loneliness, fear, hurt, shame, or sadness rather than hurt yourself, hurt others, or let others hurt you."*

A person can be clinically depressed, alcoholic, have diabetes, have a growth hormone disorder, have Asperger's syndrome, be schizophrenic, have bipolar disorder, have been sexually abused as a child, have been beaten or abandoned as a child, have been spoiled and entitled while growing up, lost a leg in a skiing accident, or participated in the Iraq or Afghanistan wars; and the quote still applies. But each person has a greater or lesser challenge to "act from their best selves," depending on their life circumstances, and no one ever fully completes the personal growth process. Jim Maddock often told us, "Fusion is easy, and statistically normal. Differentiation is difficult, and a lifelong process."

Those of us who are drunks know that our alcoholism does not give us a license to inflict harm on others. Having had a bad childhood is not an excuse to be an angry, manipulative, controlling victim. Being a jerk is just that: being a jerk. Plenty of people have good reasons to be wretched in their daily lives, but they don't have a license to be so. We'd all be a lot better off if our society stopped being so confused about the difference between being a *victim of some tragedy* versus being *stuck in the victim role* as an adult.

> We'd all be a lot better off if our society stopped being so confused about the difference between being a victim of some tragedy versus being stuck in the victim role as an adult.

There is always a more interesting truth behind the surface stories that we hear on the evening news. Most of us go into shock when we see or hear or read about yet another mass shooting. Competent psychologists who work daily with family trauma understand two things:

1. There is always a very important underlying systemic reason why human beings do awful things to each other. As we said earlier in this book, human beings always do things for a reason. A man who was abused by his father will tend to either abuse his own children or he will do everything he can to be "nice"—so nice, in fact, that he might express his anger so indirectly that he becomes sarcastic and mean, thinking that he's doing it better than his dad. And maybe he *is* doing it better than his dad, but it doesn't mean that he isn't still doing some harm. Imperfect human beings do harm to one another.

2. Because we try to *understand* why people do what they do does not mean that we are *excusing* them for doing it. When wanting to understand *why*

things happen is misperceived as *excusing* what happened, the ability to improve our society goes flying out the window. It becomes a double bind in which scientists who try to fathom the darkest reaches of the human brain suddenly have to tap dance to explain that they are not justifying the behavior by their inquiry; they are simply trying to understand it. There is currently a disturbing tendency for the U.S. news media and the people in this country to desperately grasp for simplistic answers and solutions to increasingly complex human problems, and the outcome of that approach to problem solving can lead us nowhere except to a return to sixteenth-century witch hunts. *This is not a sign of modern humanity at its best.*

So when we read that a young man took all of his parents' jewelry out of their safe and ran away to South America with his girlfriend, and we learn that as a child he was double-bound by parents who spoiled and indulged him on the one hand while being emotionally cold and distant on the other, can't we at least understand how this might happen? Under those double-bind conditions, wouldn't you go a little crazy? At the same time, once having that understanding, what does that have to do with the young man's accountability and consequences? He should still do his jail time. Understanding why it happened simply gives us a chance to prevent things like that from happening in the future.

When Jesus Christ asked us to love our neighbors as ourselves for the love of him; when he demonstrated how the despised Samaritan was more holy and deserving of God's grace than all of the "holy men" of his day because the Samaritan went out of his way to help a distressed fellow human being on the side of the road; when he said that it would be harder for a camel to pass through the eye of a needle than for a rich man to enter the kingdom of God; and when he spoke of treating "the least of these" as if we were treating him that way, Jesus was telling us that in the big picture, we'd all be better off *as a species* (think, preserving the gene pool) if we showed one another some basic kindness.

While the concept is fairly simple to grasp, putting it into practice in our everyday lives is obviously a difficult challenge. Nobody can argue that, and you certainly don't have to be a Christian to embrace this idea. You could be an evolutionary biologist and embrace the same principle. That's what makes it all so intriguing.

This chapter focuses on the nature and nurture of our being too nasty or too nice. We begin with some of the biological correlates, because ignoring or minimizing their importance is often too easy. At the same time, our belief is that when you distill it all down to its basic components, *people do bad things to each other, or let others do bad things to them, because they are afraid and lack knowledge.* Our *fear* and *ignorance* get the better of us, along with the related emotions of *hurt* and *shame.*

> *People do bad things to each other, or let others do bad things to them, because they are afraid and lack knowledge.*

The Neurobiology of It All: Biological Correlates of Being "Too Nasty"

David Eagleman's quotation at the beginning of this chapter continues,

> If you are a carrier of a particular set of genes, the probability that you will commit a violent crime is four times as high as it would be if you lacked those genes. You're three times as likely to commit aggravated assault, eight times as likely to be arrested for murder, and 13 times as likely to be arrested for a sexual offense. The overwhelming majority of prisoners carry these genes; 98.1 percent of death-row inmates do. . . . By the way, as regards that dangerous set of genes, you've probably heard of them. They are summarized as the Y chromosome. *If you're a carrier, we call you a male.* (2011, p. 115; emphasis added)

Eagleman's article began with the tragic tale of Charles Whitman, who in August 1966 went to the tower at the University of Texas in Austin and began a horrific shooting spree that left thirteen people dead. Whitman had previously consulted with a doctor for two hours, he stated in his suicide note, to no avail, and in the note he specifically requested that an autopsy be done on his brain after his death to determine the cause of his overwhelming feelings. The autopsy revealed a glioblastoma, a tumor that was impinging on his hypothalamus and compressing his amygdala—a brain structure that, if damaged, can produce lack of fear, blunting of emotions, and overreaction.

Why do we do the things that we do? Is it nature or is it nurture? Science has always concluded that it is both. And the more sophisticated science becomes, our awareness of each conclusion becomes more nuanced as well.

It has long been known that the heritability coefficient for the personality dimension of extroversion-introversion is very high (see Berry, Poortinga, Segall, & Dasen, 2002). And in the twin studies conducted at the University of Minnesota and reported in *Science* in 1990 (Bouchard, Lykken, McGue, Segal, & Tellegen, 1990), the authors noted that our genes may determine as much as 43 percent of our career choices and 49 percent of our religious preferences.

It makes sense, if you stop to reflect on it. If you're more left-brained, you'll probably gravitate toward careers or religious practices that are in sync with how you think—math, science, accounting, and a more structured religion. If you're more right-brained, you'll probably gravitate toward art, design, careers that rely on pattern recognition, and religious practices that are less structured. Even within the same religion, there are those who are more one way or the other; the writings of Teilhard de Chardin, the Catholic priest, anthropologist, and mystic, must certainly appeal more to right-brained people than to left-brained people.

Most incidents of domestic violence in intimate relationships result from a combination of emotional immaturity and drug or alcohol involvement, both of which lower people's ability to restrain themselves. You threaten to leave me, I become terrified of being abandoned by you, and then I impulsively do something to prevent you from leaving me—I hit you, throw myself on the hood of your car, or block the doorway as you try to leave. As this is happening, my heart is racing and pounding, I am flooding emotionally (Gottman, 1994), and I am feeling helpless and little.

In a different and much scarier form of domestic violence, the offender's heart rate and blood pressure actually *decline* as he is beating you up, which is a frightening thought. In these cases, there appears to be an organic problem (a physical problem that could be either genetically or environmentally caused) in the prefrontal cortex of the brain, and perhaps also the amygdala. So two nearly identical violent incidents can potentially have very different causes and very different meanings—one because he cares too much but is just too little to manage his emotions properly; the other because he is essentially operating like a reptile. Being a sociopath—lacking a conscience and lacking much empathy—appears to be related to problems in the prefrontal cortex and the amygdala.

In cases like that of Betty Broderick, discussed in Chapter 2, psycho-analysis, psychiatry, and psychology routinely assume that the person with BPD is the unfortunate product of a particularly pernicious set of parenting circumstances that often leave the person reacting as if still in infancy despite living in an adult body. But even this explanation, emanating purely from the "nature" side of the argument, is not as simple as it might appear. Steven Graybar and Lynn Boutier of the University of Nevada Reno Medical School wrote a well-researched and compelling treatise (2002) on the biological precursors of BPD, in stark contrast to the prevailing theories of the day.

Some of the symptoms of clinical depression, especially in men, are irritability and anger, which are not particularly "nice." Over the past few years we've had clients who struggled with serious depression for years, going from one psychologist to another, only to find that they were suffering from an underactive thyroid, which was eventually diagnosed by a meticulous, thorough family physician. Once their thyroid levels were adjusted, all or most of their symptoms disappeared. Symptoms of hypothyroidism include fatigue, sleepiness, slowing of speech, a lack of interest in personal relationships and general apathy, which are also symptoms of clinical depression.

Recent genetic research has linked a number of genes to one's predisposition to becoming alcoholic, which validates the wisdom of the early pioneers in alcoholism treatment, especially the notion suggested by Alcoholics Anonymous that alcoholics suffer from an "allergy" to alcohol. A 2004 study done at Washington University School of Medicine has identified the gene *GABRG3* as increasing the risk of alcoholism, by increasing GABA receptor activity and thereby increasing the behavioral effects of alcohol, such as sedation, loss of anxiety, and problems with motor coordination (Dick et al., 2004). Webb, Lind, and others (2011) report that "about 10% to 20% of the population carry a version of a gene that makes their brains especially sensitive to alcohol. The gene carries the blueprint for an enzyme called *CYP2E1*, known to be involved in metabolizing ethanol alcohol as well as other molecules, such as the pain-reliever acetaminophen . . . and nicotine. People who carry the version of the *CYP2E1* gene linked to increased sensitivity to alcohol produce more of the enzyme."

Just about anything that can make a person irritable or decrease his ability to manage complex, uncomfortable emotions—that is, his ability to self-soothe—can result in episodes of nasty behavior. Too much caffeine can be a culprit. Drug interactions can be involved. Addiction to drugs can obviously be a cause. Withdrawal from *any* addiction, including spending, shopping, gambling, sex, drugs or alcohol, exercise, work, or codependency (addiction to another person's out-of-control behavior), can result in nastiness. Diabetic or prediabetic swings in blood sugar levels can also be to blame. Walsh and Roberts (2010) report that

> On the other hand, when high or low levels of sugar reach the brain, the result may be impaired memory, anger, irritability, slowed thinking, or depression. As blood sugars rise, the levels of hormones that prevent depression may be lowered. This can worsen symptoms of depression and leave a person with less interest in doing the things needed to improve control, such as thoughtful selection of food, regular exercise, and rest. A vicious cycle of growing depression and worsening control can arise.

Low testosterone, high cortisol levels, low serotonin levels, hormonal imbalances—whether associated with aging, menopause, or something else—can all make a person more irritable. One of the most common, and most commonly misunderstood, causes of irritability is chronic pain, which, as many people suffering from chronic pain know full well, is particularly difficult for everyone in a family system because it can't be seen; it's invisible (Pohl, 2008).

Biological Niceness

Testosterone, Estrogen, and Oxytocin

Testosterone evolved to increase aggression and motivate men to leave the home fires and pursue wild animals for days and weeks at a time without being overly influenced by pesky feelings that might distract from the primitive survival goal of killing the animal and dragging it back to the home base. What kind of hunter would you be if you fell to the ground and started sobbing about missing your mate and children, and crying that "I just want to go home"? You'd all starve to death.

Testosterone shuts down feelings, increases aggression, and directs the brain to pursue an essential survival goal—a ferocious bear or a wooly mammoth—and it does so while also shutting down one's fear of danger and dying. In an almost surreal sense, primitive hunting was a spiritual drama comprising the hunter, his companions, and their prey—all bound together by the hunters' vivid memories of their women and children far, far away, who were waiting for them to come back with the life-sustaining food that was the males' primary reason for existing in that dangerous world in the first place.

We have been able to help a number of transgendered clients over the many years of our private practice, and the differences between testosterone versus estrogen and oxytocin in these cases could not be more revealing. More than a few times, a client who is in the midst of the hormonal and surgical transformation from woman to man will come in for an appointment "just to check out these new reactions." He will describe a situation in which, "as a woman, his feelings were hurt, and afterward he went home and had a good cry and cried it all out, and felt much better." Now, as a man, with much more testosterone coursing through his bloodstream, he reaches for his throat in a mock choking display as he says, "Now when my feelings are hurt, I start to feel the tears well up from inside, and then everything gets plugged up and choked off right here in my throat! Is that what it feels like to be a man?" he asks. The answer is, "Yes."

The complementary biological niceness that is necessary to balance out the testosterone-driven aggression and competitiveness in a complex system is due to estrogen and oxytocin—the hormones that cause human beings, especially females, to want to bond, affiliate, strengthen, and support their social systems and structures (Lewis et al., 2000).

Oxytocin has been dubbed "the attachment hormone" by a number of scientists. While prehistoric men were out conquering and killing, women were together in familial groups, emotionally bonding, sitting together in circles, talking about their men, their children, their anxieties, and their family conflicts—all skills required to maintain social harmony while sublimating one's own individual needs. If the group can't stay together while the men are out hunting for weeks at a time, there won't be any family or group for the hunters to come back to. Imagine the hunting party returning with a huge kill, excited to share with the women and children what they'd brought home, and nobody was there. Their social structure would have disintegrated in their absence.

Discussions about oxytocin have found their way into the mainstream press, becoming a bit of a fad of late. An article by Jeffrey Kluger in *Time Health Online* states that the colloquial term for it is the "cuddle chemical" (2010). Kluger notes that psychiatrist René Hurlemann of Bonn University and neuroscientist Keith Kendrick of the Cambridge Babraham Institute performed two studies in which a sample of men were either given aerosol sprays of oxytocin or a placebo, and then tested for their levels of empathy in one study, and their social learning and social intelligence in the next study. In both studies, oxytocin had the intended effect of increasing these prosocial behaviors. In these situations, oxytocin clearly pushed men in the direction of being nicer. Of course, though, the findings are not always so clear-cut. Kluger also describes a study in which oxytocin actually increased people's feelings of jealousy in a competitive situation when their emotions were manipulated by the offer of a bigger prize to their competitors.

Worry

As Lewis, Amini, and Lannon (2000) describe so eloquently, worry—a proneness to fear—is a crucial component of a species' survival. Fear warns an animal to make self-protective maneuvers. You see a bear in the woods, and you either fight or flee. We have always said that *fear gives us wisdom*, but only if it is *balanced*. Lewis, Amini, and Lannon state, "As DNA shuffles and recombines in humanity's gene pool, the unlucky inherit

> *Fear gives us wisdom, but only if it is balanced.*

extremes of temperament" (2000, 49). We all know that some infants seem to be unflappable and easily soothed, while others are hypersensitive to outside stimulation and novelty, and very difficult to calm. The results of twin studies suggest that 40 to 60 percent of anxiety-related traits have a genetic component to them.

Some children and adults who are more anxiety-prone also tend to be more risk-averse and cautious, which sometimes means that they will have a higher tolerance for the inappropriate or abusive behavior of others, for fear of escalating conflicts and increasing the chances of harm coming to them. In the classic victim-perpetrator interaction pattern (80 percent victim–20 percent perpetrator and 80 percent perpetrator–20 percent victim), the one doing the bullying and overpowering unconsciously *depends on* and *resents* the victim's fear, the victim's tendency to back down and be nice, and the victim's unwillingness to be "mean"—in this case, to simply stand up for oneself. This dynamic keeps the pattern going.

Heredity X Environment Interactions: The Deepest Roots of Nastiness and Niceness

Another biological antecedent of nastiness versus niceness is perhaps the most important of all, but it isn't about biology alone. It is about the interaction between the biology of the human brain and the emotional environment in which the brain develops. As social animals who work daily with social animals, we are relieved at last to have access to hard scientific evidence showing that the physical, biological integrity of one's brain depends on the human interactions we experience as we grow from infancy into adulthood.

For twenty-seven years we have conducted ongoing men's, women's, and mixed therapy groups because we were convinced that the very act of sitting in a room—in a circle, around a coffee table, under conditions of therapeutic structure and safety, with rules of interaction that short-circuit the typical anxiety-reducing but intimacy-killing responses that many of us automatically employ when listening to other human beings share their distress—was having profoundly positive effects on our clients' ability to accept themselves, bond deeply with one another, and heal. As we discuss later, modern neurobiological research suggests that we may have been onto something all this time.

> *Anxiety and our ability to soothe it are ultimately what determine the integrity with which we conduct our lives.*

Anxiety and our ability to soothe it are ultimately what determine the integrity with which we conduct our lives—how we treat others, how we treat ourselves, and how balanced or unbalanced we are in our reactions to the vicissitudes of life. In all relationships, but especially in marital, romantic, and family relationships, two ongoing sources of anxiety are present until the day we die: *the fear of losing ourselves* and *the fear of losing our relationships*. Human beings have two complementary, competing drives. Sociologist David Bakan (1966) refers to these as *agency* and *communion*. Our urge to be separate, create, build, destroy, conquer, and imprint our identity on the canvas of creation is our *agentic* drive. Our urge to affiliate, to support each other, to create groups of mutual understandings and meanings, and to maintain and support them is called our *communal* drive.

The ongoing and universal challenge for spouses and lovers, parents and children, and mutual friends is to somehow regulate these anxieties within enormously complex, infinitely nuanced, and emotionally close relationships. *She wants me to quit teaching and enter the corporate world, and I don't want to. Do I lose a bit of myself if I comply with her request? Is this a question I even want to entertain?* Or *He wants to spend the evening by the fire, curled up together, and talking and sharing our day, but I have to get back to the office to finish a report that's due. Is he losing part of the relationship if I go? And am I?* Our separate abilities to regulate the complex and volatile emotions surrounding these conflicts determine the depth of intimacy that we can attain and whether our relationships survive. The ability to self-regulate determines how close we can be with others without losing ourselves in the process—and how comfortable we can be with ourselves, imperfections and all (Larson, 2010a, 2010b, 2011; Maddock & Larson, 1995; Schnarch, 1991, 1997, 2009).

From where does this ability to self-regulate originate? It comes from an incredibly complex and awe-inspiring social and biological system of interconnections between the brain of a developing infant and the brain of her primary caretakers. Most dog lovers know that dogs' evolutionary survival strategy over thousands of years was to focus on the subtle verbal and nonverbal cues coming toward them at light speed from the humans to whom they were attached. Dogs sense and react to our moods: they worry about us if we are crying and sad, they despair when they are separated from us for too long, they have been known to embark on journeys of a thousand miles or more to find us with few scientific explanations for how they were able to do it, and now we know that they can even sense seizures, diabetes, and cancer in us. The more cynical among us argue that they do these things for purely selfish reasons: we feed them. But few of the sane among us can argue that some kind of emotional bond is present between a dog and his best friend.

The same holds true for humans. During our graduate-school days in the early 1970s, we learned of the famous studies by Rene Spitz (1946), of infants raised in "foundling homes" in which the prevailing germ theories suggested that the infants be fed and diapered appropriately but not held and touched too much for fear of spreading disease. The unexpected outcome of this grand medical experiment was that many more infants died for lack of human warmth and attachment than from germ-born disease. It reminds us of the revelation mentioned earlier in Dean Ornish's book

(1998) that more people die because of the lack of truly intimate relationships in their lives than from smoking cigarettes.

Somewhere between 150 million and 200 million years ago, a new part of the brain evolved that came to be known as the *limbic system*. This brain structure changed how some animals related to their young and to each other. It allowed for nurturing, caretaking, play, mutual interaction, more complex emotions, and more sophisticated linking up between animals and their young—and between each other. This part of the brain is most implicated in the complex attachments that we experience with one another, and between us and other animals possessing the same brain structure, like dogs. In the most complex mammals of all—humans—the role of the limbic system is unparalleled when it comes to our early brain development and our later emotional and mental health.

Lewis, Amini, and Lannon (2000) describe the process of *limbic resonance* as follows:

> The limbic brain is another delicate physical apparatus that specializes in detecting and analyzing just one part of the physical world—the internal state of other mammals. . . . Emotionality enables a mammal to sense the inner states and motives of the mammals around him. . . . A mammal can detect the internal state of another mammal and adjust its own physiology to match the situation—a change in turn sensed by the other, who likewise adjusts. . . . Within the effulgence of their new brain, mammals developed a capacity we call *limbic resonance*—a symphony of mutual exchange and internal adaptation whereby two mammals become attuned to each other's internal states. . . . When we meet the gaze of another, two nervous systems achieve a palpable and intimate apposition. . . . So familiar and expected is the neural attunement of limbic resonance that people find its absence disturbing [as might happen with someone who has suppressed most of his emotions]. . . . *To the animals capable of bridging the gap between minds, limbic resonance is the door to communal connections.* . . . Limbic resonance supplies the wordless harmony we see everywhere but take for granted—between mother and infant, between a boy and his dog, between lovers holding hands across a

restaurant table. . . . Those who spend their days without an opportunity for quiet listening can pass a lifetime and overlook it [the deeply intimate experience of limbic resonance] altogether. (2000, pp. 62–65; emphasis added)

This purely evolutionary, biological process determines so much of how human beings treat themselves and each other. Infants who experienced adequate amounts of these kinds of sophisticated neurological connections with their caretakers grow up to be adults who have a hardwired ability to connect at deeper levels with other human beings, and through repeatedly experiencing this limbic resonance with caretakers throughout their early lives, they eventually learn to soothe themselves in the same way. *Infants who didn't, don't.*

When a family system has inherent rules such that limbic resonance is a valued, accepted, and essential part of the interactional pattern within the family—that is, when family members unconsciously learn to pay attention to one another, to listen to one another, to hang out together while they simply and comfortably care about one another without having to fix or rescue one another, and to therefore sync up with one another in this way—then the evolutionary need that all mammals have for this life-sustaining and brain-developing experience simply happens, without another thought about it.

The animal and human research on the consequences of a lack of this limbic resonance are both dramatic and deeply disturbing. In the beginning of the next chapter, we present a few of these findings, along with some of the more complex cultural causes of our nasty and nice behavior.

CHAPTER 10

LIMBIC DISTORTIONS, PAINFUL CHILDHOOD EXPERIENCES, CULTURAL DENIAL, DOUBLE BINDS, AND THE BATTLE BETWEEN THE SEXES

The mutual attraction of the sexes is so fundamental
that any explanation of the world (biological, philosophical or religious)
that does not succeed in finding it a *structurally essential*
place in its system is virtually condemned.

—*Pierre Teilhard de Chardin*, Human Energy *(1969, p. 15).*

Biology may be destiny, but so is environment. We devote this chapter to some of the life experiences that can determine how well we are able to manage our emotions, and therefore what things might contribute to our being too nasty or too nice. One caveat applies in dividing causes into heredity or environment. Science has progressed far enough that it isn't always easy to divide the antecedents of our behavior neatly into one or the other. We now know that certain experiences—environment—can activate certain parts of certain genes at certain times in our lives (Sroufe

& Siegel, 2011). Also, for the purposes of this chapter, we are going to look at the battle between the sexes as more of an environmental (i.e., cultural) phenomenon than a genetic one, knowing full well that gender is determined by genes.

Destructive Limbic Distortions

William Wordsworth wrote that "The Child is father of the Man." The more shortages you experience in childhood, the harder it will be for you to have trust in yourself, others, and the world in general. When we don't trust ourselves or others, we tend to be cynical, defensive, irritable, and angry. As Duke University professors Redford Williams and Virginia Williams wrote (1998), when we are cynical, defensive, irritable, and angry, we tend to do a good deal of harm to ourselves and others.

If you have read this far, you may not be surprised that we strongly urge you to read *A General Theory of Love* (Lewis et al., 2000). It provides the most elegant, readable, and understandable explanation of the neuroscience underlying human attachment, bonding, and love that we have yet to encounter. In it, the authors summarize some of the most compelling research leading to the inarguable conclusion that limbic disruptions in the connections between infants and their caregivers can leave lasting scars on the neurological functioning of the young, whether they are chimpanzees, rat pups, or human infants. The antiquated notion that little children are really just little adults was simply a projection of parents' inadequacies as parents, as psychohistorian Lloyd deMause explained so well in *The History of Childhood* (1974). The belief that some parents still hold—that infants and young children are not affected by things like family trauma, conflict, or physical abuse and neglect because they are "not really old enough to be aware of them"—is equally antiquated.

Lewis, Amini, and Lannon (2000) paint a picture of limbic regulation disruptions during infancy that include infants in the Spitz studies simply dying from lack of will because they weren't touched, held, talked to, and cooed at enough, to Harry Harlow's famous studies in which baby monkeys preferred the "touch-comfort" of a furry-covered wire monkey over a wire monkey that dispensed milk. They illuminated the specific physiological reactions that various mammalian species demonstrate when separated too severely from their mothers—from increased attempts to search for the separated mother to increased heart rate, body temperature, cortisol synthesis, and catecholamine synthesis. Of perhaps most significance for human beings are the despair and eventual depression that result from the prolonged separation from, or death of, a parent figure or a spouse, which include decreased heart rate and oxygen consumption, decreases in growth hormone resulting in stunted growth, sleep difficulties, and compromise of one's immune system.

They also summarized the work of Gary Kraemer (1985; 1992) at the University of Wisconsin on *isolation syndrome,* noting that monkeys reared in isolation were not capable of reciprocal interactions with other monkeys, who tended to reject them; were not able to mate; and if they did have offspring, they alternated between severe neglect of their infants and savage attacks on them. Viciousness toward other adults, self-mutilation, and food and water binges were all typical behaviors of these sad animals that had been reared in isolation.

Psychoanalyst Erik Erikson (1963), who formulated the Eight Stages of Man and who coined the term "identity crisis," described the first psychosocial challenge of a human being, from birth to age eighteen months, as *trust versus mistrust.* Current neuroscientific findings support Erikson's theory. The challenge for parents and infants is to somehow graduate from this period with a basic sense that the world, despite all of its chaos, confusion, and violence, is basically an okay place to be—*even when at times it is not very safe at all.* The ability to find hope where hope is hidden from view is one of the more important outcomes of the successful resolution of this stage of human development, and it is mostly due to limbic resonance.

> *Hope comes from one place and one place only: relationships with other people.*

For the past three decades we have argued that *hope comes from one place and one place only: relationships with other people.* People who claim that hope comes only from God are missing the point, because they are failing to remember, or to even know in the first place, that the God of most religions suggests that the clearest path to spirituality and communion with God is through how we treat each other, which brings us back full circle to limbic resonance. It isn't "How much I can grab for myself," the American ethos described in 1835 by Alexis de Tocqueville. It is more poignantly, "What is my capacity for empathy?" and "How do I treat the least of these?"

The Centers for Disease Control Study of Adverse Childhood Experiences

In *Adult Children: The Secrets of Dysfunctional Families* (Friel & Friel, 1988), we listed a number of serious physical, emotional, and behavioral problems that adults develop as a result of growing up in a dysfunctional family, including a lot of victim-perpetrator interaction patterns. Family dysfunction can not only disrupt limbic resonance during infancy, but can also make it very difficult for people to maintain their relationships and their physical and emotional balance as adults. The way we were treated as children tends to be the way we treat *ourselves* as adults.

> The way we were treated as children tends to be the way we treat ourselves as adults.

In an effort to systematically examine the toll that childhood shortages take on later adult development, the Division of Adult and Community Health at the Centers for Disease Control and Prevention (CDC) and Kaiser Permanente's Department of Preventive Medicine in San Diego began a collaborative investigation of the effects of adverse childhood experiences (ACE) on later adult functioning.

From 1995 to 1997, 17,337 primarily well-educated men and women in the Kaiser Health Plan agreed to participate in surveys that examined health-care utilization, numbers of prescription drugs used, diseases contracted, and causes of death—along with the assessment of ten categories of stressful or traumatic childhood experiences, which included the following:

- Three forms of childhood *abuse*—physical, emotional, and sexual
- Two forms of childhood *neglect*—physical and emotional
- Growing up in a seriously *dysfunctional household* as evidenced by:
  Witnessing domestic violence
  Alcohol or other substance abuse in the home
  Mentally ill or suicidal household members
  Parental marital discord as evidenced by separation or divorce
  Crime in the home as evidenced by having a household member in prison

The initial findings confirm what so many clinicians have suspected for at least four decades. In the executive summary prepared for the National Association of Children of Alcoholics (NACoA), Robert Anda (2006, p. 3), coprincipal investigator, wrote,

> ACEs have a strong influence on adolescent health, teen pregnancy, smoking, alcohol abuse, illicit drug abuse, sexual behavior, mental health, risk of revictimization, stability of relationships, performance in the workforce; and they increase the risk of heart disease, chronic lung disease, liver disease, suicide, injuries, HIV, STDs, and other risks for the leading causes of death.

In addition, the research confirms that the greater the number of ACEs in one's childhood, the greater the number of adverse mental and physical consequences; also, the presence of one ACE greatly increased the probability that other ACEs would be present in that child's family. For example, of those reporting substance abuse in their households, 81 percent reported at least one additional ACE, and most of those had experienced two or more. "In the entire study population, 81%–98% of respondents who had experienced one ACE reported at least one additional category of ACE (median: 87%)" (Anda 2006, p. 8).

Nice-Nasty (Victim-Perpetrator) Interaction Patterns: An Elegant Snapshot

Maddock and Larson (1995) noted that the child who tends to protect himself (and, often, herself) from familial shortages by shutting off his feelings and getting "tough" tends to move in the direction of the perpetrator role. He may bully his little brother, get in fights at school, or, in a dominance/power move, sexually abuse his little sister—all in the service of strengthening his suit of armor, which protects him from being further hurt by the family. He gradually moves toward the *perpetrator role* as an adaptive response. As he grows older, his role solidifies, and in his mid- to late twenties, when he perhaps first gets married, his survival strategy has become a solidified part of who he is—at least for the time being.

The child who gravitates toward the *victim role* is the one who feels her (or his) feelings too much. She worries about everyone in her family, tries to mediate parental conflicts, tries to be "good" and "perfect," sets her own feelings aside for the sake of worrying about everyone else's feelings, loses her identity and her "self" in the process, and eventually finds herself in relationships with boys or men who take advantage of her, leaving her to be victimized and feeling like a victim. She is too nice and cares too much, and is unwilling to stand up and assert her identity and herself in a close relationship. These two people—the boy perpetrator and the girl victim— often create the "perfectly, destructively balanced" partnership.

Noel Larson (1995, 1999) created an elegant visual aid to help people understand what is happening in an unhealthy family. She called it the victim-perpetrator "container." A family system plagued with lots of victim-perpetrator behavior but not nearly enough "other" behavior (i.e., healthy, grown-up, psychologically differentiated behavior) might look as follows (where V = victim behavior, P = perpetrator behavior, and o = other behavior):

```
┌─────────────────────────────────────────┐
│   V   o   P   V   o   V   P   P   o       │
│       V   o   o   V   P                   │
│   P   o   P   V   o   P   V   o   P   V    │
│           V   P   o                       │
└─────────────────────────────────────────┘
```

As you can see, when these are the patterns of behavior to which you are exposed, day in and day out, over the course of twenty years, you don't get much of a chance to see or practice those other behaviors.

Many people don't realize that conflict is a normal part of daily life, or they are reluctant or even fearful to label it as such: *I want the thermostat up, you want it down; you want to go to a movie, I want to see a play; I want to sleep on the left side of the bed and so do you; you want the television louder than I do.*

The crucial question is not *if* they have conflicts, but how people manage their conflicts. If you witness your father giving in to your mother's wishes 99 percent of the time because she has a temper or because she uses mock fragility to manipulate him (the martyr role is a perpetrator role covered up by a victim cloak), then you will only see her perpetration and his victimization, *for which they are each responsible.* How will you ever learn what the other (non-V, non-P) behavior even looks like? How will you ever learn how two strong, competent adults resolve their conflicts without bullying each other or caving in?

In systems, the *patterns* are the most important. They are passed down from one generation to the next. And because it is a pattern—and not necessarily a perfect, exact match—that is passed down, it is sometimes easy to believe that the pattern isn't being repeated. You may have grown up in an alcoholic family and told yourself that you will never date anyone who drinks alcohol. But from a child's perspective, the actual painful patterns underlying parents' alcoholism include things like family instability or rigidity, high conflict or avoidance of conflict, suppression of feelings or emotional flooding (see, e.g., Gottman, 1994), and financial impoverishment or workaholism and material excess.

Because these patterns are less obvious, less visible, and less concrete than someone being drunk a lot, we end up focusing too much on one thing (drinking) and missing what's right there in plain sight for someone who grew up witnessing lots of "other" behaviors; we end up with someone who is emotionally unavailable, addicted to something else, like sex or work or exercise, or someone who is emotionally volatile and manipulative without alcohol being present.

This is especially true because if the pattern you experienced was extreme, then you may go way over to the other extreme in order to try to balance or repair the dysfunction. Because the opposite of dysfunctional is dysfunctional, then you may become excessively nice after having been physically or emotionally abused as a child.

Children who witness their parents having conflicts and getting them resolved, even with loudly raised voices at times, unconsciously and automatically learn how to be in a close, intimate relationship without losing themselves and without doing great harm to the other person. *Rage isn't measured by volume. Nor is kindness.* When Mom raises her voice and tells Dad, "I love you, and I always will. But you have to stop controlling me so much! You're driving me crazy with your anxiety!" it isn't rage. When she whispers to him with a tone of disgust in her voice and gritting her teeth, "I regret the day I ever met you," that's rage.

> *Rage isn't measured by volume. Nor is kindness.*

Sexual Abuse:
See No Evil, Hear No Evil, Speak No Evil

In systems thinking, context is everything. Light is a wave, but then it's a stream of particles, depending on the context and the observers' point of view. Similarly, the culture and the era in which a person grows up can be crucial factors in how life stressors are managed from the individual, family system, and societal perspectives.

Some significant contextual changes occurred in the psychotherapy field and in U.S. society at large between 1975 and 2000. In the 1940s, 1950s, and 1960s, "neurotic" was the buzzword among professionals and the general public; the term "codependent" had yet to be coined. And while we now seem to be living in an age of public testimonials and self-disclosure, in 1958, when actor, writer, pianist, and all-around bon vivant Oscar Levant joked about his electroconvulsive shock treatments (ECT) and other emotional problems with Jack Paar on the *Tonight Show*, it was stunning and shocking. Although Alcoholics Anonymous (AA) had been founded in 1935 and the divorce rate in 1950 (number of divorces divided by the number of marriages in a given year) was 23 percent, the words "alcoholism" and "divorce" carried so much cultural shame that they were hardly ever uttered. Children from *broken homes*, as they were called, were pitied and scorned rather than understood and supported.

During the 1940s, 1950s, and 1960s, it was still the norm for children to be spanked or hit with objects in ways that would now be considered child abuse (Miller, 1983; deMause, 1974). If an elementary schoolchild had a problem reading a passage from a book in front of the class, she might be laughed at, ridiculed, criticized, and even forced to sit in a corner in the front of the room to further humiliate her for her intransigence.

Society's handling of the sexual abuse of children and domestic violence demonstrates the importance of cultural and societal contexts in the handling of complex systemic dysfunctions. The thought of incest was so horrifying to professionals and the general public that Briere and Runtz (1991) noted,

> As recently as 1975 . . . a chapter in the *Comprehensive Textbook of Psychiatry* reported the incidence of incest to be approximately one in a million cases (Kaplan and Freedman, 1975). The same author later stated that "research is inconclusive as to the psychological harmfulness of incestuous behavior" (Henderson, 1983, p. 34). As a result of this delay in professional awareness, clinical data on the effects of sexual abuse are quite new.

In attempting to explain why "it is also now generally recognized that from Freud's time until the mid 1970s, most professionals simply did not regard adult sexual abuse of children as a serious problem," Conte (1991) wrote,

> Acknowledgment that large numbers of children are sexually abused by family members or persons known by the child is anxiety producing and emotionally difficult. It requires confrontation with potentially threatening phenomena, such as sexuality, deviant behavior, abuse and terror of children, and the violation of social norms. Inherent in the human species, psychologi-

cal defenses protect us from the anxiety-producing and painful knowledge that older persons regularly abuse younger persons. . . . *What is problematic, however, is the extent to which professional knowledge appears to be defensive in nature.* (pp. 87–88; emphasis added)

The ability to sit in the middle of one's uncomfortable emotions—well aware of them but not acting them out—is a critical skill in working with difficult human systems, and those of us in the helping professions are not immune to having blinders surrounding these issues. People whose careers depend on being highly competitive critical thinkers sometimes have difficulty experiencing and managing their own emotions—that is, having *emotional intelligence* (see, e.g., Goleman, 1995). When family systems, social institutions, or entire cultures deny issues like physical or sexual abuse, it automatically creates double binds for the child, and double binds are some of the most common causes of people's nasty or nice behaviors.

Double Binds and Crazy-Making

Gregory Bateson was the first to coin the term "double bind." One of his colleagues, renowned family therapist Virginia Satir (see, e.g., *Peoplemaking*, 1972), made the term a bit more user-friendly. She called it "crazy-making" because double binds cause people to feel anxious, agitated, and then either depressed or rageful. Some examples of crazy-making are as follows:

- A child *hears* one thing but *sees* the opposite. For example, Dad says, "I love all of you kids so much," as he is beating your brother and terrifying the rest of you.
- A parent stating, "Why are you so angry at your brother? He's your brother. You should love your brother," followed by "You need to get your feelings out. It's not good to hold them all in. Express them!" followed by "I don't want to hear anymore about it! Now stop it!"
- The complex double bind of the following situation: A child gets the lesson, "Don't question authority" (which can be explicit or implied, in that

the parent is seen as weak and therefore any questioning of the parent's authority would hurt the parent's feelings or "crush" him); followed by "Get this yard work done by Friday"; followed by the fact that it is impossible to get it done by Friday, unless, of course, it is in violation of some *other* command by the parent, such as "Be sure to study hard enough for that test you have on Friday so that you get an A on it. You know how it will cripple your chances to get into Harvard if you don't." Add the fact that the child never wanted to go to Harvard in the first place—it's for the parents' aggrandizement rather than the child's well-being—and a follow-up statement such as, "Honey, we're only pushing you because we love you and care about you. You know that, don't you?" If your head is spinning after reading this example, imagine how much confusion, agitation, and internal rage it might cause in a child or adolescent.

- The day after her anxious parents told Susan that she needed to slow down and relax and take some time for herself so that she didn't burn out, her parents said, "Susan, you need to study harder this week so you can get an A on your physics test because you want to get into a good university, don't you?"

Many double binds occur by the very nature of children being vulnerable and naturally dependent upon those who take care of them. A child should be able to trust that his parents have his best interests at heart, except that in some cases, for some reason, they don't. This leaves the child filled with confusion, doubt, and shame. If he is more on the perpetrator side in terms of self-defense, it may leave him angry and defiant. If he is more on the victim side, he may move inward and feel depressed and confused.

For example, it is reasonable for a child to expect that her parents will provide food, clothing, shelter, attention, affection, guidance, structure, and love, among many other human needs. But her parents are not capable of meeting the needs of their dependent child because their own needs weren't met when they were growing up, so they find the dependency needs of their child overwhelming. She is left with contradictory beliefs that "my parents must love me because they are my parents and I am a dependent child" while also believing that "my parents must not love me because they meet so few of my basic human needs."

In families that are in the top 16.5 percent of emotional health based on the normal curve, crazy-making is not a substantial part of the fabric of the family. Therefore, when a child in that family is faced with the countless double binds that life presents on an almost daily basis, the family responds in a way that ensures that the child is quickly able to find his way out of the bind. Many stories and examples sprinkled throughout this book, if you ponder them carefully, provide some road maps so that both you and your children can free yourselves from the confusing grip of such binds.

The Epic Struggle: Male and Female, Hormones and Power, Sex, and Limbic Resonance

The drama of circular, seemingly endless victim-perpetrator interaction patterns can be found throughout human relationships, but perhaps nowhere as clearly and profoundly as in the relationships between men and women—because of *sex*, because their neurobiology is so different, and because the emotional stakes are so high.

According to historical facts presented in Iowa State University educational materials on domestic assault and rape, the word "family" comes from the Latin word *familia*, which refers to a group of slaves that belongs to a man. The authors go on to point out, "In 2400 B.C., if a woman was verbally abusive to her husband, he engraved her name on a brick and knocked out her teeth with it." They also noted that between 200,000 and 900,000 rapes occur annually in the United States, and that 22,000 men are arrested for rape each year. "In at least 70% of the cases the victim knows her assailant," and a "large number of reported rapists are married, and most are less than 30 years of age." In trying to understand rape, the authors finally noted, "The abuser's main motivation is not pent-up sexual desire, but aggression, domination, and power" (Osterreich & Shirer, 1992).

In ancient Greece and Rome it was typical for only one female infant to be allowed to live because females were not valued. In the edited book of scholarly articles titled *Abuse and Religion: When Praying Isn't Enough*, a number of articles point out that families at high risk for domestic assault, violence, and child abuse are patriarchal families in which fear and hatred of women are present. The authors of these articles, who represent various religious faiths, all seemed to concur that many people, both men and women, have misinterpreted the Bible to use it to justify abuse and hatred of women (Horton & Williamson, 1988).

While some men's fear and hatred of women may have some biological explanations (for reasons explained later), there is no personal integrity in it for a modern human being. We believe that the confusion between men and women about sex ultimately goes back to the differences in testosterone, estrogen, and oxytocin, on the one hand, and the need that all human beings have for limbic resonance—that is, to be in sync with another human being at an emotionally intimate level—on the other.

Thousands of men with whom we have worked over the years have struggled with this problem. Many men appear to have only one way to feel truly in sync with anyone: via a sexual connection with their sexual mate, whether they are straight, gay, or bisexual. After spending a year or two in a men's therapy group, where they experience this limbic resonance in nonsexual ways with other guys, it takes a tremendous amount of pressure off of the sexual component of their marriages and partnerships, which ultimately enriches their emotional and sexual lives with their partners.

Because testosterone shuts down emotions, and because testosterone drives men to have intercourse and achieve orgasm with women in order to propagate the species, it wasn't long before the more physically powerful male simply took, as his own, the right to have sex when he felt he needed it. Today, this inappropriate sexual neediness tangles up many contemporary couples. In the past, this dynamic meant that the woman typically had to succumb to the drastic physical power imbalance in the relationship and simply accept that she was there to serve and to soothe her mate's pervasive male loneliness and emotional disconnection by surrendering sexually, often losing herself in the process. This loss of self included loss of dominion over her own body, her own sexuality, her identity as an adult woman, and her spirit—that is, the expression of her creative life force in the universe. As for the men involved in these scenarios, it is important to highlight that the term "neediness" translates easily into the term "emotionally little," which is not something that most men in the United States would be proud to claim as applying to them.

As human relationships and cultures became more emotionally complex, sex became more than just a vehicle for procreation. It became a vehicle for the deeply intimate limbic resonance between two lovers. We have maintained for years that it is a great sex life that allows the best-adjusted couples to get through many of the normally occurring crises and tragedies in life. In *With Pleasure: Thoughts on the Nature of Human Sexuality*, Paul Abramson and Steven Pinkerton of UCLA argued that sex evolved in humans not just for procreation, but also to make peace after conflicts, to strengthen the bond between partners, and to enhance love. Catherine Johnson's compelling book titled *Lucky in Love: The Secrets of Happy Couples and How Their Marriages Thrive* (1992), describes the results of her in-depth verbal interviews with 100 very happy couples. She noted that a good sex life is such an important yet "normal" feature of great marriages, that at first it wasn't apparent how deeply woven into the fabric it was in each happy marriage that she studied.

Physical anthropologist, Jesuit priest, and Catholic mystic Pierre Teilhard de Chardin rattled the Roman Catholic Church hierarchy when he suggested that because of the evolution of the human spirit, which parallels the physical evolution of all creatures on Earth, sex can no longer be considered primarily for procreation. He argued that it had evolved into a highly spiritual vehicle for expressing love between two people. In his thinking, sex for procreation was a secondary function. Not surprisingly, the Roman Catholic Church hierarchy looked at this forward-looking line of intellectual thought and tried to suppress his writings. Teilhard, for example, wrote,

That the dominant function of sexuality was at first to assure the preserva-
tion of the species is indisputable. This was so until the *state* of personality
[i.e., a separate, differentiated, identifiable sense of self—an identity] was
established in man. But from the critical moment of hominization [when
Homo sapiens first emerged on Earth], another more essential role was developed for love, a role of which we are seemingly only just beginning to feel the
importance; I mean the necessary synthesis of the two, male and female
[whether gay or straight], in the building of the human personality. No mor-
alist or psychologist has ever doubted that these partners find a mutual com-
pletion in the play of their reproductive function. But hitherto this has been
regarded only as a *secondary* effect, linked as an accessory to the principal
phenomenon of reproduction. In obedience to the laws of the personal universe, the importance of these factors is tending, if I am not mistaken, to be
reversed. Man and woman for the child, still and for so long as life on earth
has not reached maturity. *But man and woman for one another increasingly
and for ever.* (1969, pp. 72–76; emphasis added)

Sexuality is such a powerful and vulnerable part of being human that
we have tried to control it in ourselves and others for millennia. Chastity
belts, which were used not during the Crusades but during the Renais-
sance, were designed both for men and women in attempts to enforce
sexual fidelity. Trying to enforce something
that is essentially an act of love and free will
is a contradiction and a double bind. Like-
wise, the infamous mind-body dualism pro-
moted so fiercely by St. Augustine of Hippo
included the belief that using one's mind to
completely control one's body was the ideal,
and that the body was inferior to the soul. The body includes our sexuality,
our emotions, and many of the determinants of our mental and spiritual
health, so to delegate the body to such an inferior position in the scheme
of things is also crazy-making.

James Nelson, professor of Christian ethics at United Theological

> *Trying to enforce some-
> thing that is essentially
> an act of love and free
> will is a contradiction
> and a double bind.*

Seminary of the Twin Cities (Minneapolis-St. Paul, MN), pointed out in his groundbreaking book, *Embodiment* (1978), that much of our confusion about sexuality and our bodies *comes from* the many "dualisms" of thought that have plagued humans for centuries. Whatever we do to dissociate ourselves from our feelings, our senses, and thus our bodies will also cause us to dissociate from ourselves and others. Dissociation is just another way to say "alienated from," and for what appears to be many modern theologians, alienation is another way to say "sin." The belief that our bodies are evil is perhaps one of the leading causes of evil in the world today, if one defines "evil" as the trauma, family dysfunction, or psychological pain inflicted on one human being by another. In *The Divine Milieu*, Teilhard wrote,

> In their struggle towards the mystical life, men have often succumbed to the illusion of crudely contrasting soul and body, spirit and flesh, as good and evil. But despite certain current expressions, this Manichean tendency has never had the Church's approval. (1960, p. 105)

Certain attempts to control female sexuality today in many of the world's nations are considered to be grotesque. Confusion about a woman's role within society, and attempts to severely control and limit that role, is evident in the practice of female genital mutilation—clitorectomy—which is still common in some nations. A woman who advocates the practice explains it this way:

> The purpose of the cutting is to help ensure a woman's fidelity to her husband and her family. It's a tradition from antiquity. A woman's role in life is to care for her children, keep house, and cook. If she has not been cut, a woman might think instead about her own sexual pleasure. (quoted in Barbeau, 2004)

The paradoxical adoration of, desire for, and sanctification of women juxtaposed with the fear, hatred, and totalitarian control of women and women's sexuality evident in so many patriarchal societies seems to be in part the result of male fear and ambivalence: he is wildly attracted to her, and he wants to be inside of her and possess her mind, body, and spirit. This attitude removes the existential loneliness and disconnection that a man feels within himself due to his testosterone-suppressed emotions; however, focusing only on sex causes him, right after orgasm—right after he gets what he wants—to despise her for having that kind of power over him when in all other ways he mistakenly believes that he has total power over her. Thus, right after sex, he feels little, powerless, guilt-ridden, and ashamed.

To explain further, if a man believes that women are inferior, unnecessary, and powerless—and if he needed her for just a moment of sexual release because he was feeling so emotionally vulnerable—then the man is in a quandary. Now that he's demonstrated how much he needed her momentarily for that one portion of his psychological well-being, his vulnerability is more than he can handle, so he becomes disgusted and enraged with himself, and then blames *her* for being the party who exposed that vulnerability by doing what he demanded of her. She unknowingly exposed that he was not all-powerful *by being the very person who met his seemingly insatiable need.* It becomes a very confusing and powerful double bind for the woman, *but also* for the man. He temporarily satisfies his neediness and then goes back to his totalitarian, invulnerable self, denying that he was ever that needy to begin with—until the next time his loneliness or his hormones call.

This pattern can become a circular cycle of victim-perpetrator interactions that is quite familiar in systems theory, and it can go on indefinitely unless something within the system disrupts the very system of which it is a part. In contemporary patriarchal societies, the first women to try to disrupt these patterns by running away or by publicly speaking out against the system often pay with their lives.

With the advent of effective birth control and women's decreasing economic dependence on men, a heretofore unknown level of mutual resistance and struggle began. She no longer must have sex as part of her duty and as part of the survival of her children and herself, and he can no longer simply demand sex as his biological right. This leaves them both with the most challenging and rewarding dilemma of all: *How does one create balance, harmony, and sexual joy within a romantic marital system without being either a bully or a victim—without being too nasty or too nice?* How does a man tame his testosterone enough, without also becoming ineffective in the world, so that he is still desirable as a competent man? How does a woman embrace her estrogen and oxytocin

> *How does one create balance, harmony, and sexual joy within a romantic marital system without being either a bully or a victim—without being too nasty or too nice?*

and her innate desire to care for the family, while embracing her femininity, sexuality, and feminine power? And how does she do that without scaring him away?

We believe that David Schnarch's statement about the importance of sexual conflict in intimate relationships will always be a compelling aspect of all romantic-sexual relationships, whether straight, gay, or bisexual:

> A couple's sexual repertoire grows through conflict rather than compromise. Sexual conflict in marriage is not just inevitable—it's important . . . [because it] . . . makes both people grow up. (1997, p. 259)

When a man or a woman—plenty of women are more in the bullying role while their partners are more in the victim role—who tends to be more of a bully can be vulnerable for a moment and tell her how much he loves and desires her, can sincerely apologize when he has hurt her without losing his sense of self, and can be empathic and kind rather than narcissistic and small, things start to change. When someone who was formerly caught in the victim position is willing to embrace her (or his) own power without becoming a bully, and is able to manage her anxiety about rejection or retribution, can embrace her own sexuality as a grown-up woman, and declares with abandon that she wants to make love to him as well, then things can suddenly change.

As we pointed out earlier in this book, excluding damage to the frontal lobes of the brain, the primary dynamic in domestic violence situations is a man or a woman, or both, who are emotionally too little to tolerate the uncertainties present in all romantic relationships; who have a hard time soothing their own anxiety, loneliness, shame, and hurt feelings; and who then try to manage those feelings by being too nasty or too nice. If they can both tolerate the ambiguity of having a willing and lustful lover while acknowledging that they have no legitimate control over their partner or their partner's genuine sexuality, then things can change in positive ways that neither of them ever imagined possible.

Adult Children of Alcoholics

Another framework that many of our clients have found helpful in identifying why people may be too nasty or too nice comes from the adult children of alcoholics (ACoA) movement.

Minnesota was endearingly referred to as "The Land of 10,000 Treatment Centers" because for quite a while in the 1980s and early 1990s it seemed as if there was a chemical dependency treatment center on every street corner in the state. What has come to be known as the "Minnesota Model" of drug and alcohol treatment was developed there during the 1950s (Andersen, McGovern, & DuPont, 1999), where it was eventually used as the core for the treatment program at the Hazelden Foundation. The model began to spread around the world due to training and consultation provided both by the Hazelden Foundation as well as the Johnson Institute, which was a pioneering drug and alcohol teaching and training organization in Minneapolis that began its work in 1966.

In 1981 Claudia Black published *It Will Never Happen To Me!*, about children from alcoholic homes. Sharon Wegscheider-Cruse wrote *Another Chance: Hope and Health for the Alcoholic Family* that same year. Then in 1983 Rutgers University professor Janet G. Woititz released a little book titled *Adult Children of Alcoholics*, which detailed her groundbreaking research-based observations that men and women who had grown up in alcoholic families tended to have several painful characteristics in common. Her original list, below, is now familiar to millions of people around the world (Vegso, 2007). Over the years we have expanded the list to include the "other side" of each item, in recognition that children in painful families do not just acquire *victim behaviors*, but also *perpetrator behaviors*. Our additions are in brackets:

1. Adult children of alcoholics guess at what normal behavior is [or assume that everyone else is abnormal].
2. Adult children of alcoholics have difficulty following a project through from beginning to end [or are so overly task-oriented that their relationships suffer dearly].
3. Adult children of alcoholics lie when it would be just as easy to tell the truth [or are compulsively honest to the point of naïveté and harm to self].
4. Adult children of alcoholics judge themselves without mercy [or don't judge themselves at all, while judging others mercilessly].
5. Adult children of alcoholics have difficulty having fun [or have a hard time taking themselves or anyone else seriously].
6. Adult children of alcoholics take themselves very seriously [or not at all].
7. Adult children of alcoholics have difficulty with intimate relationships [or focus too much on intimate relationships and not enough on other aspects of their lives].
8. Adult children of alcoholics overreact to changes over which they have no control [or don't react enough, saying "no problem," when in fact there is a big problem].
9. Adult children of alcoholics constantly seek approval and affirmation [or are shameless and don't care at all about what others think].
10. Adult children of alcoholics usually feel that they are different from other people [or that everyone else is just wrong].
11. Adult children of alcoholics are super responsible [or super irresponsible].
12. Adult children of alcoholics are extremely loyal, even in the face of evidence that the loyalty is undeserved [or are not loyal at all, acting out their pain and anger by breaking rules and having too little guilt].
13. Adult children of alcoholics are impulsive. They tend to lock themselves

into a course of action without giving serious consideration to alternative behaviors or possible consequences. This impulsively leads to confusion, self-loathing, and loss of control over their environment. In addition, they spend an excessive amount of energy cleaning up the mess [or they are so deliberate and overly cautious that projects that should normally be completed in a day or two can take weeks]. (Woititz, 1983)

Since publication of Woititz's first book, there has been a proliferation of research on the impact of familial alcoholism on later development, much of which has supported Woititz's original assumptions and, as is often the case, some that has not (e.g., Griffin & Amodeo, 1998; Harter, 2000; Hunt, 1997; Menees & Segrin, 2000; Velleman & Orford, 1999). When compared to adults who did *not* grow up in alcoholic homes, ACoAs are more likely to become substance abusers themselves (e.g., Boyd, Plemons, Schwartz, Johnson, & Pickens, 1999); are more likely to become the victims of partner abuse (e.g., Griffin & Amodeo, 1998); have lower self-esteem, higher neuroticism scores, and are more likely to suffer from depression (e.g., Beaudoin, Murray, Bond, & Barnes, 1997); are at greater risk for mood disorders and eating disorders (e.g., Cuijpers, Langendoen, & Bijl, 1999); are more likely to become nicotine-dependent (e.g., Cuijpers & Smit, 2002); and are more likely to experience stress in life (e.g., Fischer, Kittleson, Ogletree, Welshimer, Woehlke, & Benshof, 2000).

When individuals decide that they want to understand why they are acting more from the stance of a bully, more from the stance of a victim, or acting in both ways—which is quite common—we encourage them to begin finding their answers in this chapter, in Chapter 9, and in the references and citations throughout the book. Above all, we encourage such individuals to (1) admit that they are doing things that they are not proud of, (2) search for the reasons that they are doing them—both biological and environmental, and (3) look for ways to act from their best selves, even if they never saw how to do that when they were growing up. We present more examples of how to accomplish these tasks as this book unfolds.

Part Four:

STAYING AFLOAT AMIDST A SEA OF CONSTANT CHANGE

My very top priority is for people to understand that they have the power to change things themselves.

—*Aung San Suu Kyi, Burmese opposition politician*

S uu Kyi received the Rafto Prize and the Sakharov Prize for Freedom of Thought in 1990 and the Nobel Peace Prize in 1991. In 1992 she was awarded the Jawaharlal Nehru Award for International Understanding by the government of India and the International Simón Bolívar Prize from the government of Venezuela. In 2007 Canada made her an honorary citizen of that country, one of only five people ever to receive the honor. In 2011 she was awarded the Wallenberg Medal, a humanitarian award given for actions taken on behalf of the oppressed and defenseless.

In the 1990 general election, her National League for Democracy Party won 59 percent of the national votes and 81 percent (392 of 485) of the seats in Parliament. She had, however, already been detained under house arrest before the elections. She remained under house arrest in Burma for almost fifteen of the twenty-one years from July 1989 until her most recent release in November 2010.

CHAPTER 11

Patience, Self-Restraint, and Genuine Self-Esteem

The difference between a child batterer and a
non-batterer is often just a split second.

—*John and Linda Friel*

Citing the work of coauthors Jean Twenge and W. Keith Campbell in *The Narcissism Epidemic*, psychotherapist Lori Gottlieb—in a cover story in the July/August 2011 edition of *The Atlantic* titled "How to Land Your Kid in Therapy"—noted that since the 1980s (and we have seen it at least since the 1970s), rates of narcissism among college students have been consistently rising right along with what we later explain to be rather faulty interpretations of "self-esteem":

> Narcissists are happy when they're younger, because they're the center of the universe. Their parents act like their servants, shuttling them to any activity they choose and catering to their every desire. Parents are constantly telling their children how special and talented they are. This gives them an inflated view of their specialness compared to other human beings. Instead of feeling good about themselves, they feel better than everyone else. . . . [Then when they grow up,] they get out into the real world and they start to feel lost and helpless. Kids who always have problems solved for them believe that

they don't know how to solve problems. And they're right—they don't. (from Twenge & Campbell, 2010)

In *The Soul of Adulthood* (Friel & Friel, 1995, pp. 84–85) and *The 7 Worst Things (Good) Parents Do* (Friel & Friel, 1999, pp. 20–21), we described an early 1970s university preschool one of us had encountered in which a few of the three- to four-year-olds seemed to be paralyzed as a result of parents who rewarded them for every little move that they made. When immediate reinforcement for each little behavior was not forthcoming in the preschool setting, these little ones simply ceased to respond to even the slightest challenge. Ever since then, we have stressed how critically important it is for parents and children to learn to *value struggle and disappointment* in daily life.

We believe that for more than forty years, various segments of U.S. society have misapplied and misinterpreted the self-esteem movement, which has caused a great deal of damage to children, families, and the nation as a whole.

Big Fraud at the Self-Esteem Store: The Furnace Repair Man

Imagine that you live in Minnesota, it is the end of January, and your furnace just stopped operating. It is –15 degrees Fahrenheit outside with wind chills hovering around –50 degrees Fahrenheit. You call three or four furnace repair companies to get on their waiting lists, and then you and your family pray that someone comes to the house before you freeze. After forty-five minutes, the doorbell rings, you run to the door and fling it open, and there stands a very neatly dressed, very pleasant, polite young man with a large toolbox in his hands. He makes good eye contact, shakes your hand, and says he'll have your furnace going in no time. He goes down to the basement's mechanical room and starts working.

Thirty minutes have elapsed, the other three repair shops have called to see if you still need help, and you have said "No," releasing them to go on to the next houses on their lists. You hear your guy rattling around in the furnace. You're all smiling, anticipating the sound of the furnace coming back on. Then you hear his footsteps coming up from the basement. With a "gee-shucks," folksy kind of confidence, he shakes his head emphatically and says, "Gosh. I'm really sorry. That thing has been jury-rigged so many times by other guys over the years that I can't figure it out."

"What?" you exclaim. "But we just released the other three repair guys! We'll freeze to death!"

"I'm really sorry," he says, with such a friendly, kind tone of voice that all you can do is shake your head in disbelief as you close the door behind him.

He walks to his truck, gets in, turns on the engine, and then before he goes to his next call, he looks at himself in the rearview mirror and says with the utmost sincerity, "I didn't fix that furnace, but I'm good enough, I'm smart enough, and doggone it, people like me," just like current U.S. Senator Al Franken (D-MN) used to say as his character Stewart Smalley on *Saturday Night Live.*

And then he goes to the next house, and then the next, and then the next. Eventually the people of his community angrily run him out of town on a rail. So he moves to a neighboring state and tries to set up shop there. But now he finds himself feeling depressed. So he goes to a therapist, who, thank goodness, is a self-esteem therapist. After every session the repairman feels wonderful, because the therapist says things like, "You're a wonderful person," "I just know you're going to make it," "Every human being is good to the core," and "I like you." But within twenty-four hours, Mr. Can't-Fix-It feels awful again. This pattern continues with three more therapists, and still no change.

Then he stumbles onto a psychologist who works with these kinds of problems in a different way. The psychologist listens to how depressed he feels, then does an extensive intake interview, including asking for the minute details of what happened at that first stop at that first house. "Tell me exactly what happened from the time you rang the doorbell until you got back into your truck and drove away," he said.

"Well, I shook the man's hand and made good eye contact, just the way I was trained to do."

"What HVAC school did you go to, by the way?" the psychologist asked.

"It was the Self-Esteem School of Heating, Ventilating, and Air Conditioning," the man answered. "So after I shook his hand, I went downstairs and opened up the cover of the furnace, and there in front of me was a tangle of wires that I'd simply never seen before."

"Did you do the mandatory four years of apprenticeship required to become a licensed HVAC repair person?"

"What's *that*?" the man answered.

The psychologist then administers a number of personality, clinical, and ability tests. After they are all scored and evaluated, he sits down with the furnace repair guy and has a follow-up session that goes like this:

"You have the intelligence to handle the job. That's good. You don't have any serious personality problems. And interestingly, you are not clinically depressed, even though you feel like you might be."

"Oh," the man responds. "Then what's going on?"

The psychologist takes a deep breath, leans toward the man in a firm but kind way, and says, "This may be hard for you to hear, and therefore I would like you to hang in here with me until I've had a chance to explain everything, and to make my recommendations. You are not clinically depressed. *Your problem is that you don't know how to fix furnaces.*"

The man looked stunned. Shell-shocked.

The psychologist continued. "You have been duped, lied to, fooled, sold a bill of goods. The program you went to was *designed to make you feel good, not to make you competent*. And here is the hard part, and where I see our therapy going, should you decide to continue. If you truly believe that you would enjoy being an HVAC repair person—"

"Oh, yes. Yes, I do. I think I will really love it," the man interjected.

"—then the first thing I need to help you with are the feelings of betrayal and incompetence that you feel. Then I will need to help you move toward reenrolling in a *real* HVAC school, and while you're redoing your entire training, I'll need to help you manage the understandable recurring anger and frustration that you have about having to do it all over. If you're willing to follow this plan, I can help you. And if you do, I can assure you that you will one day have a successful career as an HVAC repair expert."

The man looked stunned again, but he felt the genuine kindness and professional competence emanating from the psychologist. Deep inside, he knew the psychologist was right, and that the psychologist had his best interests at heart. "Yes. That's what I want to do."

"Okay, then. Let's get started," the psychologist replied.

The Self-Esteem Movement

The self-esteem movement began several decades ago in response to the terrible discipline practices that were considered proper at the time. It was culturally acceptable to belittle and humiliate children "to teach you a lesson," and it was always done "for your own good." Alice Miller's groundbreaking book on child abuse had the same title: *For Your Own Good: Hidden Cruelty in Child-Rearing and the Roots of Violence* (1983). To put a dunce cap on a child's head and then make her sit in front of the classroom to be laughed at by all of the other children because she has a hard time reading aloud is unquestionably a cruel, hostile act, and any social movement designed to stop such practices is to be applauded.

The problem is in what happened next. As the self-esteem movement grew, psychologists and educators won more and more grants, did more and more research, and wrote more and more articles on self-esteem. What began as a useful, hypothetical construct suddenly took on a life of its own. To many, *self-esteem is a living entity inside of each child*—an entity that has mass and weight and measurable dimensions—*except that it isn't, and it doesn't*.

The trouble with the whole concept is that self-esteem is neither an entity inside of us nor does it cause anything. In fact, self-esteem is *itself* caused by something else (Baumeister, Heatherton, & Tice, 1994; Baumeister, Smart, & Boden, 1996; Bushman & Baumeister, 1998). It is simply a summary variable, a descriptor that helps scientists talk to each other in shorthand.

Little Bobby

To say that Little Bobby is doing poorly in school because he has low self-esteem is like saying that Little Bobby's grandfather can't remember where he left his false teeth because he's ninety-two years old. It's nonsense. Grandpa can't remember where he left his false teeth because he has lost a certain number of brain cells, or because the blood circulation to his brain has been restricted due to arteriosclerosis or the ravages of diabetes, or because he has Alzheimer's disease. But not all ninety-two-year-olds have severe memory problems, and *age itself does not cause anything just by itself,* as gerontological psychologists Warner Schaie (1965), Paul Baltes (1968), and John Nesselroade (1970) so wisely warned more than forty years ago.

The truth is that Little Bobby may be doing poorly in school because no one at home is encouraging him to learn anything, or because nobody is at home, period. He may be doing poorly because of one of the following issues:

- He has a mistaken belief that he isn't capable of learning.
- No one at home knows how to learn things, and so he has no one to observe in order to see how to learn things.
- He has a learning disability.
- He isn't getting enough sleep due to his parents fighting every night.
- He isn't getting enough to eat.
- He has some kind of chronic illness.
- He has paralyzing anxiety due to being screamed at and criticized at home all the time.

If we say that Little Bobby has trouble learning because he has low self-esteem, then we might think that we can solve his learning problem by raising his self-esteem. How have experts typically tried to do that? By praising kids a lot and teaching them to tell themselves that they're wonderful. What happens if kids don't know anything but are continually encouraged to see themselves as the greatest? The result is narcissism, grandiosity, incompetence, and eventually failure, none of which do much for a child's self-esteem.

If we say that Little Bobby has trouble learning *because he doesn't know how to learn,* then our strategy will be to *teach him how to learn.* If he's having trouble learning because no one at home is encouraging him to learn, then we could either work with the people at home to teach them how to value learning, or we could make sure that we make the classroom really interesting for Little Bobby while making it worth his while to learn.

Roy Baumeister's Work: Self-Esteem Myths

Perhaps the first serious research psychologist to bring this issue into the academic world was Roy Baumeister, who, along with his colleagues, has been studying self-esteem myths for a number of years. In one laboratory study, he demonstrated that college students who have falsely inflated self-esteem are actually more prone to violence, not less (Bushman & Baumeister, 1998). In an exhaustive review of more than 170 primary books and research articles published in the *American Psychological Association*'s refereed journal *Psychological Review*, Baumeister, Smart, and Boden (1996) carefully developed the hypothesis that *violence and aggression are directly correlated with inflated self-esteem*. In the conclusion of their review, the authors wrote,

> As compared with other cultures and other historical eras, modern America has been unusually fond of the notion that elevating the self-esteem of each individual will be best for society (e.g., see Huber, 1971). America is also, perhaps not coincidentally, one of the world's most violent societies, with rates of violent crime that far exceed even those of other modern, industrialized nations. The hope that raising everyone's self-esteem will prove to be a panacea for both individual and societal problems continues unabated today (e.g., California Task Force, 1990), and indeed the allusions in the mass media to the desirability of self-esteem suggest that it may even be gaining in force. In this context, the notion that low self-esteem causes violence may have been widely appealing as one more reason to raise self-esteem.
>
> Our review has indicated, however, that it is threatened egotism [we read this as "a threat to falsely inflated self-esteem, also known as a person's pathological *narcissism*"] rather than low self-esteem that leads to violence. Moreover, certain forms of high self-esteem seem to increase one's prone-

ness to violence. An uncritical endorsement of the cultural value of high self-esteem may therefore be counterproductive and even dangerous. In principle it might become possible to inflate everyone's self-esteem, but it will almost certainly be impossible to insulate everyone against ego threats. In fact, as we have suggested, the higher (and especially the more inflated) the self-esteem, the greater the vulnerability to ego threats. Viewed in this light, the societal pursuit of high self-esteem for everyone may literally end up doing considerable harm. (1996, p. 29)

Competence and Real Intimacy: The Cures for the Self-Esteem Dilemma

In light of so many competing definitions and interpretations of the term "self-esteem," let us briefly summarize how we are choosing to define the concept in this book:

- "Self-esteem" refers to how one evaluates one's own worth or value—how you feel about yourself.
- *High self-esteem* means that you feel good about, and highly value, yourself, your abilities, your skills, and your competencies—*whether justifiably or not.*
- *Low self-esteem* means that you feel bad about yourself, and that you do not have a very good appraisal of yourself, your skills, and your competencies—*whether justifiably or not.*
- *Inflated self-esteem* means that you have a high appraisal of yourself, your skills, and your competencies, but it is inaccurate; you are not nearly as good at certain things as you think you are. This is called *pathological narcissism.*
- *Deflated self-esteem* means that you have a low appraisal of yourself, your skills, and your competencies, but it is inaccurate; you are more competent than you give yourself credit for. In some circles, this is called *codependency* or a *deficient sense of entitlement.*
- *True, genuine, healthy self-esteem* means that you know what your strengths are, and you know how your skills and competencies compare with others—

that is, where you "fit in." Healthy self-esteem also means that you know what your weaknesses are, and where you fit in when compared to others, on those aspects of yourself.

For example, one might say, "I know I do a great job fixing cars, and I am proud of my skills, and I also know that I'm not as good as those factory-trained guys who have memorized every nut and bolt and wire in the cars that they repair." Or, "I know I am horrible at repairing holes in sheetrock in my house. The guys who do this for a living do a much better job than I do. I also know that there are some guys who are even worse than me." In both cases, what defines healthy self-esteem is that *you know the real you, you are okay with who you are, warts and all, and you feel good about yourself for the right reasons.* This might be called being a competent, psychologically differentiated adult.

> *What defines healthy self-esteem is that you know the real you, you are okay with who you are, warts and all, and you feel good about yourself for the right reasons.*

With those clarifications in mind, here is the secret formula: for anyone who feels that he suffers from low self-esteem, there are only two things that will make a difference, and they will both make all the difference in the world, *if they are both present.*

Competence

First, we have to become *competent.* Every human being has the potential to become competent based on her age and intellectual strengths and limits. We know a man who is twenty-six years old and has Down syndrome. He has an IQ of about 50. He is one of the most competent people we know. Is he limited in ways that you are not? Yes.

Neither of the authors will ever become astrophysicists because neither of us has the kind of intelligence that would allow such an accomplishment. One of us likes to read popular articles about the universe but readily acknowledges that his understanding of those articles is limited primarily by his scientific IQ, and secondarily by his academic training, which in turn is limited by his scientific IQ.

Over the many years of our private practice in psychology, we have worked with doctors, lawyers, plumbers, geneticists, psychiatrists, electricians, investment bankers, teachers, laborers, accountants, retail clerks, psychologists, housewives, real estate agents, bank tellers, students, construction workers, stay-at-home dads—you name it. No matter who it is or what they do for a living, we find ourselves silently telling ourselves, *This person knows so much more than I do about . . .* People come to us for *our* expertise, but they each have *their own expertise,* for which we honor them, and hold them in the highest esteem. When it's −15 degrees Fahrenheit outside and your furnace is broken, which repair person do you want: the one who feels good about himself but doesn't really know much about furnaces, or the one who can fix your furnace faster than you can say "igloo"?

Being Seen, Heard, and Understood—aka Acceptance and Belonging

It has been said that if you are a member of Alcoholics Anonymous, and if you went home earlier that day only to find your wife in bed with the next-door neighbor, and if in a fit of blind rage you reached for the pistol in your nightstand that you swore you'd never buy, and you shot both of them and killed them—and then, stunned and dissociated, you wandered into your AA meeting, pale, ashen, and disoriented, and announced that you had just killed your wife and her lover in your bed, the first thing that people would do would be to surround you, put their arms around you, bring you over to one of the chairs in the circle, be with you, ask you how you are doing, and encourage you to talk about it.

In healthy families, people *talk it out* and *work it out,* not *act it out.* You would cry, sob, cry some more, tell the story, sob, feel remorse, regret, rage, anger, shame, fear, sadness, loneliness, emptiness, hurt, terror, cry some more, and then gradually begin to calm down, knowing that all of those warm, living, loving human beings who are surrounding you have been, and always will be, there for you.

After a time, someone would gently, compassionately, firmly, and lovingly say, "You need to call the police now. You need to know that each of us is here for you right now, and that we will be there for you if go to court, and if you go to prison; and that we will all be here when you are eventually released, because we love you and care about you, and we always will, no matter what happens, from this moment forward."

That is the second key to repairing low self-esteem: We need to be around people who can accept us for who we truly are instead of for who they think we should be. For sure, we need to find and develop our competencies. But there are so many competent people in the world who feel lonely, angry, worthless, empty, and lost. *Just* being competent doesn't cut it—at all. But if we have *competency*, *and* the sense of *truly being seen, heard, and understood*, then we have it nailed down.

> *We need to be around people who can accept us for who we truly are instead of for who they think we should be.*

In healthy families, people are accepted warts and all, but surely are not allowed to get away with murder, or become spoiled, or require nonstop, constant praise. In healthy families, each person is *seen, heard,* and *understood* on a regular basis. In twenty-first-century America, this is much easier said than done. In her book *In the Middle of Everywhere: Helping Refugees Enter the American Community* (2002), psychologist Mary Pipher described the sabbatical she took from her private practice in Lincoln, Nebraska, to help the many recent immigrants adjust to life in the U.S. Midwest. She humbly described how her initial intention was to help *them* adapt to U.S. society, only to find that she learned as much, if not more *from them* by observing how they lived their lives and solved their problems.

Acceptance and Belonging

In a healthy family, everybody fits in no matter how different they might be—the tall ones, the short ones, the males, the females, the old ones, the young ones, the ones who struggle with their weight, the ones with high metabolism who can eat whatever they want and never gain a pound, the ones who are good at math, the ones who can't add fractions, the artistic ones, the loud ones, the introverts. They all fit in and belong, and all are valued. Each is seen as contributing a unique, important piece of the complex systemic puzzle that is their life together as a family and as members of the broader community.

In describing his childhood, a man might say, "My parents have been very understanding as I've grown up. My math difficulties showed up pretty early. They had me tested, I got some tutoring, and I struggled my way through it. They never said that I didn't have to learn math, because they knew I needed to learn it. So we'd have a lot of battles about it as I grew up. But they never said that I was stupid, and I always felt like I was okay—you know—an equal member of the family. They didn't need me to be great at math any more than they needed my sister to be great at art. They just wanted to make sure that each of us had the basic skills we needed to get along in the world."

A sense of belonging is one of the most important and powerful forces in any human being's life, and yet it is conveyed in such a quiet, simple way in most cases. There are those dramatic moments, like when you win the art contest or get a scholarship to study math in college. In these cases, family members shout excitedly and celebrate. But those events don't happen very often. A sense of belonging is a pretty constant experience in a healthy family. It is conveyed in a lot of ordinary, matter-of-fact ways that, when combined, add up to the foundation for everything else in our lives.

This is why we have said repeatedly over the years that the little things in life—the ordinary, everyday things—are usually the most important. A good film director knows that. He'll focus on a look, a glance, a pat on the back, an upturned brow, or a tiny gesture of kindness. After being around the same people for a while, we know whether it's safe to let down our guard. That's another way to measure whether you feel like you belong. If the people in your family are critical, nitpicking types, then after a while you'll know deep down inside that it just isn't safe in the same way it's safe at your best friend's house. At first, it's hard to pin down what's going on in a family like this. But if you get good at what we call "noticing and listening," you'll be able to discern what the pattern is.

Mom asks, "Are you going to wear *that* to the party?" You reply that jeans and a sport shirt with a button-down collar are what most of the guys wear to parties these days, yes. Your dad asks why you thought you wanted to major in chemistry when you get to college, but it isn't an innocent curiosity that underlies his question. You can tell from the tone in his voice that he's disappointed in your choice of chemistry. You don't know why. You don't know why it should matter to him. It's your life. You ask yourself, *Why can't they just accept me for who I am every once in a while?*

When a family comes in to do some therapy work, one of the things we often try to do is to help them see these "invisible" patterns that exist in all families. Invariably, as Dad and Mom begin to see the level of negativity and criticism that they have created, they will say that they never intended it to have that effect. They'll say that they were just trying to be concerned, loving parents. That they were just trying to be helpful. That *their* parents were that way, and they didn't mean any harm by it, either. If they stay with it and struggle through until they can let their defenses down a little more, they can eventually get to a place where they can say that they let their *anxiety* take control of them, and that no excuses justify their children having to walk on eggshells all the time because of parents' anxiety, and that they are sorry.

When we worry about our kids, it shows that we love them. When we worry too much about them, it shows that we aren't confronting ourselves enough. When parents can hear, acknowledge, and embrace both of the statements above, then an infinitely positive, therapeutic double bind has taken hold. *Then* we have great hope for the family.

> *When we worry about our kids, it shows that we love them. When we worry too much about them, it shows that we aren't confronting ourselves enough.*

One of the most important things that happens after a man or woman has been in one of our therapy groups for about nine months is that this deeper sense of belonging begins to appear. You might think that nine months is a long time, but when you realize what a pervasive phenomenon we're dealing with, and how deep into our souls it goes, nine months isn't long at all. And even though we've seen it appear in hundreds and hundreds of people over the years, when this sense of acceptance and belonging begins to appear, it feels like a miracle is happening right before our eyes. There are no bells and whistles, no fireworks, no sirens, no orchestras or choirs accompanying this event. It appears in a look, a glance, a new level of comfort, a willingness to experience feelings more openly, or in giving more appropriate feedback to other group members. *It shows up in small, ordinary, everyday ways, and when it does, the person begins to heal with a depth she never knew was possible.*

When they finally believe, right down to their toes that they are at last being seen, heard, and understood, then there is nothing that they can't go out into the world and accomplish, within the limits of their competencies—which is, of course, the other component of true self-esteem.

Patience and Self-Restraint: The Mother(s) of All Virtues and the Keys to All Success

While a psychologist at Stanford University in the 1960s, Walter Mischel (e.g., 1968) conducted a series of elegant, groundbreaking studies on the relationship between four- and five-year-olds' tendencies to either accept a smaller reward immediately or to wait a few minutes for a larger reward. It came to be known as the study of *delay of gratification*. We have cited his work for decades because it describes a persistent, pervasive flaw in U.S. parenting practices. Mischel found that twelve to fourteen years later, those four- and five-year-olds who chose to wait a few minutes longer for the larger reward

- Were more socially competent.
- Were superior in school performance.
- Were superior in coping and in dealing with frustration and stress—less likely to go to pieces, freeze, or regress under stress.
- Embraced challenges and pursued them and didn't give up.

- Were more self-reliant, self-confident, trustworthy, dependable, attentive, reasonable, resourceful, and cooperative.

Those who chose the immediate reward in the experiment:

- Were still unable to delay gratification.
- Were aggressive, restless, and unable to deal with stress.
- Were sulky and whiny.
- Were prone to feelings of victimization.
- Were stubborn and indecisive.
- Overreacted to irritations with a sharp temper.
- Were easily upset.
- Were prone to jealousy and envy.
- Shied away from social contacts.
- Thought of themselves as "bad."
- Were mistrustful and resentful of "not getting enough."

We thank John's doctoral advisor and behavior modification expert par excellence, John D. Cone, Ph.D., for continuing this research and for keeping it in the forefront of our minds as we got bogged down with other topics and subjects during our graduate training. Dr. Cone's work continued long after the original delay of gratification studies had first been done, and he made significant contributions to this area of research and inquiry for many years after those original studies were done by Mischel (e.g., Cone, 1977, Cone & Hawkins, 1977) Now, almost half a century later, it appears that Walter Mischel hit upon a truth that is one of the most important factors in whether we as a nation will ultimately survive—whether our marriages will fail, whether we can adapt to the rapid changes that are coming at us at warp speed, and whether we will even be able to hang on to the system of government that only fifty years ago was seen by the entire world as the best system that had ever been created.

How could delay of gratification matter this much? Everything has accelerated so fast that the thought of slowing things down and becoming *more thoughtful, more reflective,* and *self-limiting* seems counterproductive.

But when things move fast and then eventually get out of control, the ones who emerge in positions of leadership after all of the dust of chaotic change has settled are the ones who can *think, reflect, self-limit,* and *wait* before they act.

A summary in the American Psychological Association's *Monitor on Psychology*, from the Proceedings of the National Academy of Sciences, noted,

> Self-control measure scores from children as young as age 3 could predict those children's health and legal troubles in adulthood, according to Duke University psychologists Terrie Moffit, Ph.D., and Avshalom Caspi, Ph.D. The researchers looked at longitudinal data from more than 1,000 New Zealanders, about whom self-control information had been collected from parents, teachers, observers and the children themselves. By the time they reached age 32, those with the lowest scores on self-control measures were the most likely to have breathing problems, gum disease, sexually transmitted diseases, high cholesterol and high blood pressure, as well as financial and legal problems such as massive debt and criminal records. *However, those who improved their self-control scores throughout their young lives escaped that trend.* (American Psychological Association, 2011, 16–17; emphasis added)

Pamela Druckerman (2012) wrote an insightful essay in the usually conservative *Wall Street Journal* praising the parenting methods of French parents, and bemoaning the way that many children in the United States are raised. The majority of the essay, excerpted from her book, *Bringing Up Bébé: One American Mother Discovers the Wisdom of French Parenting* (2012), focuses on delay of gratification—the simple act of waiting instead of demanding everything immediately. In a glowing response to Druckerman's essay, retired Marine Corps major and Vietnam F-4 Phantom jet pilot William A. McIntyre (2012) wrote us:

> I was far from a perfect parent, but this article makes me feel better. I had this old-fashioned idea that "no" should mean no, that parents had a right to be able to talk to each other without being interrupted. I thought my wife and I had a responsibility to have a relationship with each other rather

than being slaves to kids. I thought we couldn't be good parents without that relationship. I thought that the kids would be better off having a model of a man/woman relationship that they didn't control or unduly interfere with. I thought that they would actually be frightened if they realized that they were in control, and they didn't know WTF they were doing.

One of the major problems plaguing so many U.S. families today is that when parents and children are overextended and overscheduled with activities, it prevents them from forming proper emotional bonds with each other, which then prevents them from taking the time to reflect and analyze, which then prevents them from learning to identify and express their feelings, and to learn the complex rules of human interaction that are so crucial for thriving in a complex global society. Add in the physical and emotional isolation caused by computers, video games, and handheld devices that distract from time family members actually spend interacting with each other face-to-face, and the toll is silently and invisibly overwhelming.

As a result, these overextended and emotionally disconnected families are unable to give children guidelines for how to *soothe themselves appropriately*, which then hobbles them to the point that psychologists are seeing more and more twenty-somethings, thirty-somethings, and forty-somethings coming down the pike who are suffering from severe personality disorders. For the past thirty years, when presenting at professional training conferences around the United States and the United Kingdom, we have been hearing more and more professionals talking about the increase in the incidence of personality disorders among adults raised after 1970.

"Americans Are Forever Brooding"

Perhaps the most troubling aspect of all, because of how it speaks to the enduring depth of the problem, is the following quote from Alexis de Tocqueville's *Democracy in America*:

Americans are forever brooding over advantages they do not possess. . . . It is strange to see with what feverish ardor the Americans pursue their own welfare, and to watch the vague dread that constantly torments them lest they should not have chosen the shortest path which may lead to it. (1863b, vol. 2, p. 164)

Contrary to what those who have a very limited—or befuddled— knowledge of recent U.S. history would prefer to believe, our national focus on material wealth to the exclusion of our emotional and spiritual depth is not something that grew out of the boom years following World War II. It is something that has been in the fabric of our national character far longer. The "vague dread" about having more and more and getting it faster and faster that Tocqueville observed in 1831 America is what nearly bankrupted the United States in 2009 and 2010.

This is simply the part of the American Dream that has always been at the core of a much darker American nightmare.

Self-Restraint, Self-Control, Competence, and Books: One Simple (and Very Challenging) Way to Dig Ourselves Out of Our Troubles

In November 2005 two daughters of Korean immigrants, Dr. Soo Kim Abboud and attorney Jane Kim, published a book titled *Top of the Class: How Asian Parents Raise High Achievers—and How You Can Too* (not to be confused with the wonderful, controversial, and more recent book by Yale Law School professor Amy Chua, which in our opinion the general public and the press have grossly misinterpreted and misunderstood). Abboud and Kim noted that while Asian Americans comprised only 4 percent of the U.S. population at the time, they represented 20 percent of students attending Ivy League universities. Contrary to what many Americans assume is simply a genetic advantage, these sisters argued convincingly that the way they were raised made the difference. In a promotional interview on *Good Morning America* around the time of the book's release, the sisters described their mother buying each of them a candy bar, setting each one aside, and then telling her daughters that they could have their candy bar after reading an entire book.

The sisters' book is filled with the practical wisdom of the specific family in which they grew up. Coincidentally, that wisdom is in perfect sync with what academic researchers in the United States have known since the 1960s: kids excel in school if they learn to delay gratification, if they live in a family that values and is genuinely excited about education, and that parents' genuine love of learning *as demonstrated by their actual behavior, not by lecturing*, is key.

It reminds us of the study done prior to the 1960s in which it was discovered that, after basic raw intelligence, the best predictor of academic success in children was the number of books in the home. As we recall, the researchers went into people's homes and actually counted the number of books and then correlated that with each child's academic performance, controlling statistically for intelligence test scores.

In a May 21, 2010, article in the *Chronicle of Higher Education* titled "Want Smart Kids? Here's What to Do," which summarized a research article published in the journal *Research in Social Stratification and Mobility* (Evans, Kelley, Sikora, & Treiman, 2010), Tom Bartlett wrote:

> Buy a lot of books.
>
> That seems kind of obvious, right? But what's surprising, according to a new study published in the journal *Research in Social Stratification and Mobility*, is just how strong the correlation is between a child's academic achievement and the number of books his or her parents own. It's even more important than whether the parents went to college or hold white-collar jobs.
>
> Books matter. A lot.
>
> The study was conducted over 20 years, in 27 countries, and surveyed more than 70,000 people. Researchers found that children who grew up in a home with more than 500 books spent 3 years longer in school than children whose parents had only a few books. Also, a child whose parents have lots of books is nearly 20 percent more likely to finish college.
>
> For comparison purposes, the children of educated parents (defined as people with at least 15 years of schooling) were 16 percent more likely than the children of less-educated parents to get their college degrees. Formal education matters, but not as much as books.

From the paper:

Thus it seems that scholarly culture, and the taste for books that it brings, flows from generation to generation largely of its own accord, little affected by education, occupational status, or other aspects of class. . . . Parents give their infants toy books to play with in the bath; read stories to little children at bed-time; give books as presents to older children; talk, explain, imagine, fantasize, and play with words unceasingly. Their children get a taste for all this, learn the words, master the skills, buy the books. And that pays off handsomely in schools.

Even a relatively small number of books can make a difference: A child whose family has 25 books will, on average, complete two more years of school than a child whose family is sadly book-less.

Patience, self-restraint, and genuine self-esteem are critical factors in the success of any civilization, but especially in the United States, where, since perhaps the 1600s, we have been a people who have had too much anxiety about *acquiring* land, wealth, and power (as Tocqueville observed in 1835), and too much emphasis on the importance of *individualism*, as opposed to the warmth and buoyancy that come from close personal relationships. *When any system gets this far out of balance, something has to happen. The problem is, no one can really predict what that will be until it happens.*

As an ending to this chapter, and a counterpoint to these characteristically American traits, we were especially heartened by our dear Irish friend, London actor Dearbhla Molloy, who was in Minneapolis to star in artistic director Joe Dowling's innovative production of *Much Ado About Nothing* at the Guthrie Theater in the fall of 2011. Two days after her last performance in November, she said that she was flying back home to Dublin before returning to London. Her ninety-year-old mother's eyesight was nearly gone, so she was going to take her on a holiday driving trip around various parts of the very familiar southwest of Ireland, staying in B&Bs along the way, and spend the evenings reading a good book to her mother as they sat together by a warm fire. She said that both she and her mother would very much like that.

CHAPTER 12

CARE:
GIVING US THE BUOYANCY
TO HANDLE ALMOST ANYTHING

Its inhabitants are, as the man once said,
"Whores, pimps, gamblers, and sons of bitches, by which he
meant Everybody." Had the man looked through another peephole,
he might have said "Saints and angels and martyrs and holy men,"
and he would have meant the same thing.

—*John Steinbeck,* Cannery Row

The Buoyancy Effect that Comes from Human Care

The care we have for each other, and the human buoyancy that results from it, is what underlies the fundamental difference between people who are *powerful and gracious* and those who tend to be *too nasty* or *too nice*. It isn't difficult to understand, but it can be perplexing and easy to avoid altogether, because people in the United States struggle with being emotionally intimate. It simply isn't our strongest suit.

Given the obvious limitations of being human, each of us retains the ability throughout our lives to be both "sons of bitches" and "saints and angels." In those two sentences from the first page of *Cannery Row*, John

Steinbeck captured the essence of what it means to be human. To embrace that paradox one must understand that each of us is, at the same time, terribly flawed and also capable of awe-inspiring acts of integrity, kindness, courage, and wisdom.

People who can embrace that paradox appear to be physically and psychologically the healthiest; and they know that it can't be done without having some deep relationships that they consistently nourish. As Urie Bronfenbrenner wrote so eloquently,

> Witness the American Ideal: the Self-Made Man. But there is no such person. If we can stand on our own two feet, it is because others have raised us up. If, as adults, we can lay claim to competence and compassion, it only means that other human beings have been willing and enabled to commit their competence and compassion to us—through infancy, childhood, and adolescence, right up to this very moment. (1977)

A former men's group member came in for a check-in appointment a few years ago, and halfway through the session he paused for a moment and then thoughtfully began, "I know how much men's group helped me to heal and grow up. It was a lifesaver for me. But I have pondered this for all these years since I finished with group, and to this day, I can't figure out *how* group worked. What is it about group that made such a difference in my life? I just don't get it." Given all that we have discussed in this book thus far, the simplest answer is "limbic resonance."

A man we know was experiencing a dark period in his life. He had a strong connection with the Catholic Church, and especially admired the writings of Karl Rahner, one of the most gifted and prolific theologians of the twentieth century. Rahner was one of the driving forces behind the revolutionary thinking of the Second Vatican Council (1962–65). Behind the scenes, in several volumes of exceptional theological discourse, Rahner argued for a church that was as close as possible to the original teachings of Jesus Christ, and he did it in the logical, analytical argumentation that was the only way it could be heard and accepted by the contemporary church hierarchy.

In one of his darker moments, this man sent a letter halfway around the world to this famous man, describing his personal struggles as well as his admiration for Rahner. Our acquaintance was wise enough to realize that he would probably not receive a reply from such a great man. It was enough just to share what was in his heart.

Many weeks later, with no anticipation or expectation whatsoever in his heart for anything more, this man received a long, handwritten letter addressed from Innsbruck, Austria, from Karl Rahner, who responded to this man's heartfelt letter in a personal, warm, accepting, and loving way.

We recall that upon Rahner's death, one of the major news magazines in the United States wrote a very complimentary memorial to Rahner. In that essay, which we have been as yet unable to locate, the author noted that upon his retirement, Rahner retired to his role of parish priest in Innsbruck, Austria; and that it was said of Rahner that throughout his distinguished and prolific career as author and Vatican politician, he made a point of *personally responding to every single letter that had ever been sent to him,* because he always humbly viewed himself as a parish priest, ministering to his parishioners, first and foremost.

Buoyancy and the Paradoxical Ambivalence About Attachment and Our Dependency Needs

If you don't put on your life jacket or get into the lifeboat, the only things that will keep you afloat will be your body's relative density with respect to water, your ability to tread water, and your physical endurance. This may work fine if you jumped off the side of the boat for a relaxing swim in a calm Pacific Ocean. But if your boat was flipped over by a rogue wave and then sank, and you've been treading water by yourself for six hours, a little help might be nice. In Garrison Keillor's first novel and bestseller *Lake Wobegon Days*, there is a footnote that goes on for several pages, listing the "95 Theses 95," a takeoff on Martin Luther's Ninety-Five Theses, except that this list was supposedly written by a resident of Lake Wobegon, Minnesota, who nailed it to the door of the local Lutheran Church, and consisted of his complaints about his upbringing and its lasting effects on him:

23. Two years ago I carried a box-spring mattress up four flights of stairs, declining offers of help, and did something to my back which still hurts. I didn't see a doctor but did buy a different mattress (orthopedic). Someone helped me carry it up and I felt guilty and kept saying "No. Really. I got it now," all the way up as my back killed me and my eyes filled with tears. (1985, pp. 259–60)

We all have ambivalence about our dependency needs. During the autonomy vs. shame and doubt stage (one and a half to three years) in Erik Erikson's stage theory of human development, our challenge is to learn to stand on our own for the very first time. We say "No!" a lot, which is our way of asserting our newfound separateness from our parents; we get stubborn; we try to do many things by ourselves. This struggle for autonomy is incorporated into each of the later stages, but it is especially prominent again during late adolescence and early adulthood when we are trying to find our own identities and separate even more from our parents—at least in theory.

So at age three, I am at the park with Dad and Mom, and I decide to venture out on my own. There are three kids about my size playing together about twenty yards away, and so off I go. I start to play with the kids, and one of them shoves me. It startles me, I fall down, I am frightened, and then I get up, turn around, and hightail it back to Dad and Mom to have my tears wiped away and my bruised ego soothed, and to affirm that I'm still okay.

The paradox, of course, is that if there is no one *physically or emotionally present* to run back to, and I am only three, then a big problem will develop. My mistrust of myself and the world at large will cause me to take one of two paths: I will either get overly tough and tell myself that I don't *need* others, or I will become fearful and timid, afraid to leave the safety of my ironfisted grip on Dad's or Mom's leg—that is, I will either become *needy* or *need-less*. We said before that if you want to make someone chemically dependent or codependent when he is an adult, be sure to not *let* him be *dependent* when he is a child.

The opposite of dysfunctional is dysfunctional, and this ambivalence about our dependency needs—this swing back and forth between "I need this person" and "I don't need this person"—is a lifelong challenge for every one of us. It is a central theme in any psychotherapy, whether the client or the therapist is aware of it. "If I get too close to you and you don't meet my needs, I will be disappointed. If I stay back far enough to protect myself, I won't heal, and I will be disappointed."

The Minnesota Longitudinal Study of Parents and Children, currently directed by Alan Sroufe, began in 1975 at the University of Minnesota's Institute of Child Development. Their methodology is described in detail on their website (http://www.cehd.umn.edu/icd/Parent-child/), (see e.g., Sroufe & Siegel, 2011; Sroufe & McIntosh, 2011; Kovan, Levy-Chung, & Sroufe, 2009; Carlson, Yates, & Sroufe, 2009; Sroufe, Egeland, Carlson, & Collins, 2005; Sroufe, 2005, 2007; Weinfield, Sroufe, Egeland, & Carlson, 2008)

Among many research results, they found that, later in life, infants who were *comfortably attached* to their caregivers

- Are more comfortable with autonomy.
- Are more self-reliant.
- Are better able to regulate their emotions.
- Have greater stress tolerance.
- Demonstrate more competence with their peers.
- Are better able to handle life's turning points, such as graduation from high school or college, marriage, and birth of children.

The researchers also discovered that by age three, the quality of a young child's care could predict with 77 percent accuracy the child's high school dropout rate, and that stress and social support are two of the biggest factors in how well a caregiver is able to meet the needs of the child.

The ability to self-regulate is especially important in the functioning of a healthy person, family, or society, and it is impossible to have deep relationships unless one can sit in the middle of one's loneliness, fear, hurt, shame, and sadness without acting out. "Acting out" might mean hurting oneself, hurting others, or letting others hurt you. It might mean becoming addicted to a substance, person, or activity. The human brain is wired to become addicted to things. Some people are more susceptible to addictions because of genes, and some of the emotions

> *The ability to self-regulate is especially important in the functioning of a healthy person, family, or society, and it is impossible to have deep relationships unless one can sit in the middle of one's loneliness, fear, hurt, shame, and sadness without acting out.*

necessary for our survival can be so uncomfortable at times that some of us find it easier to push them away or act them out rather than feel them.

At the same time, we have a *universal human need for emotional connection with other members of our species, because we are pack animals.* Like dogs, wolves, porpoises, and chimpanzees, our survival strategy, which evolved over millions of years, includes relying on one another and pooling our respective skills and talents, which is why we experience the emotion of loneliness. *Loneliness is the emotion that evolved to make us so uncomfortable when we are apart from each other that we eventually reach back to join with one another.*

An intriguing, normal bind occurs whenever we face another person, especially one we don't know. Any unknown creature, human or otherwise, elicits another very important survival emotion known as *fear,* which is a survival mechanism that puts us on alert until we are sure that it is safe to let the new person into our world. Some people have more of this fear than others due to genetically higher anxiety levels or difficult life experiences, such as an abusive childhood; some have even greater fear because they have both these issues.

It is easy to see how bound up we can get with these feelings. I fear the pain and discomfort of loneliness. It is a cellular reaction for pack animals, especially the species with the longest period of dependency in childhood—which would be us. But I also fear what might happen if I leave myself open to attack from another creature, including another human being. And so I get bound up because *I fear getting close to you and I fear being separated from you.* That is the ambivalence, and the paradox.

What complicates the situation further is that it isn't just a physical threat that elicits this fear. It can also be a threat to our sense of self, our sense of identity and our sense of being okay in the world, and to our being accepted by the pack. Psychologist Gershen Kaufman (1980) wrote that the powerful emotion of shame is induced when we are denied the right to depend on others—when the interpersonal bridge between two people is broken. Therefore, it isn't just the fear of being physically hurt that drives us. It's also the fear of being emotionally hurt. Groups of human beings have long used cutting others off from the group—*ostracism*—to enforce taboos and rules. Under harsh conditions, being banished into the wilderness meant not just unimaginable loneliness but often death.

If you're an American who subscribes to the national need for *excessive* self-reliance, you'll do just about anything other than admit that you might need someone's help. You'll medicate yourself one way or another—rage, pout, manipulate, isolate, and do all the work yourself—then burn out while secretly resenting everyone else for not helping you. The ambivalence is at times exquisitely painful for everyone, as you say things like this, sometimes in the same moment, "No, no, don't worry about it; I'll do it," followed a few minutes later, in an exhausted and disgusted tone of voice, "I don't know how I ever married someone who is so helpless and unhelpful!"

In your distorted belief system, admitting that you need others' help would be a sign of weakness—except that it isn't. It is only a sign of weakness if it is excessive. The other paradox, of course, is that if you are *excessively independent*, then inside, you are really just as needy as someone who appears needy and clingy on the outside. People who are excessively independent are at high risk for depression, anxiety disorders, drug and alcohol addiction, spending or shopping addiction, gambling addiction, work addiction, exercise addiction, and perhaps more than anything

> *... if you are excessively independent, then inside, you are really just as needy as someone who appears needy and clingy on the outside.*

else, getting into an intimate relationship with someone who is addicted to something herself or who uses, exploits, or takes advantage of you.

Personality Theory and Buoyancy

The struggle to be gracious, powerful adults, rather than victims or perpetrators, can also be seen in many of the major theories of personality and psychopathology. Each in their own way highlights the importance of learning to get along with one another and to rely on one another.

Sigmund Freud argued that neurosis was the unavoidable result of living in a civilized world; we have to learn how to control our biological impulses in order to get along with one another in social groups. Alfred Adler saw neurosis as stemming from social inequality and disconnection from community. Abraham Maslow saw lack of belonging as a key contributor. In *Childhood and Society* (1950), Erik Erikson wrote, "Personality can be said to develop according to steps predetermined in the human organism's readiness to be driven toward, to be aware of, and to interact with a widening social radius, beginning with a dim image of a mother and ending with an image of mankind."

In other words, it's all about connections with others. When a human being is unable to, is prevented from, or does not know how to connect with other human beings with sufficient emotional depth, he suffers both physical and psychological damage and eventually tries to fill up the "hole in his soul," as Minnesota poet and University of Minnesota professor Robert Bly is wont to say, with something destructive instead of with the warmth and support of human companionship. Relationships give us buoyancy. They keep us afloat when times get tough. Without them, life is experienced as unbearably stressful.

Stress, Health, and Relationship Buoyancy

Today, the major stressors in people's lives are not things like being chased by a hairy mammoth, but they are still about survival. For many people, some of the major stressors in their lives are other people—the vice president of the company where you work who is trying to push you out, the next-door neighbor who has built a fence that encroaches a foot over your property line, the marriage that is in serious trouble. Just as our buoyancy is increased by positive, close relationships, it can be threatened by negative, painful ones. If the stress is too great and too enduring, then it can wreak havoc on our health.

Stress has clearly been proven to affect the immune system, as the following studies indicate:

- A standardized wound placed on the hard palate of medical students three days before a major exam *healed 40 percent more slowly* than an identical wound on the same students during summer vacation (Marucha, Kiecolt-Glaser, & Favagehi, 1998).
- Pervasive differences in endocrine and immune function were reliably associated with hostile behaviors during marital conflict among diverse samples (Kiecolt-Glaser, Robles, & Glaser, 2002).
- Mobilization of natural killer (NK) cells into the circulation is arguably the most reproducible cellular, immunological response to acute physical and psychological stressors in humans. Individuals engaged in marital conflict exhibited greater increases in NK cell cytotoxicity than those not in conflict (Dopp, Miller, Myers, & Fahey, 2000).
- Psychological and physical health clearly fare better when we have good social and emotional support (e.g., Taylor, 2007; Uchino, 2009; Herbert & Cohen, 1993).
- In a study of 259 males and females ages fourteen to twenty-three, all living at home, those who ate *fewer* than five meals per week as a family, versus those who ate *six* per week, reported much more family dysfunction and were more likely to need to utilize community mental health clinics for anxiety and depression (Compañ, Moreno, Ruiz, & Pascual, 2002).
- Medical students with good social support mounted a stronger immune response to the hepatitis B vaccine than those who did not have good social support (Glaser, Kiecolt-Glaser, Bonneau, Malarkey, Kennedy, & Hughes, 1992).

- Having a good support system is correlated with lower levels of inflammation, as measured by C-reactive protein, a marker of cardiac inflammation (Loucks, Berkman, Gruenewald, & Seeman, 2006).
- People with more social support even have a lower susceptibility to the common cold (Cohen, Doyle, Skoner, Rabin, & Gwaltney Jr., 1997).
- Social support has also been linked to lower cortisol levels in response to stress (Turner-Cobb, Sephton, Koopman, Blake-Mortimer, & Spiegel, 2000; Eisenberger, Taylor, Gable, Hilmert, & Lieberman, 2007).
- Social support lowers blood pressure and heart rate (Unden, Orth-Gomer, & Elofsson, 1991).

• • •

All of the above point to the fact that we human beings do much better when we let our *need* for support from one another override our *fear* of getting close to one another. When we make that positive choice, then we are much more likely to act from "the better angels of our nature." John Steinbeck's iconic quote captures not only the essence of Christianity, Buddhism, and many other religions, but of the human condition itself—that each of us is capable of horrible acts of cruelty as well as uplifting acts of grace, love, and kindness.

In describing her friend, Judi Dench, in *Darling Judi: A Celebration of Judi Dench* (2005), Irish-born Dearbhla Molloy, and a London and Broadway stage actor, wrote:

> *"But her real generosity is not in giving things, but in giving those parts of herself that are far more valuable and cost her far more. She gives time, and commitment, and passion, and loyalty, and her word. In the deepest sense of the word, what she gives is love."*

CHAPTER 13

LOVE, POWER, AND GRACIOUSNESS

It is not ill-bred to adopt a high manner with the great and
powerful, but it is vulgar to lord it over humble people.

—*Aristotle,* Nicomachean Ethics

There are many ways to help people with their problems. In our esti-
mation, the deepest are ways that help people find new meanings and
new ways to change; they are about developing new resources to solve
problems in new ways. The templates that we use to attach meanings
to the myriad complexities and ambiguities in life are what define us as
individuals. [*Authors' note*: This chapter synthesizes many ideas from our
book, *The Soul of Adulthood,* to help explain some of the principles.]

A man screams at his children in the grocery store, and five different
observers attach five different meanings to what they see and hear. To one,
it means that the man has an anger problem. To another, it means that the
man is exerting proper control with unruly children. To yet another, it
means that the children need positive attention, and have settled for acting up in the grocery store to get at least some kind of a connection with
their father.

A woman stops in the middle of making love and says, "I just can't go
on right now. Maybe we can try again later." The meaning that the two

lovers attach to that experience will determine whether they have a deeply intimate marriage or one that is about to heave silently onto a rock-strewn coast. If it means that she is simply tired, that's one thing. If it means that she's frustrated with how he meets her sexual needs, but is afraid to tell him what she needs, that's another thing. If he interprets it to mean that she is simply tired, and that they will make passionate love again another time, that would be very different than if it means to him that she is no longer interested in sex, or that she is no longer interested in having sex with *him*. And there *is* no way for two lovers to clarify the meanings of these things without talking openly and candidly about the intimate details of their emotions and the intimate details of their sex lives, in ways that will by nature be uncomfortable for both of them. So, if there is no willingness for either of them to say what they really want, need, or mean, then of course there is no way for either of them to have any kind of truly worthwhile, passionate, intimate sexual relationship.

This book is about people whose lives are joined together in one way or another over many decades—as brothers and sisters, parents and children, lovers and friends, or romantic partners. It is about the joys and heartaches and battles that normal parents and stepparents have as they struggle to remain deeply, intimately connected amid competing forces that from time to time lean into their relationships with relentless ferocity. This book is about the older man with whom we have worked who still "smells her perfume and feels the same 'pitter-patter' in his heart that he felt the day they first kissed," and of the woman who looks into her partner's eyes while she's still mad about the mess in his office and says, "I don't understand it at all. After all these years, no matter how mad I get at you, all I have to do is look into those big brown eyes of yours, and I know I love you. But I still don't know why!"

Confucius wrote, "Only the truly kind person knows how to love and how to hate," which for some of us is as perplexing today as it was in 500 BC. Maintaining the fragile balance between love and hate, grace and power, revenge and forgiveness is a fundamental aspect of being a joyous, fully competent adult. For many years we have suggested that love and hate are part of the same complex bond that connects us to each other, and that without our healthy anger it is difficult to experience deeper intimacy with another. The closer we get to each other, the more likely we will step on each other's toes, and the more likely we will lose our identities in the attempt to fuse with our beloved, unless we have access to our anger. Anger is there to protect us, to set boundaries, to provide resistance, to say "no," and as such, it is essential for deep love. We fully affirm, embrace, and define our identities when we can say both "yes" and "no."

Many years ago, we defined "intimacy" as "the ability to maintain a close relationship with another person without losing our identities in the process" (Friel & Friel, 1988, p. 133). We have often said that deep love occurs only when we connect with each other at the level of our weakness, but this is true only as long as we do not expect our loved one to repair that weakness. A man confides to his partner that he feels frightened of an upcoming meeting with an associate, thus exposing his vulnerability. This man is a powerful person at work, yet he is a human being just like his partner, with fears and vulnerabilities. He has let down all of his normal self-protections and has opened himself up to shame, criticism, and rejection. This man's partner acknowledges that this man is scared, and that this man feels little, but this man's partner does not try to remove it, belittle it, compare it, or imply that this man is weak and that his partner is strong, because his partner respects this man's vulnerability and trusts that this man simply needs his partner to hear him. They both maintain their power and dignity in this tiny moment of deep intimacy, and they set the stage for this man's partner to share a moment of weakness with this man in the future. This man takes care of his fear in his own way, as an adult, but with the added confidence of knowing that his partner *does not view this man's vulnerability as a defect.*

Love is an ongoing dance, struggle, and balancing act between self and other, between lover and beloved. Too little resistance and the relationship quickly degrades into smothering and fusion; too much resistance and it ricochets into isolation and emotional poverty. Too much care results in helplessness and resentment; not enough care results in emptiness and shame. In the end, two people who "do everything right" but who are unable to share at the level of their weakness live in a practical yet life-less void.

Graciousness

There are many meanings for the word "gracious," but here we wish to focus on two from the *Oxford English Dictionary* (1971). The first is "Disposed to show or dispense grace; merciful; compassionate," and the second is "Characterized by or exhibiting kindness or courtesy; kindly; benevolent; courteous." Some would say that we have sadly lost the capac-ity for graciousness in our society, and that we are so literal and practical that we have driven the magic and tenderness right out of our lives. But then we encounter a person who is deeply gracious and we are startled by our appreciation of that person, which shows that we long for gracious-ness in our lives even as we fumble for the words and images to describe it. We do not take graciousness lightly. We just aren't sure what it is or how to do it because we lacked models of graciousness when we were young.

A woman prepares her home for holiday visitors and reflects with care on the personalities and idiosyncrasies of each guest without judging them. One likes fine wine, another exercises regularly, another requires extra privacy, and another likes to meet new people and engage in spir-ited conversation. *She would never assume that each of her guests was just like her.* She puts her special touches all around her home because it is an expression of her inner self and thus a subtle way of reaching into anoth-er's consciousness without intruding. When her guests arrive she makes them feel at home by her kindness, and paradoxically by her detachment. She doesn't hover because it makes people uncomfortable to be overly solicitous. She remains unobtrusively and intuitively attuned to the needs of her guests without sacrificing her own needs.

She includes her guests in her own holiday plans and celebrations whenever it is fitting to do so, but does not push her plans on others, always leaving each guest plenty of room to say, "I'd love to join you and your friends for dinner, but I think I'd like to take some time for myself

this evening." She is kind and courteous. When someone oversteps his
bounds, she is able to respond without hurting his dignity. A guest who
tries to stay too long would not be confronted and told that he is being
rude. She might simply use her own vulnerability to avoid exposing the
obvious vulnerability of her inappropriate guest by saying, "I'm having a
wonderful time talking with you, but I think I'm losing some of my youth-
ful stamina. Would you mind terribly if I retired for the evening, and we
could continue our conversation at a later time?" Perhaps John Milton
described this woman best with these words from *Paradise Lost*:

GRACE WAS IN ALL HER STEPS, HEAVEN IN HER EYE,

IN EVERY GESTURE DIGNITY AND LOVE.

Of course, graciousness can be an insincere, affected performance
intended to make oneself appear superior rather than as a genuine expression of respect for the dignity of other souls, but then it would not be
the kind of graciousness that we have defined here. Anyone can read an
etiquette book, which can be a helpful way to learn how to put one's graciousness into practice, but it is the struggle to acquire empathy, respect,
maturity, and depth of soul that allows us to be truly gracious. Following
the rules of etiquette without developing one's inner graciousness would
be a hollow gesture at best.

Graciousness is essential in love relationships. A man and woman are
having a disagreement about something, and as it becomes more heated
the man suddenly becomes aware that the woman is tired and that her
emotional reserves are low. He detects a point of weakness in her that
could give him an edge in the argument, but instead of trying to *win* he
abruptly changes course and says to her, "You know, I think you're right
about this. I wasn't looking at it from the same angle that you were. It
makes sense to me now." Suddenly the argument is over as his graciousness releases the tension between them and allows her to feel heard and
understood, which is exactly what people need when they are tired and
their emotional reserves are low. He could have won but decided to exercise tact, compassion, and mercy, which is what being gracious is all about.

The great issues of the day can be debated later. *Hurting a person's spirit is not worth needing to be right all the time.*

It is said that we always hurt the ones we love, a statement we see confirmed with unnecessary frequency in our culture. But as people mature and deepen in spirit, they are able to take to heart and put into practice these wise and gracious words of Oliver Wendell Holmes Sr.:

> Don't flatter yourself that friendship authorizes you to say disagreeable things to your intimates. On the contrary, the nearer you come into relation with a person, the more necessary do tact and courtesy become. Except in cases of necessity, which are rare, leave your friend to learn unpleasant truths from his enemies; they are ready enough to tell them. ([1888] 1955, p. 45)

Graciousness and Power

Graciousness and power are inextricably intertwined. The power to which we refer is not necessarily measured by wealth, status, or political influence, although these may be a part of one's overall power. This kind of power is measured by the clarity of one's spirit, the openness of one's heart, the depth of one's soul, the strength of one's character, and the quality of one's mercy. A truly gracious person is powerful, while an artificially gracious person is not,

> *Power is measured by the clarity of one's spirit, the openness of one's heart, the depth of one's soul, the strength of one's character, and the quality of one's mercy.*

even though she may appear to be. A powerful person does not use her power to harm others or to gain unfair advantage over them, whereas a weak person is always looking for a way to diminish others or elevate herself in some fashion. Mature power is about protection, integrity, honor, respect, care, wisdom, tenderness, and compassion. Immature power is about fear, greed, revenge, narcissism, harm, selfishness, want, getting even, and bitterness. One of the most dynamic and energizing aspects of adulthood is our struggle to balance power and graciousness, to temper one with the other.

Graciousness Without Power

When a person tries to be gracious without first having tapped into the protective power of his soul, he may find himself feeling angry and bitter much of the time. Anger empowers and protects so that the kind person is not taken for granted—not taken for a fool. Without healthy anger, our attempts at graciousness fall short and come to rest at the more immature level of indiscriminate, unsolicited, unmitigated niceness. This distortion of kindness directly contradicts the wisdom of Confucius cited above. Graciousness does not flow from our fear of rejection. *Graciousness flows despite our fear of rejection.* True kindness is not a cleverly disguised attempt to prevent others from hurting us, nor is it an attempt to buy affection or admiration. It is simply an attempt to affirm the spirit of another human being for no reason other than because we care about each other's dignity. Erik Erikson wrote,

> We must stand ready to expect and to respond to human love in any of our fellow men so long as they do not set out to kill that human dignity in us without which we could not really love anybody. For only people with equal dignity can love each other.

Graciousness without power is just another way to describe victimhood or martyrdom. A grown-up adult does not feel comfortable around someone who has sacrificed her identity for the sake of a relationship and who therefore fawns, hovers, or grovels in the name of "niceness." The recipient of such behavior is placed in the unwanted and painful position of having to bear witness to and participate in the other's unacknowledged embarrassment. It is also a double bind, in which we find ourselves angry at someone who appears to be nice on the outside, until we unwind the bind by recognizing that the other person is actually manipulating us, as in the following interchange:

"Can I wash your car for you?" (with no legitimate social context for him to be offering to wash your car in the first place, which is the tip-off that something isn't right).

"No, actually, I was looking forward to doing it myself. It's one of those personal things I like to do on my own."

"Really, it's no trouble at all. I enjoy washing cars. Why don't you just rest up for the party this evening?"

"Well, I was rather looking forward to washing my car."

"But I'd really like to do it for you."

"That's very kind of you, but I think I'll do it myself."

Power Without Graciousness

An old folk saying goes, "Never judge a man by how he behaves outside of his own hut," which is just another way of saying that we tend to hurt the ones we love—and then proceed to look good in the public eye. Graciousness is not confined to how we treat people in public. When it is, then we are really talking about an artificial performance rather than a characteristic of soulfulness deep within ourselves. A truly gracious person with a clearly formed identity responds to the human dignity inside of each person he encounters, whether at home or in public. If he detects weakness, ineptness, or vulnerability within you, he will respond in a way that honors who you are, not who he would like you to become, as long as you do not "set out to kill that human dignity" in him, which is required for love.

During a therapy session, a man told us of a transforming experience he had while at a cocktail party connected with his job. He was very uncomfortable in social settings, and this one was especially painful for him because most of the people were much more powerful and better educated than he. He felt very much out of place as he wandered from group to group, trying to find a way into one of the conversations but never succeeding. He felt like running away as he stood at the bar and ordered another ice water, when out of nowhere a well-dressed gentleman appeared next to him and said, "I'm always uncomfortable at these blasted things. I'd much rather be at home watching a movie with my wife." Our client immediately felt at ease and struck up a pleasant conversation with this man that lasted until the man had to go up to the podium to receive an award. It turned out that this gracious gentleman was the most powerful person in the room, and our client's brief encounter with the man transformed his beliefs about people who possess wealth and power. With an innocent and grateful smile our client said, "I once believed that all powerful people were arrogant, aloof, greedy, self-centered, and hurtful, but this man showed me otherwise."

Power without graciousness is patronizing and condescending, and is therefore just another way to describe an offender, perpetrator, bully, or manipulator. With every ounce of newly acquired power comes greater responsibility to treat the less powerful with respect, compassion, and care. An ungraciously powerful person plays on the power differential between the two of you. She will be an emotional or physical predator, preying on your weaknesses and belittling your strengths until you are drowning in a pool of shame. She will always be right even when she isn't, by simply intimidating you. She may cleverly treat people outside of her own hut with artificial respect, but in her very intimate relationships she will be overbearing, controlling, ignoring, or worse. If you are in love with such a person, you will quickly find that she never shows her own weakness, and it is never safe for you to show yours. To use our words from earlier in this chapter, the two of you will be unable to connect at the level of your weakness, and so you will be unable to enjoy the experience of deep love for each other. The relationship will soon be lonely, hollow, and superficial at best.

Love, Power, and Graciousness

Graciousness requires time, effort, and thoughtfulness, which are at a premium in our fast-paced, competitive society. When we are always in a hurry, we don't have the time to stop and notice how other people are reacting or what they might want or need, and we certainly won't notice what we feel, want, or need, either. The result is that we feel shortchanged and empty in our relationships, which eventually turns into feelings of powerlessness, bitterness, and vengefulness.

Compassion, mercy, kindness, and love must be nurtured like rare orchids in a tropical nursery. One of the mysterious paradoxes of life is that powerful lovers *cherish their dependency* upon each other *while protecting their independence* at the same time. They fight fairly and openly, stopping short of capitalizing on the other's vulnerability. They treat each other with kindness and respect, and they harbor a deep, abiding appreciation for the mystery of the love that they share. As Samuel Johnson wrote in 1773, "Gratitude is a fruit of great cultivation; you do not find it among gross people."

Each of us struggles with the relationship between power, love, and graciousness, whether in a marriage, a business partnership, a friendship, or a more distant association. Sometimes we must take Confucius's words to heart and be angry, dispensing with the tact and courtesy suggested by Holmes, especially if our deepest dignity is at stake. Sometimes we need to express the outrage in our hearts for the sake of our own or others' security. Love is complex, and human relationships are sometimes unfathomable. The soul is not black and white, it is not linear, and it is not static. But without an ideal for which to strive, we are like ships adrift in a sea of emotion and primitive, reactive, defensive urges. Thus, regardless of how confusing our relationships with one another may get, and no matter how hard it is to know the best way to treat one another at times, we still find ourselves gently charting a course back toward the timeless description of love that Paul wrote in his letter to the Corinthians. In these words we find welcome direction and comfort:

> Love suffers long and is kind; love does not envy; love does not parade itself, is not puffed up; does not behave rudely, does not seek its own, is not provoked, thinks no evil; does not rejoice in iniquity, but rejoices in the truth; bears all things, believes all things, hopes all things, endures all things. Love never fails. (1 Corinthians 13:4–8)

Part Five:

KEEP YOUR BALANCE, KEEP YOUR POWER

When a family member asks for help, the professional must exhibit the skill of a tightrope walker in taking the necessary steps to protect the minors while simultaneously avoiding any confirmation of the splitting of the family into "bad guys" and "good guys."

—*Stefano Cirillo and Paola DiBlasio,*
Families that Abuse *(1992)*

CHAPTER 14

ACTING FROM YOUR BEST SELF

> We will punish the guilty. The punishment will be more
> generosity, more tolerance, more democracy.
>
> —*Fabian Stang, mayor of Oslo, Norway*

Oslo, Norway, July 22, 2011

"Tonight the streets are filled with love," Crown Prince Haakon told the vast crowd massed on the banks of the Norwegian capital's fjord after the car bombing of ministries and mass shooting of Labour Party youths on Utoya island.

"Those who were in the government district and on Utoya were targets for terror. But it has affected us all," he said to applause.

Prime Minister Jens Stoltenberg then addressed the crowd, saying: "Evil can kill a person but it cannot kill a people."

The mayor of Oslo, Fabian Stang, said: "We will punish the guilty. The punishment will be more generosity, more tolerance, more democracy."

Central Oslo streets were closed to traffic because of the vigil, which had originally been planned as a "flower march" but it was decided that people should stay in one place because of the large numbers turning up.

"We came out of solidarity, to all be together and share our pain," said Tone Mari Steinmoen, 36. "This is a time of important communion for our country."

"We're here to show that we're an open-spirited and respectful society," said Roy Kvatningen, 37, who came with his six-year-old daughter.

"And to support the victims," added his friend, Ger. (*Sydney Morning Herald*, July 26, 2011)

Keep Your Balance, Keep Your Power

Keep your balance, keep your power. Whether you are a therapist working with a complex family system or a member of a complex family system who is struggling to "hold on to yourself" while remaining connected to a family that makes it difficult for you to maintain your balance, this statement offers not only a great challenge but it is in fact the only way that human beings remain connected at all. Maddock and Larson wrote,

> The ultimate goal of ecological therapy is transformative growth, not fixing or curing. . . . Within families, these transformations are directed at creating dynamic balances that simultaneously
> (a) maintain the autonomous identities of individual members,
> (b) allow members to relate to one another in mutually helpful and meaningful ways,
> (c) preserve the family as a functional system, and
> (d) contribute to the integrity of the larger community and physical environment. (2004, p. 373)

The four points above look like so many graduate-school textbook lists that we memorize for the final exam and then quickly forget. But those four items actually challenge each of us as much as Jesus Christ challenged us when he asked us to throw out all of the compulsive detailed rules of his time and then embrace the much more difficult ones that simply asked us to love God and love our neighbors as ourselves—leaving us to *think* for a change.

The paradox is that the simpler the rules, the more powerful and harder they are to follow. On the other hand, complex but picayune rules are "easy" to follow but leave us lost, empty, shallow, and filled with fear, bitterness, competitiveness, and smugness; nowhere are we feeling love, warmth, connection, or spirituality as a result. The limbic system of the brain dies under these compulsive black-and-white rules.

We have worked with hundreds of families, especially of Greek, Italian, Middle Eastern, and Irish origin, in which certain pairs (dyads) of people haven't spoken to each other for decades. Mom hasn't spoken to daughter-in-law; Dad hasn't spoken to son; grandfather and grandson are mute. In our terms, these are inflexible yet enmeshing strategies that, far from protecting family members from each other, actually wrap them all around the axle of a big four-by-four truck and then tie them in knots. In very few instances do we ever support our clients' *total*, absolute disconnection from their families. If a family is particularly abusive or dangerous, the contacts with the family that we support might be as simple as a Christmas card and a birthday card each year. But to end *all* contact doesn't seem to work for anyone. It only serves to keep everyone tangled up and unable to grow.

Systems Constantly Try to Maintain Balance: A "Simple" Birth-Order Example

When teaching graduate classes on family health and dysfunction, we often begin by saying that during the many hours in the classroom, we will attempt to construct and then gradually fill in a "three-dimensional holographic image"—shaped like a globe—of the many interrelated forces, factors, causes, and variables that describe how a family system works, and how each part is related to all of the other parts, and to the system as a whole.

We ask that the students give us and themselves the courtesy of realizing that we might spend three entire class periods talking about the effects of birth order on people's personal development. We say that we will later ask them to plug that block of information into one part of the holographic globe, and that the very act of plugging that block of information into the larger "globe" of the system can alter one's understanding of the entire system, as well as their deeper understanding of the effects of birth order, because it then links that information to all of the other components in the system. Understanding and working with the linkages within a family or societal system is crucial.

Students who need a nice, neat, tidy, linear explanation of how things work struggle greatly with this aspect of the class, because in systems theory, all of the separate parts are related to all of the other parts; they are mutually influencing (Maddock & Larson, 1995), and they often operate at several different levels of influence at the same time.

For example, the birth order system that we have used for decades, created by brilliant Minneapolis psychiatrist Jerry Bach and described in *Birth Order Roles and Sibling Patterns in Individual and Family Therapy* (Hoopes & Harper, 1987), combines birth order theory with the various functions required in a family system, making it extremely helpful in generating hypotheses about what is happening in a family, but also makes it much more complex at one level. At another level, it makes understanding things much simpler.

During our ClearLife Clinic lecture on birth order, we tell the participants that they may be able to intellectually absorb the material right away, but that it may take them one to two years to digest it emotionally, and in terms of their own family structure and history.

For example, Bach suggests that the second-born child tends to have a little more of a "connection" or "identification" with the "themes" (not necessarily the actual observable behaviors) of the mother. What can make this confusing in some family situations is that the way this bond between second-born and Mom gets played out may make it look as if the second-born is actually more bonded with the father.

If Dad is more on the "overpowering" and even "nasty" side, it is most likely that Mom will be more on the "nice" and "yielding" and more "compromising" side in their power struggles (remember, power struggles are a given in all relationships, even with couples who believe, mistakenly, that they don't have any power struggles). If the children, especially the second-born (and in this situation, some of the children may typically side with Dad and see him as "The Good Guy" and Mom as being ineffectual), who is more attuned to Mom's issues, perceive Dad as being a bit of a bully and Mom as a bit of a victim, then they will "feel sorry for" and "feel protective of" Mom, and feel "annoyed" or "angry" toward Dad. The second child often feels this in a profound way—which may cause her to become "the feisty one" who takes on Dad. And then Dad often finds her to be endearing for her feistiness. In many families, she is the only one who "gets away with" being feisty. When the other children try to confront Dad, they may immediately be crushed by him, verbally or otherwise.

When this second-born comes into therapy at age thirty-five, she doesn't know it yet, but she's angrier and more self-protective than is good for her; she is consistently unhappy in her successive romantic relationships that keep failing; and she is fraught with ambivalence about her parents and her own role in the family. She says that she is angry at Mom for not standing up to Dad, but she does not yet see that a significant percentage of her own "ambient anger" is a carryover from her expressing Mom's anger *for her*; she became the "standard bearer" for Mom while Mom sat back and avoided standing up for herself. At a deeper level, she is also very angry at Dad for being such a bully to Mom, and even deeper, for seducing her onto his side by overvaluing her "feistiness" instead of dealing with his conflicts and disappointments directly with Mom.

She is bonded with Mom in a very deep way, and yet she strongly identifies with Dad as someone who is not letting himself be a victim, which, as a second-born who is connected to Mom, is her greatest fear—of being a victim just like Mom. Unconsciously she is saying to herself, *I hate how Dad treated Mom. I hate how Mom didn't stand up for herself. I'll be damned if I'm going to be a victim like Mom, because the pain of identifying with Mom's plight is more than I can bear, so I'm not going to ever let anyone bully me like that. Plus, even though I feel sorry for Mom, I like the fact that I am the only one in the family who Dad admires, and so I simply can't give that up. It's too seductive.* In other words, her ambivalence about her unmet dependency needs, and her desire to love two parents who are not grown-up enough to resolve their own power struggles appropriately, leaves her in an emotional quandary.

And what of their son, the oldest child? Bach suggests that the first-born child tends to have a little more of a "connection" or "identification" with the "themes" (not necessarily the actual observable behaviors) of the father. In these situations, the oldest child—son or daughter—tends to have that special connection with Dad. And if Dad is perceived as excessively negative, one way the oldest may play it out is to try to become *the exact opposite of Dad*. In this family, it means that when you ask him who he is more like, he'll quickly say, "My mom." But is he more *bonded* with Mom? Or is he being more like Mom because he is being the opposite of Dad, due to his bond with Dad? If so, he is more bonded with Dad than perhaps anyone else in the family.

It all sounds so complicated because, at one level, it is. But what would happen to every single person in this family system if Dad and Mom were so passionately in love with each other, and so grown-up, that they were able to confront their own selves rather than their partner? What if they were able to deal with the ambivalence and anxiety that comes with *all* romantic relationships rather than acting out by being a bully or a victim? What if they were able to keep their children out of their own obvious marital conflicts? What if Dad didn't use the second-born daughter as his little "ally" and Mom didn't use their firstborn son as her little "ally"? It would then be so simple.

Poof! Dad and Mom have a great marriage; they have a great sex life that is none of their children's business; and each one of their kids gets to grow up safe and secure in the knowledge that their parents' marriage is more important than them. Those kids will be assured that their parents will always have the kids' best interests at heart, which frees up each child to become his or her own self, free from the double-binding entanglements with their parents' unresolved conflicts.

The son no longer has to protect Mom, so he doesn't have to grow up and get into one relationship after another in which he is rescuing women and feeling manipulated by them at the same time. Second-born daughter no longer has to be angry "for" Mom, and doesn't have to be seduced into protecting an emotionally inadequate dad, so she can grow up and have healthy relationships with men, resulting in a long-lasting, highly reward-ing, passionate relationship with a guy toward whom she doesn't have to be angry all the time to protect herself from being vulnerable. After all, the ability to be vulnerable without losing yourself in the process is what makes for great sex, enduring love, and unending passion in a long-term romantic relationship (Schnarch 1997, 2009; Maddock & Larson 1995; Maddock 1999; Larson 1999, 2010b, 2011).

We just spent several pages explaining one tiny little corner of that great big holographic image that is filled with enormous amounts of data, link-ages, and interactions within a system. We demonstrated what happens when individual parents become more balanced within themselves; their parental balance flows out to the family system, allowing more balanced relationships within and between family members, and then that flows out to the broader society in the form of healthy marital relationships for the children, which presumably will eventually flow out to society at large in terms of those grown children's contributions to the world. We can't cover everything within that large holographic image in just one small chapter, but we hope you have an idea of how this systemic approach can work, if it is worked properly.

In the next section, we present a larger societal issue of victim-perpetrator dynamics that has plagued humanity for millennia, how one small Minnesota community finally stepped forward and decided to do something about it, and what has evolved from that since its early beginnings.

An Ecologically Balanced Approach to Psychotherapy: Domestic Violence Treatment as a Case in Point

All families, no matter how healthy or troubled, have strengths and limitations. As most therapists are already aware, wondering whether a client experienced childhood family dysfunction isn't a matter of "if they did"; it's a matter of "how much and what kinds of dysfunctions did they experience?" What happened in the therapy world over the past forty years can be considered revolutionary because it represented an inarguable shift from denial to acknowledgment, followed by treatment for a large number of individual and societal ills that had been ignored due to professional and societal fear and shame. In our experience, the ensuing professional dramas and struggles over the treatment of domestic violence provide a unique opportunity to see the value of thinking ecologically, regardless of one's other theoretical orientations or methods.

The field of domestic violence treatment followed a timeline similar to other awakenings in the mental health field, with increased societal attention beginning in the early 1970s. The reader may not be aware that until this time, if a man shattered all of a woman's teeth, broke her jaw, and damaged her kidney with a violent punch, society in general, and law enforcement in particular, turned a blind eye, just like mental health professionals turned a blind eye to incest and the sexual abuse of children.

What revolutionized everyone's thinking about domestic violence in the United States was the organized, formal treatment program called the Duluth Model, begun in 1981, in Duluth, Minnesota, and described in *Education Groups for Men Who Batter* (Pence & Paymar, 1993). This model was based on the input of a group of battered women's activists who were invited to advise the program's developers. It includes the belief that abuses of power and control, and a societal tendency to blame the victim, are what contribute to domestic violence. By learning to challenge their attitudes and beliefs about their victims, perpetrators would supposedly stop battering. Based on their recommendations, in most criminal jurisdictions and among many therapists who treat domestic violence, it is also believed that victims and perpetrators should not be in treatment together, as in couples therapy, *because doing so would in and of itself imply blaming the victim to some degree.*

It was a revolutionary program at so many levels, including a reversal of the thousands of years of violence, torture, humiliation, and subjugation of women by men. With the introduction of this program, a group of concerned, courageous human beings in northern Minnesota was willing to right a wrong and begin to balance a terrible imbalance in the human ecosystem, despite the fears, prejudices, and potential repercussions from men who had claimed an entitlement over women that went back millennia.

In our experience, many of us who work as therapists have a tendency to lean toward erring on one side or the other of this complex dynamic; based on ecological-systemic principles, this tendency creates paralyzing imbalances in the marital or family system. We believe that criminal prosecution is often a critical component of treating domestic violence, and that imprisonment is necessary in more severe cases. *We also believe that victims' advocates serve a crucial role in helping victims of violence find shelter and legal protection.*

We also believe that for the *psychotherapist* (*not* the victim's advocate) to lean too heavily on a perpetrator of domestic violence is no more helpful than if he errs in the direction of rescuing the victim. We draw a clear, boundaried distinction between victim advocacy, which we wholeheartedly support without reservation, and *psychotherapy* with a victim, which is a whole different issue.

Of course, no program, no matter how excellent it may be, is without opposing points of view. Regarding couples therapy, for example, studies by Goldner (1998), Goldner, Penn, Sheinberg, & Walker (1990), and Maddock and Larson (1995), among others, show that treating couples, and entire families, can be a more successful way to treat domestic violence issues, *if done properly*. If not done properly, it can prove absolutely disastrous, and therein lies the rub. If there is a surgical procedure that can cure an intractable physical problem, but too few surgeons are even capable of learning how to do the procedure properly, we have a problem. Then we must convince the medical community at large that the procedure is the best way to fix the problem, and *then* we must find people capable of learning the procedure.

The Maddock-Larson ecological approach, along with components of David Schnarch's Sexual Crucible® model, both of which rest on the principle of increasing a client's psychological differentiation (i.e., being grown up enough to stand up as a separate, autonomous adult, while remaining connected in constructive ways to one's partner) as an overall therapeutic goal both for victims and perpetrators (and for all couples), was used for several years at one of the most successful and highly regarded domestic violence treatment programs in the United States: the Tubman Alliance in Minneapolis–St. Paul (formerly the Harriet Tubman Center). It has since merged with Chrysalis in Minneapolis and, due to budgetary and ideological concerns, has lost the Maddock-Larson focus after twenty-five years of their stunning successes in treating domestic violence couples.

Several years ago, the Tubman program caught the attention of the producers of the *Oprah Winfrey Show*. They sent a team to film what was happening at the Tubman Alliance, and halfway through the filming the team was so upset that they started to pack up their equipment and leave because they thought that what they were seeing was the staff "babying the perpetrators" and "blaming the victims" of domestic violence. The executive director at the time, Resmaa Menakem, personally trained and guided in this therapeutic model by Maddock and Larson, convinced them to stay. By the time they were through, they were so impressed with the program's success that Oprah Winfrey devoted three entire shows to their program (Menakem, personal communication, 2006).

Their model of treatment assumed that the victims of abuse as well as the perpetrators of abuse were in need of intensive psychotherapy to heal the wounds of their respective childhoods, and to learn new cognitive templates—new patterns of responding to uncomfortable and anxiety-producing situations. In other words, as children, they had both been exposed to *few* "other behaviors." In the program, perpetrators' violent behavior was contained, they were taught self-soothing strategies, and they were taught how to be powerful without being perpetrators. Clients who were caught more in the victim position were taught to have a voice and to become empowered without becoming perpetrators; they learned how to self-soothe their destructive anxieties and how to stay connected in romantic relationships without losing themselves in the process.

James Maddock created a simple and powerful list for the Tubman Alliance website that describes for both men and women how to have a nonabusive relationship. For many years, we have handed out this list to our couples clients, whether they have abuse in their relationships or not, because it is a brilliant template for anyone in a marriage to improve the dynamic between them by improving each partner separately:

For Men
- Work on self-control.
- Practice assertiveness without aggression, and seduction without coercion.
- Give respect to women regardless of what you think of women in general.
- Increase your involvement in the everyday lives and experiences of children.
- Practice open communication in all close relationships.
- Support and nurture other men as well as women.
- Simplify and clarify your roles at work and home.
- *Get the right kind of help.*

For Women
- Practice self-empowerment.
- Work on recognizing your own needs and desires.
- Set limits without being judgmental.
- Give respect to men regardless of what you think of men in general.
- Increase interactions with adults of both sexes.
- Learn to compete comfortably.
- Practice open communication in all close relationships.
- Support and nurture other women.
- Simplify and clarify your roles at work and home.
- Appropriately advocate the importance of female perspectives and experiences.
- *Get the right kind of help.*

We have been presenting Maddock and Larson's model of treatment for twenty-seven years on the professional training circuit, and we still encounter a certain percentage of participants who become angry at what they think is a stance of blaming the victim and coddling the perpetrator. But the more sophisticated among them, and among the therapeutic community at large, understand that this model is much more challenging for therapists, perpetrators, and victims, because it is truly an ecological-systemic model, meaning that it is harder to work with up front, but in the long run it is so much simpler and easier once its subtlety and sophistication are understood and digested. And it is infinitely more successful than traditional methods of treating these complex cases.

A traditional victim-perpetrator model of treatment (victim advocacy) assumes that there is a good guy and a bad guy, and that all we have to do is rescue the good guy and incarcerate the bad guy. But that approach does not take into account the ecology inside of each family member, the ecology of the family itself, nor the ecology of the family within the larger community. Neither does the traditional model take into account the fact that in the majority of cases in which there *is* imprisonment of a convicted offender, the person waiting outside the gates of the prison to take the offender home is *the victim*. As Noel Larson warned so solemnly at a large professional training conference that we chaired in Las Vegas a few years ago (U.S. Journal Conference on Sexuality and Intimacy, 2003):

> Doing this kind of work—and it's a dramatic statement on my part—can steal your soul. You can lose your integrity relatively easily, in either direction. I do evaluations for the Social Work and Psychology Boards in Minnesota on therapists who have gone astray in various ways, and gotten themselves in trouble, and I also do supervision—not with the ones I evaluate—and these are individuals who have lost their souls in the process of this kind of work. And remember, I said that [perpetrators] need to figure out your vulnerabilities and go for them. [Victims] will do the same, because they believe their survival depends on you, and they'll start tying you up, in some ways, where you lose your flexibility as a therapist. Once you do that, your integrity starts to go. And the same is true with [perpetrators]. They will try to bring you into their system, and figuring out a way to stay connected and attached but not joining their system becomes enormously important.

Maddock and Larson also cautioned that

> the naivete of many victim advocate therapists has led some well-intended interventions to devastate the lives of families in ways that might have been avoided by a more balanced approach. Some therapists who are themselves incest survivors have failed to distinguish their own motives for revenge or repair from the needs of their clients. (1995, p. 17).

To summarize the underlying principles of useful ecological-systemic interventions, we offer the following examples from Maddock and Larson (1995) and Maddock, Friel, and Friel (2009):

Goal: Maintain the autonomous identities of individual members

Balanced approach

Sue can decide to go to a trade school rather than medical school.

Dad can vote for a different candidate than the rest of the family and still be "okay."

Unbalanced approach

If Sue goes to a trade school, certain family members may belittle or shun her.

Dad votes for a different candidate, and it starts an internal battle that splits the family apart.

Goal: Allow members to relate to one another in mutually helpful and meaningful ways

Balanced approach

When a family member has a personal crisis, the unconscious rule is that others listen and are supportive, but don't often give advice or analyze unless it's really warranted.

Unbalanced approach

When a family member has a personal crisis, the unconscious rule is that Dad "falls apart" and Mom "scurries around anxiously," trying to come up with "solutions" that will reduce Dad's distress.

Goal: Preserve the family as a functional system

Balanced approach

Differences between family members are valued; everyone feels loved and
valued; parents' conflicts are dealt with in the marriage so that children
do not have to act them out.

Unbalanced approach

The underlying belief is that there will never be "enough" to go around, and
that Dad's and Mom's attention and approval will be divvied up to various
children in ways that ultimately tear the family apart.

Goal: Contribute to the integrity of the larger community and physical environment

Balanced approach

The family is connected to the community in various ways, such as neighborhood groups, church groups, AA and Al-Anon, political involvement,
and service organizations.

Unbalanced approach

The family tends to be isolated as a whole, even if individual members are
connected to society in certain ways. The sense within the family is that
"we are 'terminally unique'" and "the rest of the community consists of
outsiders."

• • •

In the next two chapters we present two actual clinical situations in
great detail so that the reader can see exactly how the actual process of
personal change occurs, as opposed to the fast, artificial, television-
produced "instant pseudo-change" that many of us are exposed to much
too often, and not in our best interests.

As you read through these cases, see if you can detect the internal
structure of the change within each person, and how the *structure* of those
changes will apply equally to the struggles encountered by men, groups of
friends within a neighborhood, the relationships between neighborhoods
and voting districts and the state and the nation as a whole, between
nations, and to the world itself as it continues to evolve, day after day, one
foot in front of the other, for as long as the world exists.

CHAPTER 15

ECOLOGICAL-SYSTEMIC MAGIC:
When the Mother from Hell Simply Becomes the Mother Who Cares

Is it True?

Is it Kind?

Is it Necessary?

—*Rules for feedback in Linda Friel's women's groups*

Releasing old struggles can be especially challenging. In our twenties it is natural to seek the perfect mate who will completely understand us and meet all of our needs without effort or disappointment. This is natural because we do not let go of the myths of childhood easily. Children want to believe that their parents are flawless despite their flaws, so that is what children believe. When in the mother's womb, everything is taken care of without struggle, and we hang onto this myth for quite some time.

As we move into our thirties or forties we slowly learn that this *is* a myth. We discover that our parents weren't perfect, but with that discovery comes acceptance of our own shortcomings, as well as theirs. We realize that being in the womb was perfectly safe, but it had its limitations—after all, how much wisdom, consciousness, identity, and deeper intimacy did we have when we were still in the womb? The risks of coming out into the world and facing reality are great, but the rewards are even greater.

The rest of this chapter is intentionally detailed because in our clinical practice we have found that when people are creating new templates for handling old problems, in many cases, it will happen more effectively if they can *see* what the *process of creating that new template* actually looks like.

The "struggle for intimacy while holding on to one's identity" described in the rest of this chapter is quite common in families—perhaps more common than the reader is willing or able to acknowledge. As with all of our clinical work, whether in session in our office, or in our books and seminars, we don't expect anyone to accept what we say without challenging it and struggling with it, and we certainly will not be offended if the reader thinks that it is pure bunk. All we ask is that you consider the possibility that what we are describing might be helpful to you in some way, and if so, that you be somewhat open to the possibility that a seemingly impossible relationship can be repaired with heartwarming results.

Alicia and Phyllis: A Mother and Daughter Struggling to Find a Connection

Round One: The Face-Off

"Mother, this has to stop!"

Alicia, a successful forty-two-year-old CEO and entrepreneur shot a fiery glance at her sixty-seven-year-old mother, Phyllis, took a deep breath, and then screamed again, "Mother! Stop it! Don't *ever* snoop in my purse again! I have had it! Do you hear me? I have *had* it! Just stop!" They were both stunned and silent as her angry words ricocheted off the walls of her kitchen.

Alicia Loring maintained an intense, angry, rebuking stare at her mother as her mother looked away and then down at the kitchen floor. Then her mother took a deep breath, sighed, looked up with a hint of seductive, puppy-dog woundedness, and calmly replied, "Honey, I didn't mean any harm, I was just—"

"I don't care. I don't care! You always have a pathetic excuse for your snooping, your controlling, your manipulations, your bossiness, your intrusions into every crevice of my being," Alicia interrupted. "I am *so* tired of your excuses! Just stop! I mean it!" Then she asked her mother to leave. "I'll call you in a couple of days, Mother. I just need to compose myself. I have too many things I have to get done before I leave town again on business."

Her mother said, "I understand, dear," as she headed toward the front door to leave. Alicia noted the telltale, hangdog look on her mother's face, masked by the equally confusing attempt to be strong and understanding, which was her mother's modus operandi.

"Oh, brother," Alicia said under her breath. "Here we go again. I am *so* exhausted by this. *Ar-r-r-g-g-h-h-h!*"

Round Two: *The Anatomy of a Family Seizure*

Alicia started getting ready for her business trip, finalized two reports to the best of her abilities, paid four nearly overdue bills, packed, watched the 10 o'clock news, fell into bed and into a deep, exhausted sleep—all the while dreaming fitful, conflicted dreams that she didn't need to bother to interpret. She awoke feeling relieved and exhilarated, momentarily, followed by feeling vaguely guilty and even more vaguely anxious. She'd been through this too many times before. As she was racing between planes at O'Hare, her cell phone rang. It was her brother, Tom, calling from his law office in Manhattan.

"What were you thinking, Alicia? You *know* Mother is sensitive. Can't you just contain yourself now and then? We all know she's difficult. Why do you have to stir things up so?

"Tom, I can't take it anymore. You and Sarah live 1,000 miles away. You don't have to deal with it every day. Don't call me and take me down every time this happens. Why don't *you* confront Mother when it's necessary?"

"Sarah and I just don't think it's worth it. She's old. She's not going to change. Why can't you just play along? Be a good sport, will ya?" He was annoyed and condescending.

"Don't patronize me, Tom. That's bullshit and you know it. I can just as easily ask you why you can't back me up when Mom pulls this manipulative crap. Why are you calling me? What is it you want?"

"We want you to back off, Alicia. Just let her be the pathological mother that she is. She isn't going to change. She's sixty-seven years old. What do you expect? Let it go, Alicia. Let it go, for God's sake!"

"Sixty-seven? Sixty-seven? She doesn't have Alzheimer's. She's not ninety! She's not that old. Sixty-seven is *not* helpless and unable to change. Are you kidding? You're assuming she can't change because it's convenient for you to let *me* struggle with it. That doesn't cut it, Tom. I'm not buying it." Alicia's call to board her plane was announced, and she hurriedly ended the call.

Thank God for airplanes, she told herself. *This needs to stop. Let them stew in it for a while.*

As her plane hit the runway in Miami, she activated her cell phone and noticed a phone message from her sister, Susan, who lived in Los Angeles. She ignored it. Then her sister's second call came in. She answered it.

"Alicia, it's Susan. Mom's in hysterics. She's in the ambulance on the way to the ER. She thinks she's having a heart attack. It's the same old thing. Bob and I understand how hard it is for you, honey. If we were there instead of in L.A., we'd try to take some of the pressure off of you. But we aren't. You know how fragile Mom is. But she's *always* been this way. You know that. We *all* know that. Why do you have to stir these things up like this? Just let her be Mom, y'know? It's so much easier that way. When you get settled in Miami, call her and apologize and say that you were just under a lot of stress and you're sorry for the misunderstanding, and you'll take her to lunch when you get back and have a nice time, and then everything will be back to normal. That's all any of us want . . . to just manage her so that there aren't anymore storms like this."

"Susan," Alicia began with a somber, resigned tone in her voice, "after *you* move here for a year and have her rifling through *your* mail, going through *your* purse, asking why there's a condom in *your* bathroom, writing notes on *your* personal mail that she has opened without permission, then *you* tell me how I should handle it. You don't get it. This *is* going to change, even if it means that she spends the rest of her life in a mental hospital. I've had it, Susan. None of you get it. *I . . . have . . . had . . . it!*"

Everyone was upset now. The seizure had gone full circle and had gathered up as much familial energy as it possibly could. They were all flooded and out of control. Mom was resting peacefully in a hospital room, under the influence of some relaxing medications, getting wonderful care and attention from a competent, caring hospital staff, with no diagnosis that would require her to stay for more than a nice forty-eight-hour rest, during which time she felt pampered, cared for, listened to, and understood, in only the superficial way that would be possible in an ER situation. Nothing would be diagnosed. No therapy would be recommended; no changes would be in the offing. It was a perfect end to a perfect *recurring family seizure*.

Everybody is upset and agitated . . . except Mom . . . who is resting comfortably, relaxing up for the next round, which she expects to win with equal ease. Sadly, she's not even aware that what she's doing is making herself lonely and alienated from her family, and making her family feel lonely and alienated from her. Nobody wins. Nothing changes. The system is perfectly intact and stable in its chaotic instability.

Round Three: Assertiveness Training

When Alicia returned to Minneapolis from her business trip, she immediately went to Frank Seltzer, Ph.D., the director of her Human Resources Department, and sat down with him. It was her company. She had built it from the ground up. She had taken it from herself and three hourly employees fourteen years ago to a multinational corporation doing sales in excess of $500 million as of last quarter. She oversees 1,500 employees in five states and two foreign nations. She is considered to be one of the finest CEOs in the United States—smart, strong, tough, competent, compassionate, fair, and above all, kind.

"Frank," she began, "my mother is going to be the death of me." He'd heard bits and pieces of the story for the past three years, but this felt different. Alicia appeared to be at the end of the line with her mother. "I need some help. I need some serious help. And I need it now."

"Let's start with the basics and see what happens," he began. "Try an experiment. If it doesn't work, we can go to Plan B." He wasn't exactly certain what Plan B was, but she understood. He was a traditional HR guy, and she trusted him. He was solid and had kept the company out of many a personnel problem over the years.

"Okay. Tell me what I should do."

"Anita Thompson has another Assertiveness Training class beginning next week. If you're comfortable being in a class like that here on campus, then that would make the most sense to start with, given your hectic schedule. You could pop in for two hours every week for four weeks and be done. It sounds like you and your mother get so revved up that neither one of you can hear the other. It might just be that some careful, rational phrasing and pacing could change the whole picture."

"Okay. Sign me up," Alicia replied.

And so she did. For two hours, four weeks in a row, Alicia and the other participants chose scenarios that were uniquely emotionally charged for each of them, and then worked on finding more balanced ways to express their wants and needs in those situations.

Two weeks after the class was over, she had her chance to try out her newly acquired strategies. She had given her mother the garage door opener to her house so that her mother could bring in the mail and water the plants. Fortuitously, she told herself, her mother was just finishing up at the house when Alicia returned from her travels. She was excited, and nervous, as she entered the house and cheerfully greeted her mother.

"Hi, Mom! How are you doing?" Her mother was adjusting some papers on the built-in desk on the east wall of the kitchen as Alicia entered. She turned and smiled confidently as she said, "I brought in all of your mail and watered all of the plants. Everything is under control and just fine, dear."

Alicia glanced down at the papers her mother had been tidying up, and noticed that it was her mail. She breathed a sigh of relief. And then she looked closer. Her mother had opened all of the mail and had written notes and comments on each piece. Alicia moved in to look at what her mother had done as her mother unobtrusively moved to the side. Then Alicia felt her blood begin to boil. She felt fire in her belly. She felt her teeth clench. "Mom, what have you done here?"

"Oh, I know how busy you get, and how stressful these details are for you after you've been gone on one of your business trips, and so I've tried to organize the mail for you, and have made suggestions that I think will make it easier for you to respond."

"O-o-o-kay-y-y-y," Alicia began, very cautiously, trying to use her self-soothing techniques to stay in charge of herself and not overreact. She began to sift through the mail, and then her blood began to boil again. "I see what you've tried to do here . . . and here. . . ." Then the next one was like a knife in the stomach. "Mom! What is *this*?"

Her mother responded innocently, "What, dear?"

"This is a letter from a guy I've dated three times over the past three months. You've written on it, 'This guy sounds like a loser. Why are you still in a relationship with him?'" She glared angrily, impotently, at her mother.

"Well, honey, I mean—"

"Are you kidding me? You mean what?" Then her four weeks of training started to kick in. She took a deep breath, calmed herself, and relaxed. "Look, Mom. I really appreciate your help. It's just that my personal life has to remain personal. Do you know what I mean? I sincerely appreciate your watering my plants and bringing in the mail, but it just doesn't feel right that you actually *open* my mail and then comment on it. I guess I could find a way to accept your trying to prioritize my bills and other business correspondence, but for you to open a piece of personal mail and write comments on it is more than I can handle. I want your help, but I need you to know that I feel violated when you open my personal mail, and I feel doubly violated when you write comments on it. I need you to know it makes me angry and ashamed and little. And I would like you to stop doing it. I love you, but that just feels too invasive." *There, I said it*, she told herself. *Not exactly as we role-played it in class, but close enough*. She stood back, proud of herself, and waited for her mother's response.

Her mother, Phyllis, took a deep breath, sighed, looked up with a hint of seductive, puppy-dog woundedness, and calmly replied, "Honey, I didn't mean any harm. I was just trying to be helpful."

"Oh, Mother, but of course you were. I understand that. It's just that I need to have a part of my life that's just mine. You just can't do that with my personal mail." *We're finally getting somewhere,* she told herself. *I think Mom is finally going to get it. Thank God for Frank Seltzer and Anita Thompson!* Her heart was soaring.

Then her mother put on her coat, and as she walked toward the front door to leave, she half-turned toward Alicia and said in her most exquisitely wounded tone, "I just don't know how to make you happy, dear. I have never known. You were always the one I had the hardest time connecting with." And with that, she closed the door behind her, got in her car, and drove home. Alicia immediately felt the urgency, the anxiety-producing inevitability of a volcano preparing to erupt, of an earthquake preparing to rumble to the surface. She felt another family seizure coming on. And this one was going to be a *doozy.*

Round Four: Two-Plus Years of Psychotherapy

This time, the family seizure was, indeed, a doozy. Phyllis went home and quickly proceeded to melt down. At the time, she had no idea that there might be other ways to get her needs met. She just did what she'd learned to do as a child, long ago, in a family that was indescribably painful. First, she flooded with feelings of shame and hurt, followed by rage. Then she allowed her mind to escalate it into a catastrophe. Then she called Tom and Sarah in Manhattan and burst into tears, wailed, hyperventilated, and sobbed uncontrollably (at least, that's how it appeared). She explained how reasonable she had been, how helpful she'd tried to be, how she just meant well, how she was concerned about the man Alicia had dated three times; after all, he seemed weak and manipulative in his letter to her, and what was a loving mother to do, just let it play out without trying to help? Tom and Sarah were so limited in their ability to soothe themselves in the face of another's emotions that all they could muster were ineffective attempts to take Phyllis's side in the hopes that it would calm her down, not knowing that by doing so, they were feeding right into the family seizure—pouring kerosene onto a fire.

Once they took Phyllis's side, they were ensnared in ways they didn't want to be, but by then it was too late. As they were sucked in even more, their unsoothed anxiety caused them to make the "choice of death" when it comes to family seizures. They sealed the deal by buying in hook, line, and sinker. They dialed 911 and said that their mother in Minnesota was either having a heart attack or a nervous breakdown. As the sirens screamed down the street near Phyllis's house, we can imagine someone wondering how different it might have turned out had they simply said, "It sounds confusing, Mother. Maybe you two should cool off and talk about it again in a couple of days. We're sorry it's so painful right now for both of you, but we believe you're both able to work it out. It's really late here on the East Coast. We're going to go to bed now. Call us tomorrow night and let us know how it's going."

But that's not what happened.

Still on the telephone with Phyllis, and having called 911, Tom and Sarah heard the sirens approach the house and the paramedics enter and begin questioning Phyllis. Phyllis handed the phone to the paramedics, and Tom and Sarah filled them in on the demographics and their take on the circumstances surrounding the crisis. As the ambulance sped away from Phyllis's house, Tom and Sarah, still agitated and unable to soothe themselves, did the only thing that *they* knew to do to try to self-soothe; they called Susan and her husband, Lance, in Los Angeles.

"Lance," Sarah began, "Phyllis is on her way to the ER again. Tom and I think it might be the big one. She's gone way over the edge."

Lance put Susan on the other line, and Susan jumped in, "What the hell is going on, Tom? We thought this was all under control! What happened? Is it Phyllis and Alicia again?"

Tom said, "I haven't talked to Alicia yet, but it sounds like she and Mom had another row over Mom's intrusion into Alicia's life, and Alicia let her have it, and Mom fell apart and ended up in the ambulance on the way to the ER."

"Damn!" shouted Susan. "When in the hell is Alicia going to *get it* that the only way to keep peace in this family is to let Mom have her quirks? She's not going to change. But she's surely going to die if it keeps playing out this way. I'm going to call Alicia right now. Enough is enough!" She picked up the phone and dialed Alicia's number.

Alicia answered, tentatively, breathing deeply, trying to stay centered like she'd learned to do in her classes. "Hello."

"Alicia, it's Susan. Look. We know how difficult Mother can be. And we feel really guilty that we can't be there to take some of the burden off of you. But you must buck up and stop trying to change things. Change is bad. Change isn't realistic. Change does nothing but disrupt and create chaos. You need to surrender, and admit that change is simply not going to happen. Let it go, Alicia. Let it go!"

Alicia actually reflected on what her sister had said because that's what she'd learned to do in her assertiveness training class. But she found herself reflecting on it in even deeper ways than she had ever imagined possible. She reflected on it as if there truly *was* nothing more to do—that they'd reached the end of the trail—that the only emotions left to feel were grief, sadness, resignation, and acceptance. With a soft but in no way weak or resigned tone of voice, Alicia replied clearly and strongly to Susan, "Yes, Susan, I see the wisdom of what you've all been telling me. I see it more vividly than I ever thought possible. It *is* time to let go of those old patterns once and for all. It *is* time to let things heal and become normal. It *is* time for all of us to get along as things are, not as we wish they could be. Thank you. Thank you all for your love and concern and help during this latest crisis. I have a lot of changes to make now."

Alicia said good-bye to her and fell into the deepest, most restful sleep of her adult life; dreamed interesting and complex dreams; and awoke refreshed, excited, and with no anxiety whatsoever about the fact that she had no idea whatsoever what all of this meant. She just knew that there had been some kind of shift in her own psyche, and she was excited to follow it and see where it took her.

Alicia decided to dig in and get to the bottom of this seemingly hopeless and painfully sad, lonely situation. Frank Seltzer and Anita Thompson were not really aware that assertiveness training worked perfectly well under certain circumstances, but that it did not work much at all with unreasonable people. It's one of the little-known facts about such training. Being reasonable, rational, and clear works reasonably well with reasonable people, but it doesn't work at all with unreasonable, highly manipulative, or damaged people.

Alicia entered one of our long-term women's therapy groups designed for high-powered, successful women who are struggling with issues of powerlessness in closely intimate (not work-related) relationships. After getting situated for a few months she then decided to attend one of our three-and-a-half-day ClearLife Clinics where she was able to look at her family-of-origin issues, not just in depth, but also in the context of other people who were looking at the same kinds of issues. In other words, she was able to look at them in a social context. After the Clinic, she resumed her work in women's group, and some two and a half years into this process, she was finally able to master the conflict with her mother despite the well-intentioned but unhelpful, enmeshed interventions of her overly anxious family members who had been key elements in the previous family seizures.

How she did it highlights the truth about real intimacy. Real intimacy is so easy, and so simple, and so brief, and so powerful—and clearly *not* convoluted—that it is terrifying to all except those who are willing to face the challenge of growing up—which is why so many Americans are spending so many millions of dollars looking for intimacy without finding it. We tell couples that it is perfectly normal and typical to enter therapy with the unconscious, unintentional belief, "There must be a way to fix this relationship without me having to actually change." That statement is often followed by clients' sheepish smiles of acknowledgment.

Many people don't really want to be intimate. They choose to have pseudo-emotional "orgasms" with each other that include complaining about how elusive intimacy is, rather than doing the simple growing up that is required to have it. Trying to find intimacy in ways that will never pan out becomes a pointless, circular, emotionally addictive rush that feeds itself because there is never a way for it to become consummated. The *hope* that it will happen, coupled with the belief that *I don't have to change to make it so*, creates an endless, dead-end loop.

> *It takes a grown-up to be intimate. And the proper management of intimate conflicts turns a child into a grown-up.*

It takes a grown-up to be intimate. And the proper management of intimate conflicts turns a child into a grown-up.

In women's group, Alicia discovered that, for the first time in her life—she told us later—she experienced what it must be like to be a member of a healthy family. People listened to each other and avoided giving each other advice or rescuing each other. They laughed and cried together, all under relatively safe conditions, because there was someone who was in charge, but who wasn't authoritarian or manipulative. After many months in the group, she felt genuinely connected enough to make another effort with her mother. The key was going to be for her to *use the power of her own love for her mother*, and to *assume the best about her mother*—that, in some distorted way, her mother really *did* have her daughter's best interests at heart when she went through her purse.

Human beings always behave a certain way for a reason, even if the behavior isn't healthy. Our client was to assume that her mother wanted to be loved and respected just as much as the next person, and that like a child having tantrums, if someone could gain the upper hand with her without making it look or feel like a direct confrontation, she might respond well. So we helped Alicia practice being the respectful, powerful, grown-up woman that she was at work, *but in relationship with her mother*. This meant refining her earlier attempt at being assertive, and making sure to add a strong piece of affirmation for her mother, *as she gently removed the purse from the center of their relationship*.

Alicia practiced and practiced and got support from the group and shared her fears about it blowing up and resulting in a six-month alienation from her mother, and then she said she was ready. She had invited her mother over for lunch, and while she was making sandwiches at the side counter in the kitchen, she looked around and noticed her mother facing the built-in desktop on the other side of the center island. Her mother was going through her purse. Alicia made herself aware that a mother might go through a daughter's purse for many reasons, but that the most obvious one is that she is concerned about her daughter—that she actually cares in a rather distorted way.

She noticed what she was feeling, composed herself, and then in one smooth, uninterrupted, fluid maneuver, she brightly and warmly glided around the center island toward the wall where the desktop was, gently but deliberately removed the purse from her mother's hands without being the least bit snippy, curt, abrupt, or nasty—all the while saying very cheerfully, and without an iota of cattiness in her voice, "Oh, Mother, I stopped letting people go through my purse a long time ago—" As she said that, she glided right around to the cabinet on the opposite wall and put it up on one of the higher shelves, and without any disruption in the flow of her movements or conversation, she moved back next to her mother, put her arm around her, and continued, "—and besides, you're the greatest mom in the world, and I love you. It's such a beautiful day outside. Let's have a nice lunch together."

And that was that. Her mother nearly melted right there on the kitchen floor because her daughter had so deftly done two things at the same time: (1) unequivocally blocked her mother's intrusion into her purse and (2) unequivocally affirmed the lovableness and goodness of a seventy-year-old woman who had never once been affirmed in a way that could get past her very rational defenses, which were installed when she was a little girl growing up with parents who were tired, overworked Scandinavian farmers who believed that outward signs of affection were inappropriate, leaving her with only one way to show her love—inappropriate attempts to control an adult *as if* the adult were still a little child.

Our client came to group the next week with the composure and self-possession that could only be present in a grown-up woman.

The Therapists' Take on It

1. When families or family members operate from *flawed intimacy templates*, they get caught in double binds. Here's how we see Alicia's success as it might be understood—unconsciously or not—in the mother's mind. "I love you and want you to be a grown-up, separate adult. I fear you growing up because I *need* you, and I don't know how to make this work because I never saw that in *my* family when I was growing up."

2. I want to be a loving mother, but every time I try, you get mad, because the way I do it is intrusive and therefore not very loving.

3. You want to be a loving daughter, but you also need to become an autonomous adult, and then my way of meeting my needs conflicts with yours.

4. You stand up for yourself the way you should, but I am too little to handle it, so I have constant meltdowns, which include enmeshing other family members in the drama.

5. When you finally try to break out of this double-binding, crushing system, I act from my worst self—from my wounded, little self, and have tantrums that have high stakes attached.

6. The other family members who have not become as self-aware as you side with me, simply to reduce their own anxiety. They know you're right, but they are not yet ready to face their own "littleness," and so they blame you, instead of expecting *me* to grow up.

7. You finally grow enough to realize that your mental health, and your life, are more important than my acting out, and you raise the ante—you call the bluff—which is scary, because I might actually harm myself in the process.

8. At this epiphany, you call the bluff, choose your own life over some imagined disaster, and you do it in a way that is both kind and powerful, touching me with a depth and emotional honesty that I have never experienced in my life before. As a result of that huge risk, we both grow in ways we never imagined possible.

9. This approach creates a healthy, loving imbalance in the family system that leaves the others scratching their heads, wondering what *their part* has been, and what they now need to do in order to grow up as well.

CHAPTER 16

SHOULD I SIMPLY END
ALL CONTACT?

Every exit is an entry somewhere else.

—*Tom Stoppard, award-winning playwright*

Trade-offs in Families

The value of learning to accept trade-offs is especially poignant when we work with family members in conflict. A man worked very hard to make sense of his self-destructive behavior and in the process identified some painful aspects of his childhood. He understood that to simply blame his parents for his current problems would be too shallow, leaving him in a victim state with no responsibility for his own life. He also knew that to ignore his childhood pain would be unrealistic, leaving him with unhealed shame.

He decided that one way to achieve some balance between the two would be to share parts of his discoveries with his parents in the hope that they would just listen and acknowledge that some things in his childhood were less than ideal. He invited them into a therapy session, and they agreed to attend. With high hopes for a major breakthrough, the man began to share some of his early pain with them, only to find that they had a hard time listening. They hadn't done the work that he had, and so with the best of intentions they tried to explain why they had done what they had done each time he brought up an issue. It was clear that they were trying, but it was also evident that he would not achieve the acknowledgment that he sought. At his next individual session, the man was hurt and confused. He asked, "What do I do now?"

As we worked with his disappointment he began to formulate his own answer to his question. Over the succeeding months he grew to realize that he had some choices and that it was up to him to pick one of them. At first he chose to be bitter and angry, distancing himself from his parents in the hopes that they would feel the pain of his rejecting them and thereby see the light of how they had rejected him. But they just weren't getting it. He would talk to them occasionally, but they always seemed confused. They wanted to help, they told him, but they just didn't understand what he wanted. He gradually let go of this choice, and as he did, another option magically appeared.

A few months later he came in and announced that he had decided to accept them for who they were, and to get what he could from them rather than trying to get what he couldn't. His heart opened wide as tears of grief and acceptance trickled down his cheeks. He had chosen to trade a fantasy of what could be, but was unlikely, for what was real and possible—to have the relationship with his parents that was there, rather than none at all. By doing so, he retrieved his power from the tight grip of his past, allowing him to live his life more fully.

Balancing the Ecology of the Entire Family System

In the 1980s and early 1990s, it was not uncommon for some therapists to tell their clients, "Cut off all contact with your family of origin, because it is too toxic for you." A variant of that was, "Your father is too abusive, and he'll never change. You need to cease all contact with him." When it comes to human interactions, it is perhaps too extreme to always rule out extreme measures; there are usually exceptions to any rule. But this general cutoff strategy for adapting to one's rigidly unhealthy family often creates more problems than it solves.

To tell a victim of abuse to do something or not do something is considered by many experts to be a poor way of helping that victim grow up and cease being a victim (e.g., Maddock & Larson, 1995; Trepper & Barrett, 1989). Leading that client in the direction of formulating her own solution to the problem is much better because it helps the client activate her own adult problem-solving abilities—and, as the saying goes, "Blood is thicker than water." While we have encountered many families in which certain members have not spoken to other members for decades, we also find that this typically comes with an excruciating price. No matter what they tell you to the contrary, people who treat selected family members "as if they are dead to me" are not at peace with their decision. Their pain is often palpable to others, even if to them it feels as if it has long since been buried and done with.

A woman we once knew struggled with this notion of a "cutoff strategy" and eventually discovered a powerful, gracious, and respectful way to deal with a very troubled father while maintaining open lines of relationship with all of her family members, including him. Would her strategy work in your situation? Not necessarily. Every person is unique, every family is unique, and every circumstance is unique. But it is a poignant example from which you might glean some wisdom.

When she was seven, her father began to sexually abuse her, telling her that she was special, and that it was a sign of his love for her. He was such a passive, gentle man that neither she nor anyone else inside the family, nor in the larger community around them, ever thought that he could be capable of this kind of boundary distortion. She was very confused for a long time by this double bind, which was further confounded and intensified by the physical sensations in her body, her love for her father, her desire to preserve the surface calm in her family, her desire not to betray her mother, her fear for her two sisters, and her need for love and affection that grew out of the inherent emotional loneliness in the family that she felt despite the family's flawed belief that "we are a close, loving family."

By the time she was ten, she had long been displaying some of the typical symptoms of children who are being treated as sexual adults by a parent. She had become shy, withdrawn, and moody; she had difficulty concentrating and was very confused about her sexuality and about sex in general. Not knowing exactly what was going on, but knowing that she had been singled out as "special" somehow, her siblings began to resent her. Conflicts erupted. Anger, hurt, and miscommunication ensued. People, including Mom, secretly felt jealous and competitive with her for Dad's affections. It was an emotional-psychological mess.

A wise, seasoned school psychologist began talking with her about her grades, her moodiness, and how she felt about not getting along so well with peers at school. Then one day as her need to share what was happening grew stronger than her fear of what might happen if she said it, she blurted it out to her newfound ally. Fortunately, the psychologist knew how to respond. She said, "That's a lot to be carrying all by yourself." The girl burst into tears and sobbed and sobbed and sobbed. The psychologist stayed right there with her, resisting any urges to overreact or to rush in and rescue. She knew there would be a right time to do that.

Child Protective Services (CPS) entered the picture, then the court system, and the family reluctantly agreed to become involved in therapy. Her father was put on probation, and her father and mother were required to engage in ongoing therapy, which included the entire family at times, and the marriage at times. There was individual therapy for the young girl, her father, her mother, and also her siblings. Over the course of four years, the family healed many of the boundary distortions and painful rules that are so common in this kind of family.

Things became pretty "normal," and the children grew up and went out into the world and began to create their respective adult lives. But Dad and Mom stalled somewhere along the line, having made much progress, but not sticking with it quite long enough to make the changes permanent "in their insides."

At the age of thirty-six, married, and the mother of two boys and a girl (ages twelve, nine, and six), an old pattern appeared that left this woman with a perplexing puzzle to solve. How should she relate to her father, mother, siblings, and other relatives given the following scenario? It is Christmas Eve. She and her husband and three children have driven five hours to her parents' home in northern Wisconsin. A light snow has been gently falling for the past few hours. The trees and highways and byways are covered with frosting. The night is magic, cold, crisp, white, and filled with the hope and anticipation of a warm and loving Christmas Eve. She and her family pull into her parents' driveway, relieved that they made it safely with the increasingly heavy snowfall, thrilled about Christmas, and excited to see loved ones they hadn't seen for over a year. She takes the lead—it's her family, after all. She reaches the landing at the front door, rings the doorbell several times in jubilation, the door flies open, she looks into a house filled with relatives and presents and the wondrous smells of turkey and dressing and sweet potatoes; and then her father, who was the first to open the door, lunges toward her, throws his arms around her with a huge smile on his face, gives her a huge bear hug, holds her tight, leans back to look into her eyes, and then plants his mouth on top of hers, and as he does, she detects his attempt to push his tongue inside of her mouth, as if she were his wife, his lover, his spouse of so many years.

When she returned to Minneapolis, she shared her dilemma with some of her friends, but after a while they became just as lost as she was. They got seduced into rescuing her, began to give her advice and tell her what to do, and worst of all, they began to be angrier about the situation than she was. Their inevitable solutions for her were to either cease visiting her family on holidays altogether, or for her to rely on her husband as a buffer between her and her father. Her husband was to ring the doorbell and then firmly, and with some obvious "toughness," keep her father from coming near her. But this well-intentioned advice only served to reinforce her as a victim. Nothing changed. It was still a *victim-perpetrator interaction pattern*.

She got back into therapy, and after two years in a women's therapy group, she had accepted that her family of origin was not yet ready, and might never be ready, to address the boundary violations that existed in the family, despite all of the earlier work that was done when the abuse was first addressed. In doing childhood trauma resolution work, the final step is often the most rewarding to witness in our clients. It occurs when they have been able to identify how they were hurt and disappointed as children, have been able to experience and express some of the appropriate feelings about what happened, and have moved beyond responding with anger or helplessness.

During these months of agonizing ambivalence, this adult woman had been asking herself these questions: *Should I avoid my family altogether? Should I have my husband run interference for me when we first ring the doorbell and enter the house next Christmas? Should I plan a family intervention and confront Dad with all of my years of shame and rage, which I have mostly worked through anyway? Should I tell him directly to stop it, when that approach has never worked before? Should I put my head down in shame, avoid eye contact with my father, get little, pout, and remain nervous, angry, sullen, and bitter for the entire Christmas visit?*

According to Maddock (1993), Maddock and Larson (1995), and Maddock, Friel, and Friel (2009), ecological-systemic interventions are directed at *creating dynamic balances* that simultaneously

- Maintain the autonomous identities of individual members.
- Allow members to relate to one another in mutually helpful and meaningful ways.
- Preserve the family as a functional system.
- Contribute to the integrity of the larger community and physical environment.

The approach that she worked out within the context of her supportive women's therapy group accomplished all of the goals listed above. Her two years in group had created personal transformations in her that made it possible for her to carry it off as a grown-up, gracious, powerful, respectful, kind woman. In the months leading up to Christmas, she practiced her strategy in group. And then on Christmas Eve, as she and her husband and children walked up to her parents' snow-covered house in northern Wisconsin, she took the lead, rang the doorbell, composed herself, smiled warmly as the door swung open, and then when her father impulsively reached out to kiss her as he greeted them all, she gently put her hands out to grasp his biceps so that she could inconspicuously control how close he came to her, and as his mouth came nearer to hers, *she simply turned her head so that he kissed her on the cheek*, the way any adult with normal boundaries would, and then before he even knew what had happened, she *gently* moved him to the side a bit so that she could move into the house and hug her mother, and then her sister, and then her nieces and nephews.

Her father never violated that boundary again, even though he never really knew why. And their family became closer than any of them had previously imagined possible, even though most of them weren't aware of how or why it happened.

Maddock and Larson's (1995) explanation of ecological balancing is an elegant description of how this woman became empowered and grown-up without leaving an intergenerational trail of tears and alienation behind her:

> *Ecologically, balance is a process of transforming the relationships between subsystems in an ecosystem without either losing the interdependence between them or destroying the overall integrity of the ecosystem of which they are a part.* For example, throughout its life cycle a family is preserved as an ecosystem to the individuals that compose it only by permitting and encouraging continuous transformation in the relationships between the members, without destroying their interdependence as family subsystems. This ecological balance is expressed through *patterns of reciprocal interaction* between the systems. . . . It reflects the total interdependence of all systems and ecosystems on a continuous basis. (p. 25)

The magic that can happen between family members when *just one* person in the family takes the risk to grow and change will always be one of the most rewarding, surprising, and miraculous events that we are honored to witness, in the long history of an evolving family system.

Part Six:

MAKING THINGS RIGHT

People usually fail when they are on the verge of success. So give as much care to the end as to the beginning. Then there will be no failure.

—*Lao Tsu,* Tao Te Ching

CHAPTER 17

ACCOUNTABILITY, INTEGRITY, AMENDS, AND RECONCILIATION

In the world in which time is a circle, every handshake,
every kiss, every birth, every word, will be repeated precisely.
So too every moment that two friends stop becoming friends, every time
that a family is broken because of money, every vicious remark in an
argument between spouses, every opportunity denied because
of a superior's jealousy, every promise not kept.

—*Alan Lightman,* Einstein's Dreams *(1994, p. 11)*

Alan Lightman's enchanting, whimsical, deeply thought-provoking, and limbically resonant little book, *Einstein's Dreams*, imagines what Albert Einstein might have been dreaming, night after night, while working as a patent clerk in Berne, Switzerland, as he was beginning to come to grips with his special theory of relativity. In the book, his dreams were all about time in all of its wondrous possibilities, and they were out-of-the-box kinds of dreams, in which, for example, time repeats over and over in a circular fashion, or in which time stands still. Each chapter in this wonderful book describes in vivid detail what it might be like for the residents of Berne to live in a universe where time was like that. How wonderful it would be if every middle school or high school science student were required to read Lightman's book before digging into the details of their science studies. It would embed science in unimaginable ways in their hearts and souls and everyday lives.

If time *were* circular, as implied by the epigraph above, there would be no way for anything to change. There would be no way for relationships to transform and deepen. There would be no way for the wounds that each of us experience, or cause in another, to ever heal. It would be the essence of what many theologians refer to as "hell." What makes us *spiritual beings* is our ability to look back at what we have done to each other and to consider, with the wisdom of experience and age, how what seemed "normal" back then now seems cruel and inconsiderate; and then to have the chance to repair those wrongs or to forgive those wrongs done to us by others.

Each of us hurts others. We rage, we continually hide our real feelings and then let them explode years later in a nuclear fashion, when—had we more integrity, had we been more grown-up or differentiated—we could have expressed our anger in smaller, more manageable doses all along the way. We are passive-aggressive, feigning niceness when we don't really feel nice at all, and thereby denying who we are and losing ourselves, but inadvertently killing off the relationships that mean the most to us by hiding our true selves from the ones we love the most. We sabotage each other by appearing as if we are so fragile—a very manipulative stance to take, by the way—that we give others the message that we can't handle the truth. The result is that we are the most powerful ones in the relationships, even though we look like the weakest, because we bind others up so they believe they can't be intimate with us, all while we complain about having no intimacy in the relationship.

We step on each other's toes. We let each other down. We frighten each other with our ability to distance from loved ones when all we are really doing is protecting ourselves and trying to lash out at someone whom we believe has hurt us. We say mean things we can never take back, although we wish we could. We have affairs that we never thought we would ever be capable of having, and then we lie about them to protect our loved ones from the hurt, but also to protect ourselves from the intense conflict that is the only way the two of us can ever heal the wound that the affair has caused. We bind each other up in ways that are so unintentionally creative that we can barely recognize the bind at all.

We are human beings. We are flawed. That is a given. What makes us spiritual, holy, and capable of infinitely deep emotional love with one another is our ability to be accountable, to have personal integrity, and to make appropriate amends—that is, our ability to make *genuine amends*, and to be big enough emotionally to admit our mistakes, to humble ourselves, and to be grateful for the small things in life that turn out to be the most important of all. Gratitude fixes or repairs the fundamental flaw in all human beings—that we have a brain big enough to reflect on our own deaths, but no power whatsoever to prevent death.

Gratitude comes from the grace that we experience in that moment when we have tears rolling down our cheeks as we admit a terrible wrong and feel truly ashamed and sorry for what we have done, and we see the tears of relief and validation in the other person, and we realize that for an instant we are on the same page. The page that says, "Our love now transcends even this egregious offense that has been committed," which immediately transcends the hurts that I feel and the guilt and shame that you feel, and propels us upward to a new level of intimacy that says, "We can love each other deeply, from this mutual platform that we have now created for ourselves, despite how we have hurt each other over the years, and despite the fact that we will probably hurt each other in the future."

Couples often describe these moments as the moments when they fell deeply in love "for the 'real' first time," even though they may have been married for twenty or more years. These are the moments that redeem and justify years of heartache and struggle as both people are growing up, and they often occur as the couple is ready to end their relationship. But after this moment of shared but separate growth and powerful intimacy, the chances that they will actually split up decrease to near zero. Life is filled with paradoxes.

Richard Nixon had many successes while he was president of the United States, but he wasn't powerful enough—in the sense of weaving both *power*

and *graciousness* into the way he related to the world outside of himself—
to get beyond his insecurities about his own upbringing and his insecurities about the "northeastern liberal elites" that he so hated and secretly
envied. Like the Neanderthals—fighting large animals with large pointed
spears and clubs at close range—he returned to his default position when
under stress. His weakness, his littleness, his Achilles' heel, was that "when
under attack, attack back, and defend, no matter what." How different his
world and our national history might have been as the Watergate scandal
was in its infancy, had he simply said to the American people, face-to-
face, during a nationally televised prime-time presidential announcement,
"Some of the people who are overly zealous in supporting my reelection
crossed the line of propriety, and I am asking for your forgiveness. I cannot
support their efforts, I cannot endorse the criminal break-in and theft of
the campaign secrets of my opponents, and I am embarrassed and angry
about it. Most of all, I ask that you, the American people, forgive me, and
I promise you right here and right now that this will never happen again."

People are *very* forgiving if they are given a *genuine* amends. It probably would have blown over with few repercussions, and he would have
finished out what was looking like quite a stellar presidency.

What would have happened if Bill Clinton, faced with irrefutable
charges of his having had a sexual relationship in the White House with
an intern, had looked into the camera at millions of Americans and said,
"I have a problem with women. I had this problem when I was governor
of Arkansas. Everyone pretty much knew about it before I was elected
president, including you, the voters. It is a terrible flaw that I know has
hurt my wife and daughter, as well as my closest associates. And now it has
the potential to hurt my presidency, just when we have so much important
work to do. So, yes, I am sexually compulsive and, at times, reckless. And I
apologize for that. But more than anything, I admit that I did it."

Our hunch is that those millions of Americans would have looked at
their television sets, seen the genuineness of his facial expressions and
heard the authenticity of his words, realized that he was perhaps the most
intelligent president the United States has had since Thomas Jefferson,

looked at the booming economy and at his adept and strategic compromises with his political opponents on the other side of the aisle, shrugged, and then gone on with their lives. "Yeah," they might have said, "he has some real problems with women. But he's a hell of a president!" And that would have been that. There would have been no witch hunt, no impeachment trial that gridlocked Congress for two years, and no loss of power.

Genuine amends—as opposed to the myriad of artificial and insulting amends we see nowadays that are based on shallow scripts written by attorneys and expensive public relations firms—are embraced by most human beings, because we all know that we are all flawed, whether we want to admit it or not.

Every human being is vastly capable of being both nasty and nice at various times throughout our lives. We are flawed. We are both "whores, pimps, gamblers, and sons of bitches," and "saints and angels and martyrs and holy men," as John Steinbeck wrote. Our capacity for forgiveness and our capacity to make amends are boundless, if we let them be. We are the most flexible creatures on Earth, and as Gregory Bateson implied, that is our greatest strength and also our greatest weakness. More than forty years ago, he warned us, "It is doubtful whether a species having *both* an advanced technology *and* this strange way of looking at its world can endure" (1971, p. 377).

Lee Thorn's Incredible Journey of Reconciliation

In 1966 Lee Thorn was a navy bomb loader on the U.S.S. *Ranger* in the Gulf of Tonkin, near Vietnam. His job was to load cluster bombs and phosphorous rockets onto bombers and jets headed for secret targets in Laos, and then to watch filmed footage of the destruction wrought by the bombs: families, villages, children, livestock blown to shreds or burned to death, day after day. Years later, suffering from post-traumatic stress disorder (PTSD) and massive guilt, Lee Thorn was tortured by nightmares that left him "lurching to his feet, in cold sweats" (Fagan, 2003).

The secret, illegal, unauthorized bombings of these targets continued for over seven years, unbeknownst to members of Congress, under the auspices of Operation Menu, sanctioned by the Johnson and Nixon administrations. According to the Legacies of War website,

> Laos is the most heavily bombed country in history, on a per capita basis. U.S. Vietnam War–era bombings from 1964–1973 left nearly half of Laos contaminated with vast quantities of unexploded ordnance (UXO). Over 20,000 people have been killed or injured by UXO in Laos since the bombing ceased. Here are some other startling facts about the U.S. bombing of Laos and its tragic aftermath: Over 260 million cluster bombs were dropped on Laos during the Vietnam War (210 million more bombs than were dropped on Iraq in 1991, 1998 and 2006 combined); over 75 million did not detonate. During the bombing, the equivalent of a planeload of bombs was dropped every eight minutes, 24 hours a day for nine years. More than half of all confirmed cluster munitions casualties in the world have occurred in Laos. Each year there continue to be over 100 new casualties in Laos. Close to 40% of the accidents result in death, and 40% of the victims are children. Over the past 16 years, the U.S. has contributed on average $3.1M per year for UXO clearance in Laos; the U.S. spent $17M per day (in 2010 dollars) for nine years bombing Laos. The U.S. spent as much in three days bombing Laos ($51M, in 2010 dollars) that it has spent for clean up in the last 16 years ($51M). Nearly 40 years on, only a fraction of these munitions have been destroyed.

Lee Thorn's journey of redemption began in 1998 with a plea in a veterans' newspaper for medical supplies needed in Phon Hong, a village fifty miles from the capital of Vientiane. The plea was written by a woman by the name of Bounthanh Phommasathit who had fled Laos and was working as a human services consultant in Ohio. Lee Thorn called her, located 200 pounds of medical supplies, and with his best friend, Rich Stoll of Pleasant Hills, California, flew to Laos. "What he found was personal absolution" (Fagan, 2003).

Rich's wife said that they had watched Lee get on planes for peace rallies, knowing that he was on drugs and alcohol, suffering from PTSD, and wondering if they'd ever see him alive again. "But he always wanted justice. He always wanted to do the right thing. He just needed to find out how to get out of his box. He needed Laos" (Fagan, 2003). The partnership between Bounthanh and Thorn led to the Jhai Foundation, which in five years (as of 2003) had shipped ten tons of medical supplies to Laos, dug wells, installed computer learning labs for children, repaired school buildings—and now, has started shipping coffee to the United States (ibid.).

Lee Thorn was featured in Jack Silberman's PBS documentary titled *Bombies* (2001)—the Lao word for the millions of tennis-sized cluster bombs strewn across the nation of Laos—during which time he spoke of the torture and agony that he felt as a result of loading all of those bombs onto planes in the Gulf of Tonkin. In one of the more moving portions of the documentary, Thorn described entering a Buddhist temple and encountering a mural on the wall depicting many of the horrible atrocities inflicted on mankind by mankind throughout the centuries—beheadings, bombings, torture, murder, wars—and that in the midst of all that senseless violence and cruelty from human to human, floating amid all of the carnage, was a large Buddha with a tranquil, angelic smile that balanced out all of the horror, matching the terrible power of humans at our worst with a spiritual countenance that spoke of humans at our best. Lee said that he wept uncontrollably, and that for the first time since the Vietnam War, he felt whole, complete, and at peace.

Thorn began to help the locals cultivate and market their *Arabica typica* coffee beans, brought there by the French in 1930. The beans have been rated as among the twelve best in the world by the prestigious CIRAD coffee research institute in Montpellier, France. He began selling them through a fair-trade dealer in northern California under the name of Thanksgiving Coffee. Since then, the Jhai Foundation has expanded its operations extensively.

The Jhai Foundation is a non-profit organisation working mainly in Laos. One of its projects is bringing communication services to rural communities lacking electricity or telephones. To achieve this goal they have developed the Jhai PC and Communication System, a solid-state, low-energy-consuming computer that can be powered by a foot-crank generator built into a bicycle frame or solar energy and uses a wireless network to provide VoIP and Internet services. The JhaiPC runs Linux with a localised version of KDE. The hardware and software design and user documentation for the JhaiPC are completely open and have been released through SourceForge.net. With the minimal communication technology provided by the JhaiPC, small businesses, such as farmers in Ban Phon Kam, are able to get better prices for their products. Jhai is also introducing organic farming techniques, fair trade marketing and direct sales to these farmers.

(http://en.wikipedia.org/wiki/Jhai_Foundation)

After all these years of hard work and dedication on the part of Lee Thorn to make the Jhai Foundation work, including partnerships cultivated with Silicon Valley companies like Cisco and the International Finance Corporation (we urge the reader to read of the amazing accomplishments of the Jhai Foundation on its website at http://jhai.org/our-history), Lee Thorn sent an e-mail dated November 8, 2011, stating that he was retiring from the Jhai Foundation. We felt sad for the loss, as well as grateful for what he has done for the world and for what he has taught us by his dedication and willingness to correct a huge mistake that many would say was not even his fault. But for that, we admire him even more.

In Kevin Fagan's August 17, 2003, story in the *San Francisco Chronicle*, Lee Thorn was quoted as stating what we understand to be the essence of reconciliation:

> My relationship to the Lao people in the war was *abstract*. I knew I was helping defeat communism, and that I could kill them. The whole point was that we're better than them, we can defeat them. But it was stupid— thinking purely like that, with only war in mind, leads to more war, no economic development and a lot of dead people on all sides. *The only way I could heal was to see them, and have them see me, as whole human beings. When you are in a war, there is no relationship. It's all about destroying things.* (emphasis added)

Dissociation is how people manage to do horrible things to one another, and so Lee Thorn was absolutely correct in his attempts to reconcile, heal, and make amends. As long as we find a way to disconnect from the person, we can and do commit atrocities. When we connect with and empathize with the person, being a perpetrator is much harder.

Pedophilia in the Catholic Church— A Troubling Amends with Questionable Integrity

Many people in alcoholic or abusive families eventually get their realities confirmed and validated by (1) the process of first exposing the abuse and dysfunction—telling someone outside of the system who can see beyond the limited and defensive confines of the system, (2) the shining of a light on them by socially sanctioned investigations conducted by child protective services and other social service agencies, and (3) empirically validated research into the real causes and outcomes of family abuse and dysfunction.

Validating the very "craziness" that is caused by a father or mother who excuses violence, sexual abuse, and the terrorizing of children makes people feel less "crazy," and frees them to trust their own feelings and realities about the abuse.

One of the authors (JCF) wrote about one of the more stunning cases of priest abuse of children in his 1993 book, *Rescuing Your Spirit: When Third-Grade Morality Isn't Enough for Christians*. Through the excruciatingly painful and courageous initial efforts of one of the people who had been molested, Frank Fitzpatrick, it was revealed that in the 1960s in Massachusetts a charming young Catholic priest, Father James Porter, began molesting scores of children in his parish (Woodward, Friday, & Springen, 1992; Mehren, 1992; Sawyer, 1992). In several cases, Father Annunciado, a priest in the same parish, stumbled onto Father Porter in the act of sexually abusing his victims. Father Annunciado simply shut the door and went away in silence. Diane Sawyer tastefully and compassionately presented the story on *PrimeTime Live* in July 1992. During that telecast we had the privilege of witnessing the shame, outrage, healing, and love for each other of the many survivors of Father Porter's abuses who chose to come forward and participate in the program. While it was painful to

hear of the abuses, it was spiritually moving to see these honorable, courageous people support one another in their pain. It was an example of true
human healing at its best.

When the case first broke in the press, we were as shocked as anyone
else, despite our familiarity with sexual abuse cases. But what we found
unnerving and very unexpected was the public reaction by Cardinal Bernard Law of Boston, who angrily and gruffly snapped into the *10 O'Clock
News* reporter's camera something to the effect that all the press was doing
was making it hard on all of the good priests out there. His "official statement," quoted in the *Los Angeles Times,* was that it was "the tragedy of
a priest betraying the sacred trust of priestly service." But the cameras
of *PrimeTime Live* showed Cardinal Law preaching, presumably at Mass,
and thundering from the pulpit, "By all means, let's call down God's power
on the media."

If we were Catholics, and victims of sexual abuse, this remark from a
high church official in such an angry, accusatory tone would probably mes-
merize us into feeling ashamed of our outrage. We would probably nod in
agreement, our eyes glazing over in the dissociation that goes with being
abused, and then we would comfortably go back into denial about the horrors that these scores of adults experienced and are still experiencing.

But that wasn't our reaction. Our reaction was disbelief and then anger.
How dare he try to gloss over the betrayal of children's faith and innocence
by trying to dump the shame back onto those who have a duty to expose
this kind of abuse. How dare high church officials sit back and hope that it
all blows over. At that moment in his own personal journey through life,
Cardinal Law missed a powerful opportunity for accountability and healing, and therefore he missed the ultimate act of spirituality and human
kindness—especially for the survivors of Father Porter's sexual atrocities.

And so we asked ourselves—and we must be clear that the quotation
below is our own hypothetical "ideal" response that actually never came
close to actually happening—what *if* Cardinal Bernard Law of Boston had
said the following?

What Father Porter did was atrocious. It never should have happened. There is no way that we can undo it, but as a representative of the Catholic Church, I apologize from the depths of my soul for what a fellow clergyman did to you. I applaud the press for exposing these abuses so that we can all know about them, so that the survivors can feel believed and begin to heal, and so we can increase our very early, tentative efforts to deal with and treat our priests who are sexual offenders—and bring them to justice within the secular legal system.

If he had said that, he would have been a model of true Christianity. But he didn't. He chose to indirectly shame the victims by attempting to shame the press who were, by reporting these atrocities, helping the victims begin to be believed and to heal.

Cardinal Law left Boston in December 2002. In 2004 Pope John Paul II appointed him archpriest of the Papal Basilica of Saint Mary Major in Rome. In November 2011, upon reaching the age of eighty, he resigned from this position (Donadio, 2011).

As a postscript to the recently concluded drama of Cardinal Bernard Law, a May 21, 2011, editorial in the *Los Angeles Times* was titled "Report indicts '60s counterculture in Catholic abuse cases—A study links child sexual abuse by Catholic priests in the '60s and '70s to the feminist movement, a 'singles culture' and divorce. *That implausible conclusion detracts from the report's data*" (emphasis added).

Blame the flower children. That seems to be the chief conclusion of a new report about the Roman Catholic Church's sexual abuse scandal. The study, undertaken by John Jay College of Criminal Justice at the request of America's Catholic bishops, links the spike in child abuse by priests in the 1960s and '70s to "the importance given to young people and popular culture"—along with the emergence of the feminist movement, a "singles culture" and a growing acceptance of homosexuality. It also cites crime, drugs, an increase in premarital sexual behavior and divorce.

The problem with this conclusion isn't that it absolves molesting priests of responsibility. Even the study's authors wouldn't go that far. Rather, the flaw with the theory is that it's unsupported by any data or evidence. It thus detracts from the report's other findings, which are based on empirical research. Indeed, aside from its implausible indictment of the '60s counter-culture, the report is an enlightening analysis of an abominable chapter in the Roman Catholic Church's history.

Drawing partly on a 2004 study, also by John Jay College, the report provides a detailed account of everything from the incidence of sexual abuse by priests to the age of victims to the relationship of sexual orientation to abuse. Some of the conclusions it draws from its data are debatable. For example, it suggests that only a minority of the abusers should be considered pedophiles, because most priests molested children older than 10—even though most social scientists consider 13 to be a more accurate cutoff. But the data themselves are important. Especially striking is the dramatic decline in incidents of abuse over the last 25 years, a phenomenon obscured by the fact that so many examples of abuse have come to light recently. In explaining that decline, the report points to activism by victims' advocates and tougher responses to abuse by bishops.

Let's return to our brief discussion of child abuse earlier in this chapter, and draw a parallel between that and these discussions of the church's response to priest abuse. Imagine that if every time a child abuse report was sent to a state agency, the agency investigated and concluded that whatever abuse occurred was either perfectly justifiable on its own merit or excusable because of extenuating circumstances that really were not extenuating circumstances at all—just red herrings. Children and families would be left in pools of shame and self-doubt. That is what this church report has done to the survivors of sexual abuse at the hands of priests. It does not address the problem; it fabricates an irrelevant excuse that sounds vaguely plausible but is ultimately completely implausible, unsatisfying, totally unnecessary, self-serving, and lacking in any moral or theological integrity.

It is an eye-opening statement about the flaws that plague all human beings and all human institutions when the amount of power they possess is not at all in balance with their sorely limited capacity for human intimacy, empathy, compassion, and ethical responsibility. Absolute power does corrupt absolutely, and in this case, the consequences have been morally and psychologically reprehensible—and for many human beings, damaging beyond words.

Why Making Amends and Reconciliation Heals the Heart and Soul: Intriguing Biochemical Evidence

We have been conducting men's and women's therapy groups as part of our private practice since 1985, and we have also conducted a three-and-a-half-day group/lecture therapy process called the ClearLife Clinic for just as long. We are sold on groups, because we believe that the human brain cannot function optimally without experiencing limbic resonance on a regular basis. So many of us in the United States continue to grow up in a culture, and in families, that simply do not value that kind of activity. The issue goes back to the quotation from Alexis de Tocqueville (1835) that we cited in Chapter 11.

Americans are forever brooding over advantages they do not possess. . . . It is strange to see with what feverish ardor the Americans pursue their own welfare, and to watch the vague dread that constantly torments them lest they should not have chosen the shortest path which may lead to it. (1863b, vol. 2, p. 164)

What we find so exciting now is the convergence of the findings of a nineteenth-century social observer of a young nation, observations of human behavior by clinicians working in the twentieth and twenty-first centuries, and some of the hard neuroscientific evidence reported today from the emerging field of interpersonal neurobiology.

By far, some of the most powerful and inspirational experiences in which we have had the honor to participate have been moments in marital therapy, family therapy, and addiction treatment when clients finally reach the deeply intimate and terrifying point of facing each other as genuine, emotionally open human beings.

A fifty-year-old woman asks her eighty-six-year-old father to join in her therapy and tearfully shares that, when she was a child, what she needed most from her dad was some time with him. The father, who is now a retired CEO of a successful corporation that he founded, and dying of emphysema, acknowledges that he was too busy building his empire to be there in those small but crucial ways that he now knows his daughter needed. The daughter begins to shed some tears, knowing that her father is dying; the father also sheds some tears, knowing that he let down his daughter. The healing, the spirituality, and the love in the room at that moment defy description.

A husband and wife are enjoying a romantic evening at a sensuously designed and appointed tropical restaurant as the gentle surf of the Pacific Ocean washes onto the beach with a hypnotic *whoosh* beneath their perch a few feet above the water. They are deeply in love and deeply connected, and then she says, her eyes glistening, "You were really mean to me when we were first married. I know you were still drinking then, but it hurt me so much. You were so mean. I don't know what was wrong with you back then." Rather than flooding with shame and getting defensive, he calmed his insides, felt the shame, held on to his sense of self, and then reached across the table, put his hand on hers, looked her in the eyes as they both began to shed tears, and said, "I am so sorry for hurting you that way. I am so sorry." The night instantly became mystical, filled with the magic of their indescribable love for each other.

A woman who had been drinking alcoholically for twenty-five years while her husband, an attorney who had held the family together and had covered for her alcoholism just as long, attended her fourth inpatient treatment program at Hazelden in Center City, Minnesota. During the Family Program, her true self finally emerged after all those years of pain and sadness and childhood sexual abuse that she had experienced, and she looked her husband and her grown children in the eyes and declared, "I hurt you. I hurt you when I made a spectacle of myself at your wedding. I embarrassed you at your college graduation. I am so sorry that I raged at you for no reason when you invited me to your in-laws for Christmas—I was drunk, jealous, petty, irrational, and infantile. I am so, so sorry. And I own it. My drinking is no excuse."

A son says, "I have been addicted to cocaine, and I have done horrible things to you. I have stolen from you, I have lied to you, I have blamed you for my problems. I am sorry. You didn't deserve what I did."

When one human being acknowledges to another human being that he has done something that he shouldn't, and if it is done with sincerity and genuineness—and when the receiver is big enough to let it in rather than just use the apology as an opening to further rage and act like a wounded victim—then there is no relationship on Earth that cannot heal.

In an article that appeared in the July 2010 edition of *Wired* magazine titled "Secret of AA: After 75 years, we don't know how it works," Brendan Koerner (2010) wrote the following,

> After a review of nearly 200 articles on group therapy, a pair of Stanford University researchers pinpointed why the approach works so well: "Members find the group to be a compelling emotional experience; they develop close bonds with the other members and are deeply influenced by their acceptance and feedback. . . .
>
> . . . Publicly revealing one's deepest flaws and hearing others do likewise forces a person to confront the terrible consequences of their alcoholism—something that is very difficult to do all alone. This, in turn, prods the impaired prefrontal cortex into resuming its regulatory mission. "The brain is designed to respond to experiences," says Steven Grant, chief of the clinical neuroscience branch of the National Institute on Drug Abuse. "I have no doubt that these therapeutic processes change the brain." And the more that critical part of the brain is compelled to operate as designed, the more it springs back to its pre-addiction state. While it's on the mend, AA functions as a temporary replacement—a prefrontal cortex made up of a cast of fellow drunks in a church basement, rather than neurons and synapses.
>
> Finally, the 12 steps address another major risk factor for relapse: stress. Recovering alcoholics are often burdened by memories of the nasty things they did while wasted. When they bump into old acquaintances they mistreated, the guilt can become overwhelming. The resulting stress causes their brains to secrete a hormone that releases corticotropin, which has been shown to cause relapse in alcohol-dependent lab rats.

AA addresses this risk with the eighth and ninth steps, which require alcoholics to make amends to people they've wronged. This can alleviate feelings of guilt and in turn limit the stress that may undermine a person's fragile sobriety.

Bill W., as Wilson [AA's cofounder] is known today, didn't know the first thing about corticotropin-releasing hormone or the prefrontal cortex, of course. His only aim was to harness spirituality in the hopes of giving fellow alcoholics the strength to overcome their disease. But in developing a system to lead drunks to God, he accidentally created something that deeply affects the brain—a system that has now lasted for three-quarters of a century and shows no signs of disappearing.

The act of making a *genuine* amends is one of the most holy and *physically* as well as *emotionally* healing of human actions.

Integrity, Honor, and Accountability

[*Author's note*: This section is adapted from our book *The Soul of Adulthood* (1995).]

What Are Integrity and Honor?

"Integrity" and "honor" mean many things. The words strike several chords. They mean being consistent and trustworthy, having values that are on a higher plane than simply serving the self, and they include honesty, fairness, and wholeness. These are lofty ideals and it is therefore important to keep in mind that no one is perfect. Being consistent and trustworthy do not necessarily mean being punctual, although it might include that under certain circumstances.

Sometimes people confuse things like punctuality and rule following with integrity and honor. For example, a man is always on time, always tries to be nice to others, remembers birthdays and anniversaries, hardly ever raises his voice in anger, reads the Bible, espouses virtue and honor, and is liked by most of his associates. And then one day there is a conflict at work or home that requires him to act by taking a clear position on a difficult issue, but he finds himself unable to do it. He knows what his stated values are, and everyone else knows what they are, too; but he can't respond when the chips are down. We might then question his integrity when it comes to those particular values because he lacks consistency between what he says and what he does.

We recall the words of a Sufi master who said, "I no longer listen to what people say. I watch what they do." Being trustworthy and consistent in our values requires that we not just verbalize but also act according to those words.

At the same time, it is important to leave room for one's humanity. A man may have impeccable integrity when it comes to his professional life but have a deep flaw in his character somewhere else. He might be another Nelson Mandela at work but have difficulty living according to his higher values in his marriage. Do we judge him as lacking integrity altogether, or can we make room in our hearts and minds to honor his strength and courage at work despite his personal flaws? Was Winston Churchill just an alcoholic, cigar-smoking tyrant, or was he a tremendously courageous leader who helped to save the free world? Some would focus on the former, but we hope most would focus on the latter.

Integrity and honor are always developing, always in process, and ever-deepening. A woman may live a life of quiet desperation and victimhood in which she sacrifices her integrity year after year for the sake of family unity, and then late in her life she may suddenly come to life and take a courageous stand on a powerful issue. In that one courageous act she may erase an entire lifetime of moral equivocation so that her life has as much meaning as her death. It is never too late to choose wholeness over fragmentation if only we can muster the courage to do it. In *Richard II*, Shakespeare wrote, "Mine honor is my life; both grow in one;/Take honor from me and my life is done."

Accountability

When you want to know where your resources are, how they have been utilized, how much you have left, and how much you need in the future, you might hire an accountant to help you. Accountant jokes usually center on the sharp pencil used by the accountant and the fact that every penny must be accounted for when doing a formal audit—which explains why we nickname them "bean counters." When we move into the murky realm of human relationships, it is even harder to do an accurate accounting because feelings and behaviors are less quantifiable than dollars and cents. But we must try. Accountability is a crucial aspect of integrity and honor.

A woman is miserable in her marriage and then suddenly finds herself falling in love with another man. She is so lonely and empty in her marriage and so afraid of disturbing the painful balance between herself, her husband, and her children that she convinces herself to accept the affair as the lesser of two evils—divorce being the other. As she gets more deeply embroiled in the affair, it becomes harder and harder to juggle both relationships until one day the whole delicately balanced house of cards comes crashing down around her. She looks into the frightened eyes of her husband who has just asked her point-blank if she is having an affair, and as she says "yes" she realizes that the greatest damage that she has done to him is to lie when she knew that he suspected something all along, because it deprived him of the dignity of being able to respond to what was real.

We all weave tangled webs within the structure of our lives now and then, and many people fall into extramarital affairs without seeming to know how it happened. The critical question is, "How do we handle our relationship pain in the future once we have seen and felt the terrible damage caused by this kind of deception?" A woman who is open to the deepening of integrity and honor within herself will take the great risk to do a personal accounting of the experience. Her first action after doing this might be to apologize, without excuses, for interfering with her husband's reality and therefore his dignity. She might wait patiently as he expresses his shock, his outrage, his deep hurt and betrayal, and his fears. Owning up to the affair levels the playing field just as keeping it secret gives her more power than is fair. Once it is out in the open she might also act honorably by either ending the marriage if she feels it is hopeless, or by ending the affair so that she can work on the marriage and give it another chance, unfettered by the intrusion of the other relationship.

Regardless of what happens to her marriage, if this woman is becoming truly accountable and honorable, she will no longer be free to choose a hidden affair as an indirect way of dealing with relationship pain in the future. It simply won't be an option any longer because she knows from firsthand experience how much destruction it causes. As our clients move toward accountability, we liken it to being in a room with doors in each corner, and then painting themselves into the corner of their own choosing. If it is an accountable choice, they will paint themselves into the corner where the door opens up to honesty and directness in relationships so that their only available choice will be to resolve the disappointment and unhappiness in their current relationship, cleanly and respectfully, before considering moving on to another relationship.

An adult man, in this case, can weather the end of even the deepest of relationships because he knows that life is filled with endings. It is the lack of consistency, honesty, and integrity that makes him *feel* so crazy. And it is the lack of accountability that keeps him stuck in the old, painful relationship. A grown-up man can come to accept that his relationship is over if his partner is forthright and clear about what is in her heart. When she maintains her false dignity by not being honest, then he must struggle with the disrespect implied by her lack of honesty—a struggle that is harder to release.

Accountability does not mean that we continually beat ourselves up for all of our limitations. We help people see that their defenses and addictions developed as a way to protect themselves from painful circumstances when they were children, and that as children they did not have the power to protect themselves in healthy ways. This allows the person to have self-acceptance and forgiveness so that he can work through the shame of his limitations. But as retired Southern California therapist Lyndel Brennan noted many years ago, self-acceptance or acceptance of another's limitations does not mean that we condone those limitations. We can forgive another's hurting us, but we can also expect them to work on their problems so that they stop the hurt.

Cultivating Integrity, Honor, and Accountability

Jean Piaget wrote that children learn empathy more while playing in the sandbox than from being told to memorize rules. We believe by this he meant that as we struggle with each other we directly experience the impact of our behavior on others, and theirs on us. I take your toy away from you and laugh at your tears, and then a bigger or faster child takes my toy away from me and I cry. I lie about my commitment to you and it violates your trust, and then another person lies about her commitment to me and it violates my trust. These experiences can then be plugged into the moral teachings of our larger society so that we no longer behave respectfully just because the law says we must; we do so because of our deepened empathy and understanding of the reasons underlying the law.

The human brain is perfectly capable of extrapolating from a less severe example to a more severe one. If someone beats me with words and attempts to kill my spirit with emotional neglect, can I not get a strong feeling for what it must be like to be beaten with a pipe and to have my life taken from me?

We believe that each human being, no matter how much he hurts later, is born with an empathic/ethical drive, except in cases of genetic shortages or brain damage. This may sound preposterous given the violence in our world, but we don't think so. We have seen what appeared to be incorrigible offenders eventually reclaim their dignity by becoming accountable. We have seen people who were so driven by their sexuality that they never thought they could maintain a sexually monogamous relationship with their partner, but they have. Accountability is a choice. It is an attribute of the self that can be cultivated. And while being accountable means that we lose certain "freedoms," it also means that we gain immeasurable gifts along the way, which is why it is worth pursuing.

Integrity, honor, and accountability begin in our homes and then spread past those four walls into the world beyond. A little boy overhears his mother say to his father, "You hurt my feelings when you said that, and I didn't like it." Then he hears his father say, "You're right. I'm sorry.

I was out of line with that comment." Day in and day out, year after year, this little boy sees and hears his parents sticking up for themselves, fighting with clarity and respect, owning up to their faults without trying to weasel out of them, giving each other room to make mistakes without always being taken to task, taking risks, acting on their values rather than just talking about them, appreciating and loving each other, and enjoying their relationship. When this little boy becomes a man he automatically conducts the majority of his life with integrity and honor.

For those of us who lacked good examples of accountability when we were growing up, cultivating integrity and honor begins with our fearless assessment of who we are and how we affect other human beings. Sometimes life gently *invites* us to do such an accounting, and sometimes life grabs us by the throat and demands that we do it, as in the case of the man who went to prison for unintentionally killing another man in a drunken bar fight. He struggled and fought fiercely and bitterly for many years, angry at those who had imprisoned him, and even angrier beneath it all at those who hurt him when he was little. The angrier he became, the less anyone was willing to consider his parole, until one day he simply surrendered, at the age of forty-two. He entered the prison's alcohol rehabilitation program for the third time, but this time he did it voluntarily—not because his spirit was broken but because his spirit finally demanded a voice. His spirit had finally come to life after being dormant all those years.

Upon completing the program he initiated a systematic process of becoming accountable to those he had hurt throughout his life. Without any court's suggestion or request he began to make restitution or wrote contracts for restitution that he pledged to fulfill upon gaining his freedom and getting a job. The pledges were to himself alone. No one else knew about them. Upon his release from prison, he came to see us to help maintain his accountable behavior and to heal all of the old wounds that had accumulated from his painful childhood. He was a remarkable man, as close to a saint as we had ever personally encountered. After two years of intermittent work with us, he came in for a session carrying several pieces of yellowed, creased, old paper. He explained that these were the pledges of restitution he had written in prison, that he had shared them with no one, and that he had been living in near-poverty because he was putting money away and volunteering his services to make good on the pledges. He had brought them in to formally honor the people he had hurt, and to share his actions with us so that we could privately bear witness to what he had done, allowing his soul to rest at last.

Our office was filled with warmth and light and tears, and a depth of dignity that was nothing less than awe-inspiring.

CHAPTER 18

THE CONSEQUENCES OF FEAR, IGNORANCE, AND GREED

> Side by side with Crime, Disease, and Misery in
> England, Ignorance is always brooding.
>
> —*Charles Dickens*

Upon visiting one of the "ragged schools" that had been set up by Evangelicals to help teach the children of the poor, Charles Dickens wrote, "I have very seldom seen in all the strange and dreadful things I have seen in London and elsewhere, anything so shocking as the dire neglect of soul and body exhibited in these children" (quoted in Epstein, 1998).

John Walsh wrote of Dickens,

> He thought of the plot of *A Christmas Carol* on a visit to Manchester to see his sister Fanny (an Evangelical) and make a speech to the Manchester Athenaeum, a charity for educating labouring men and women. Dickens' social conscience, his disgust at the ragged school, his memories of his own childhood and the nearness of Christmas all wrestled together in his imagination.
>
> He wrote the story quickly, in six weeks flat, ending in early December. Despite a terrible cold, he became strangely elated while writing it: according to John Forster, he would weep over the manuscript, then laugh, then weep again, and take 10-mile walks through London at night, as though revisiting his life at the time of the blacking factory, remembering what he had been

and imagining what he might have become. The Cratchit family's little terrace house is similar to the Dickens family's home when they arrived in London. But when Scrooge sees the lonely, solitary figure of a boy reading near a feeble fire in a dilapidated school, and weeps for his past, that's Dickens weeping (again) for his incarceration in the crumbling blacking factory (Walsh, 2008).

The quote at the beginning of this chapter was written because "he was so appalled by the children's condition that he tried to approach the government to warn of the *abyss of ignorance future millions of children might fall into*" (Walsh, 2008; emphasis added).

In *The Friendly Dickens*, author Norrie Epstein wrote,

> Dickens had intended a tract on education for the poor, but he now decided to write a story that, he announced with justifiable hyperbole, would hit his readers over the head like a "sledge-hammer."

> The sledgehammer of a Christmas story is a reminder that Dickens is one of the few, if not the only, examples in literature of someone who did well by doing good. Like the old Scrooge, Dickens was a man of business, and like the reformed one, he never forgot that mankind was his business (1998).

The two allegorical children hidden beneath the cloak of the Ghost of Christmas Present in *A Christmas Carol* were Ignorance and Want. The childhood experiences that molded Dickens into the person who was able to write such a short, powerful story included his father's uncontrolled spending that eventually landed him in debtor's prison and the consequences of that unexpected poverty:

> [At the age of eleven] Charles was sent into a dark, miserable blacking warehouse to work. He lived alone in London in a small rented room, spent a dozen hours a day pasting the labels on bottles of shoe polish, and was thrown together with a group of coarse boys who horrified him. This terrible season of his life had such an impact on Dickens that he never spoke of it, even to his wife, and in fact the details of that period were only revealed by his biographer after his death (mgfaulkner blog 2010).

Everyone has a story, and everyone's story is important and has meaning, and is what connects one human being to another. *A Christmas
Carol* was more autobiography than anything else, but it was autobiography tempered and molded by a genuine warmth and compassion for the
human condition, despite the shame that Dickens must have felt about his
childhood, given that he never spoke of those years spent in the blacking
warehouse.

We are often asked how we can sit and listen to people's problems all day
long without burning out, and we reply by saying that hearing each client's
story and helping each client unravel the complex systemic dynamics of
their families, marriages, and other relationships is anything but boring.
Like watching a good production of *A Christmas Carol*, it is, for us, like
participating in the artistry of each human being's unfolding life, while
having the honor of being invited into the middle of those lives in order to
help each person find the patterns and the meanings in them. It is never
boring. Ever.

Dickens' story has timeless and universal appeal because it reaches into
the heart of every person who reads it or watches it being performed, and
validates our common experiences as human beings, including both our
dark sides and "the better angels of our natures." It invites us to *care* for
one another. It prods us to set aside our childhood wounds and open our
hearts to the only thing that can ever heal those wounds—the love and
comfort of warm, enduring relationships with other *Homo sapiens*. It is
what each human brain requires in order to function properly. It is about
limbic resonance.

Fear, ignorance, and want are themes that have been woven into the
complex social and genetic systems of human beings since we first walked
the Earth some 200,000 years ago. They will always be basic human
themes. George Santayana's warning, "Those who cannot remember the
past are condemned to repeat it," will always be apropos. And as is obvious in so many heartening ways, human beings in much of the world are
much more civil and civilized than ever before. But we are still human,
and we still ignore the lessons of history.

A Lesson or Two

Fear causes people to either (a) act from their best selves and become courageous and ethical, or (b) act from their worst selves and become brutal, insensitive, selfish, and greedy.

Ignorance causes people to fear things that they needn't fear. And when uninformed people who are scared begin to act, they tend to act from the most biologically primitive part of the brain—the reptilian brain. And then all hell breaks loose.

If I believe that the Earth is the center of the universe, and if I believe that any other take on it is religious heresy (thereby confounding science—facts—with theology), and if you come along and say that you have discovered that the Earth rotates around the sun, then my emotional reaction will be threat (terror), and my behavioral reaction will be to burn you at the stake for spitting in the face of God. Then, as theology catches up with scientific knowledge, I find myself in the most horrible of double binds: I have killed an innocent person because of my misunderstanding of how the universe works, and because of *the way that I was told to practice my religion* (religion per se is not the problem). Because I am too afraid to use my God-given brain the way God intended me to use it, because I can't see beyond my own nose, I have done something that yesterday was perfectly justifiable, even "holy," and now, today, is an unconscionable violation of all that is good in God's vast creation. These are the kinds of difficult double binds facing human beings today, as they always have been and always will be.

Cultural Context in the Ecology of a Human System

In *Families and Family Therapy* (1974), Salvador Minuchin, one of the founders of the family systems therapy movement, recounted the story told by José Ortega y Gasset of the time Admiral Robert Peary was mushing toward the North Pole. He took a fix on the stars, followed his compass due north all day long, set up camp, and then that night took a fix on the stars again. It turned out that he had been traveling south. How could this be? Peary later discovered that he had been on a giant ice floe that was drifting south. It is the near-perfect metaphor for how hard it can be for any of us to see how we are being affected by the system in which we are embedded.

If one of the hardest things for us to do is to see the cultural context in which we are embedded, then we certainly should be given a pass when we fail to see it. So let's all begin by giving ourselves a pass. But Peary didn't leave it at that. He had a goal—a mission—and a problem to solve, and he didn't just curl up in a ball on the ice and give up. He grappled with it, pondered it, went on, remained open "to the universe providing an answer," and soon enough the answer came—his position on a giant southward-bound ice floe. If he had stubbornly refused to be open to other explanations, he might never have figured out what his problem was. Being open to the power of the context in which we are embedded is one of the cognitive and emotional skills that separates the men and the women from the boys and the girls—and the victims and perpetrators from the competent, healthy adults.

In explaining the nature of ecosystems, Maddock, Friel, and Friel stated,

> Any given system is composed of parts—which are themselves systems. Thus, every system is an ecosystem to the systems that compose it. At the same time, every system is a subsystem within other systems that make up its environment; therefore each system has an ecosystem. *Any given system both has and is an ecosystem* (Odom, 1983). . . . A family is an important ecosystem to its individual members (subsystems); at the same time, a family is a subsystem within a larger social ecosystem. (2009, p. 23)

We have said that, in many ways, *context is everything*. I can say "I love you" because you have a gun to my head and have told me that if I don't say that, you will kill my wife, whom I love and adore. Hours later, once I am free from that terrifying situation and have been reunited with my wife, I can say "I love you" to my wife, and it will have an entirely different meaning. Words and actions mean nothing unless you know the context in which they occur.

If you are embedded in a cultural context in which everyone is a highly functioning alcoholic—and believe us, that is not an unusual circumstance —then your perception of your own drinking behavior will be very different than if you were embedded in a cultural context in which nobody drank more than half a glass of wine once a month. You would *feel* different when around the former group as opposed to the latter group, and the only difference would be the context.

Claudia Black (1981) built her career on describing the unconscious rules in alcoholic family systems and how those rules affect children as they are growing up. Her famous "don't talk," "don't trust," "don't feel" triad of painful family rules has helped millions of people begin to make sense out of the swirling confusion of emotions they feel from having grown up in alcoholic homes.

Say you live in a family context in which nobody ever talks about Dad's alcoholism because (a) they don't want to start a fight, or (b) they don't want to hurt Dad's feelings and embarrass him, or (c) they don't want Dad to have a shame attack, which will then trigger his formidable rage, or (d) it's just too scary to admit that your parent is alcoholic and may be suffering from a really serious disease that has a lot of legal and social consequences attached to it. In that case, it makes perfect sense from the point of view of the child's survival to embrace the family's "no talk" rule, *even if deep down inside, the child knows that it is wrong to be silent and to let the family go down the drain together.* The fact of the matter is that human beings are incredibly adaptive, and we will do, in the moment, whatever we believe we need to do to survive, *especially when we are vulnerable, dependent children.*

The cultural contexts in which we all live have a very strong influence on how we think and feel and act in the world, which is why subsystems within our larger ecosystems can be so troubling, depending on the context. Most certainly, in this age of cable television, film, the Internet, Facebook, texting, Twitter, and other as yet to be discovered means of communicating with one another, *context most certainly is still everything.*

News, News, News

A survey released by the Pew Research Center on April 15, 2007, indicated that regular viewers of *The Daily Show with Jon Stewart* tend to be more knowledgeable about news than audiences of other news sources. Approximately 54 percent of *The Daily Show* viewers scored in the high knowledge range, followed by Jim Lehrer's program at 53 percent, significantly higher than the 34 percent of network morning show viewers. The survey showed that changing news formats have not made much difference on how much the public knows about national and international affairs, but adds that there is no clear connection between news formats and what audiences know.

The Pew Research Center's Project for Excellence in Journalism released a content analysis report suggesting that *The Daily Show* comes close to providing the complete daily news (2008). This from a show that bills itself as a comedy, although it should be added that respectable authors with a serious book about public policy, government, science, social analysis, or economics try the hardest to get on *The Daily Show* to promote their books, because they get the best interviews, most intelligent discussion, and best exposure for that type of serious material.

The Big Lie, and the Little Big Lies That Follow

Emotional honesty and integrity—without the subtle manipulations that can sometimes seep into family dialogues—are essential to the healthy, high functioning of a family system. To say, overtly, that our family always tries to be up front and honest about our issues, while at the same time sending covert, nonverbal cues that if you are *too* honest I won't be able to handle it, is ultimately manipulative and "crazy-making," as Virginia Satir might label it. By the same token, accurate and courageously honest news reporting is as essential to the functioning of a democracy as is the right to vote. Getting accurate facts, as opposed to either no facts at all or facts that are so distorted by partisan opinion that they are no longer usable facts, is crucial. What can happen in the absence of those actual facts was no more powerfully apparent than in Nazi Germany.

The concept of the Big Lie was central to Adolf Hitler's condemnation of the Jews, claiming that *they* had used the technique to blame Germany's loss of World War I on one lone German Army officer, Erich Ludendorff (Hitler, 1925). But it was actually one of Hitler's primary techniques for taking over Germany, a technique later perfected by his Reich minister of propaganda, Joseph Goebbels, who wrote,

> "If you tell a lie big enough and keep repeating it, people will eventually come to believe it. The lie can be maintained only for such time as the State can shield the people from the political, economic and/or military consequences of the lie. It thus becomes vitally important for the State to use all of its powers to repress dissent, for the truth is the mortal enemy of the lie, and thus by extension, the truth is the greatest enemy of the State (Jewish Virtual Library, 2012)."

Contrast this with Thomas Jefferson's assertion that

> whenever the people are well-informed, they can be trusted with their own government; that, whenever things get so far wrong as to attract their notice, they may be relied on to set them right. (quoted in Padover, 1939, p. 88)

In describing Hitler's modus operandi, the U.S. Office of Strategic Services wrote,

> His primary rules were: never allow the public to cool off; never admit a fault or wrong; never concede that there may be some good in your enemy; never leave room for alternatives; never accept blame; concentrate on one enemy at a time and blame him for everything that goes wrong; people will believe a big lie sooner than a little one; and if you repeat it frequently enough people will sooner or later believe it. (Langer, 1973, 219)

This is the philosophy of a classic bully-perpetrator who is so tiny inside that his only way of holding on to himself is to never accept wrong (i.e., be shameless and unaccountable), never acknowledge any good in your enemy (dehumanize him—*dissociate*—so that you won't later have guilt about harming him), never leave room for alternatives (might makes right), focus on one enemy at a time and blame him for everything (brilliant strategy to find a scapegoat and then pillory him for all to see), and then just repeat the big lie over and over, because people are too simple and trusting to ever question a big lie. It's the perfect manual on how to create the ultimate perpetrator, sociopath, or thug,

When children lack the power to get the truth to be seen and accepted by the adults in the family system, they eventually give up and then tend to *act it out* instead. In the beginning, their senses tell them what is real. At first they trust their perceptions. They know something is wrong no matter how many excuses are proffered. But after a while, after hearing the same excuses and defenses over and over, most of them eventually succumb, go into a trance, and simply accept what is said.

"Mommy really loves you. She was just having a bad day when she bruised the backs of your legs with a coat hanger," or "Daddy's not an alcoholic, he's just under a lot of stress right now." As these children give up, one by one, their suppressed, agitated, unconscious feelings inside often translate into their trying to be perfect, getting into a lot of fights at school, getting into alcohol and drugs at an early age, becoming rageful or depressed, or any number of other ways that kids act out.

From the perspective of victim-perpetrator dynamics, there is no difference between a dictator's Big Lie and the loss of reality and self that occurs on a smaller scale among children in a painful family, who are often left with no option other than to accept the same kinds of distorted truths.

For the second year in a row, a Public Policy Polling survey gauging public trust in TV news has found that PBS is now the most trusted name in news. PBS was found to be trusted by 50 percent of respondents, and distrusted by 30 percent—*the closest any news network has come to gaining the trust of a majority of Americans*" (UPI.com, 2012; emphasis added).

And the Sun Revolves Around the Earth

Looking at other facts and statistics, it is unsettling to discover that 18 percent of people in the United States believe that the Sun revolves around the Earth. It certainly *looks* that way if all you do is get up in the morning, get dressed, tie your shoes, go to school, come home, and get on your iPhone. But think of how many centuries of painstakingly patient, detailed, deliberate, thoughtful observations it must have taken primitive human beings to figure out that they had the context all wrong. Can you imagine the first awareness of this discovery? "Hey," someone shouted. "We have the context all wrong! We were being so egocentric! The joke's on us! It's *amazing*! *We* are revolving around the Sun. The Sun is not revolving around us!" And think of the fear and anger and shame and hurt and rage that must have followed when someone first said this. He or she was lucky not to be burned at the stake, if indeed, they weren't.

And think of what an exciting lesson plan a creative schoolteacher could put together for her students that would teach not only science but also the deeply personal empathy needed to understand how people come to struggle with information that challenges their very core beliefs about the world. Instead of saying that this discovery is coming from Satan to make us doubt our faith in God, what if it were framed as "Isn't God amazing and loving and kind? He created us with a great big brain that is capable of reflecting not only on our own death but also on all the wonders of the universe that he created. And then out of love for us, and respect for our ability to manage uncertainty and the unknown, and knowing that facing challenges would be the very part of our existence that would make us unique in all of creation, and that would give our lives meaning and depth and purpose, he created a universe that is so complex—from the big bang that started it all, to evolution, and beyond—that we could spend until the end of eternity discovering more and more and more about his creation, until millions of years later, we would join him for all eternity."

Wouldn't that be a lesson plan that could get kids to start thinking across several different disciplines? And it might just get them excited enough about math and science and philosophy and chemistry and theology, all in one lesson, to move them in the direction of competing on the academic world stage again.

Good Morning America reported in January 2011 that "many high school seniors were unable to tell the difference between a planet and a star" in recent science tests. And in a 2010 University of Texas/*Texas Tribune* poll, 30 percent of Texans believed that dinosaurs and human beings lived together on the planet—as if life on planet Earth is the same as a *Flintstones* cartoon. Thirty-eight percent agreed with the statement, "God created human beings pretty much in their present form about 10,000 years ago" (Ramsey, 2010).

In Texas textbooks, Thomas Jefferson, considered to be one of the most brilliant and influential people in our nation's history, was recently removed from a list of writers who inspired revolutions because conservatives on the Texas Board of Education didn't like the fact that he coined the phrase "separation between church and state" (McKinley, 2010).

In our opinion, this increasing anti-intellectualism—*this mistrust of facts and knowledge*—is due to a number of mutually interacting factors, including the following:

- Intellectual laziness
- The state of being overwhelmed with the sheer volume of information on the Internet.
- Lack of knowledge of history
- Lack of the intellectual filters to discern information sources that are reliable from those that are not
- Anxiety fueled by rapid globalization and change
- Lack of commitment to education in American families
- Educational systems that are nearly paralyzed by parents who either *care too much or care too little*
- Political exploitation of vulnerable Americans by the wealthy and powerful

This mistrust of knowledge and of critical thinking is also one of the biggest threats to our financial stability and our national security, which many contemporary analysts have noted, but which is not a very contemporary idea. Ironically, Thomas Jefferson himself emphasized the importance of education in the maintenance of a democracy:

If a nation expects to be ignorant and free, in a state of civilization, it expects what never was and never will be. (quoted in Padover, 1939, p. 89)

Whenever the people are well-informed, they can be trusted with their own government; that, whenever things get so far wrong as to attract their notice, they may be relied on to set them right. (in Padover, 1939, p. 88)

What Are the Real-World Consequences of Fear and Ignorance?

What are the consequences of having a poorly educated and very scared populace, newspaper and television reporters who are afraid to make waves by reporting uncomfortable truths, and cynical leaders who are willing to bend the truth until it is barely recognizable, simply to achieve their own selfish aims? The answer is plain to see in the following 2003 report by Linda Feldmann for the *Christian Science Monitor*:

> In his prime-time press conference last week, which focused almost solely on Iraq, President Bush mentioned Sept. 11 eight times. He referred to Saddam Hussein many more times than that, often in the same breath with Sept. 11.
>
> Bush never pinned blame for the attacks directly on the Iraqi president. Still, the overall effect was to reinforce an impression that persists among much of the American public: that the Iraqi dictator did play a direct role in the attacks. A *New York Times*/CBS poll this week shows that 45 percent of Americans believe Mr. Hussein was "personally involved" in Sept. 11, about the same figure as a month ago.
>
> Sources knowledgeable about US intelligence say there is no evidence that Hussein played a role in the Sept. 11 attacks, nor that he has been or is currently aiding Al Qaeda. Yet the White House appears to be encouraging this false impression, as it seeks to maintain American support for a possible war against Iraq and demonstrate seriousness of purpose to Hussein's regime.
>
> *"The administration has succeeded in creating a sense that there is some connection [between Sept. 11 and Saddam Hussein]," says Steven Kull, director of the Program on International Policy Attitudes (PIPA) at the University of Maryland.*
>
> Polling data show that right after Sept. 11, 2001, when Americans were

asked open-ended questions about who was behind the attacks, only 3 percent mentioned Iraq or Hussein. But by January of this year, attitudes had been transformed. In a Knight Ridder poll, 44 percent of Americans reported that either "most" or "some" of the Sept. 11 hijackers were Iraqi citizens. *The answer is zero*. (Feldmann, 2003; emphasis added).

During the Iraq War, a majority of Americans believed that Saddam Hussein had a role in the 9/11 terrorist attacks on the World Trade Center, despite conclusive evidence from the U.S. Central Intelligence Agency disproving that belief. What a tragic, anxiety-based, uninformed failure of the people and the press in the United States to do what Thomas Jefferson admonished us to do: to be well-informed enough so that "whenever things get so far wrong as to attract their notice, they may be relied on to set them right" (quoted in Padover, 1939, p. 88). Because we were poorly informed, weren't thinking critically, were scared, weren't able to sort through relevant information amid the flood of data coming at us from every direction, and were too easily seduced by leaders we believed we could trust but shouldn't have, we continued to support a plan that led us further and further down a military rabbit hole—a $4 trillion rabbit hole that has contributed significantly to current U.S. economic woes.

Many men and women in the United States who fought in the Vietnam War, who had loved ones die in it, or who lived through the national chaos surrounding it fretted that we might be getting into the same quagmire that Vietnam represented. The gentle Vietnamese people had endured invasions and wars, the last being by the French, for centuries; we thought we could overwhelm them with our technological might. But we made the tragic error that we continue to make—*ignoring the fact that the human spirit is much stronger than a B-52 loaded with bombs*.

After we invaded Iraq, it was revealed that George W. Bush didn't have a clue about the difference between a Shiite and a Sunni, according to, among others, former ambassador to Croatia, Peter Galbraith, in his book *The End of Iraq: How American Incompetence Created a War Without End* (2007) let alone the fact that much of the Middle East is governed by tribes, not linear, structured nations like the United States and the United Kingdom. Our political leaders were trying to play the United States' version of football, the Iraqis were playing soccer, and so it didn't work out the way we had hoped.

Then General Eric Ken Shinseki appeared on the nightly news. He is the first Asian American four-star general in U.S. history, and was the 34th Chief of Staff of the U.S. Army from 1999 to 2003. He was former president Bush's Army Chief of Staff when he was asked to testify before the Senate Armed Services Committee on February 25, 2003, on his troop-level estimates required to stabilize Iraq after we were to execute our proposed "Shock and Awe" attack, which would subsequently leave much of Iraq's infrastructure in a shambles—meaning that the battered country would essentially be thrown into indefinite chaos. General Shinseki said that he felt we would need at least 400,000 troops to achieve the stabilization, because the destruction of infrastructure and government caused by our "Shock and Awe" approach, and the tribal nature of the people there, would otherwise plunge the country into chaos.

General Shinseki was right, but it didn't matter.

His testimony infuriated Secretary of Defense Donald Rumsfeld, who believed that all we had to do was attack, destroy, and then withdraw—like a U.S. football team executing a single play with no thought as to what might happen after the whistle blows. In U.S. football, you get a breather to regroup and then set up another play. In a war being conducted in a highly fluid, leaderless, tribal country that has just been thrown into total chaos by your very own actions, there are no time-outs, no whistles, no referees. Rumsfeld's strategy has proven to be both naive and grandiose, as evidenced by former president Bush's embarrassing "Mission Accomplished" performance on the U.S.S. *Abraham Lincoln*, during which he announced that major combat operations in Iraq had ended.

History sadly proved otherwise. General Eric Ken Shinseki was vindicated by his flawless assessment, and so by any measure he was a wise U.S. patriot par excellence. But bullies don't like to lose face or ever admit a mistake—that is part of the definition of a perpetrator—and so when General

Shinseki was unceremoniously "retired" in 2003 (Moulin, 2008), former president Bush, Donald Rumsfeld, and architect of the Bush administration's Mideast policy, Paul Wolfowitz, were conspicuously absent.

Four-star General Eric Shinseki is now President Obama's Secretary of Veterans Affairs, and he has been permanently honored in the U.S. Army Military Museum in Honolulu, and in the book written about the history of Fort DeRussy (Moulin, 2008).

• • •

Our national befuddlement about the proper places in the United States for religion, politics, and pure science gave actress, writer, and comedian Tina Fey (2005) one of the most memorable and powerful one-liners of her career:

> A new poll shows that 66% of Americans think President Bush is doing a poor job on the War in Iraq. And the remaining 34% think Adam and Eve rode dinosaurs to church.

That a $27 million Creation Museum was built in America is a living testament to the paralyzing anxiety—about scientific facts and data, about a rapidly shrinking planet, and about many new "foreign" influences—experienced by a significant minority of the U.S. population. We believe that people's anxieties need to be addressed in helpful and growth-producing ways. Those of us—and there are millions—who believe that God created the universe over a period of billions of years, and that He created human beings by a process of evolution over billions of years, are in awe of the vastness and near-incomprehensibility of God's work. But to reduce God's fantastic universe to such a simplistic explanation seems like an insult to God, were He capable of being insulted.

And whether one believes in God or not, how can we possibly maintain even a semblance of our waning prosperity and declining "American exceptionalism" if we lose our excellence in the domains of math, science, engineering, chemistry, physics, and creative thought? The upsurge of creation "science" in the United States, and the intolerance and prejudice that often accompany it, can't be comforting to brilliant scientific immigrants.

Few question the fact that our unbelievable achievements in science and technology since the 1940s have been due in large part to foreigners who chose to live in this country because of our climate of intellectual, religious, and social tolerance.

What will become of us now? Karen King (2011), as quoted in the *Wall Street Journal*, wrote:

> Indian, Chinese, and other foreign nationals earn 70 percent of U.S. doctorates in electrical engineering and half the master's degrees in that specialty, which usually leads to a career in information technology. Noncitizens now launch half of all Silicon Valley startup companies.

The religious fundamentalism that resulted in the Taliban's destruction of the sixth-century Buddhas of Bamiyan, carved into the side of a cliff in the Bamyan valley in the Hazarajat region of central Afghanistan, and destroyed in March 2001 on orders of Mullah Mohammed Omar, is very similar to the religious fundamentalism in the United States that accounted for the repeated vandalism of a Cambodian Buddhist temple in Rochester, Minnesota, home of the Mayo Clinic and IBM (Brown, 2010). This fear and hatred of religious and cultural differences, along with anti-immigration policies and a general tone of anti-intellectualism (Florida, 2005), may drive out or keep away the very immigrants who can help us maintain our worldwide position as strong competitors in scientific creativity and productivity.

In an excerpt from his book *Borderless Economics* that appeared on Salon.com, Robert Guest (2011) wrote,

> Until recently, America's technological preeminence was based on a simple formula: The world's best brains came to the United States. . . . American scientists, however, are more productive [than the Chinese]. They wrote 28 percent of the published scientific papers in the world in 2007, against China's 10 percent, though the Chinese share had doubled since 2002. The quality of American papers is also higher: the best crude measure of this is the number

of times a paper is cited by other scientists, and the average American paper is cited three times more often than the average Chinese one. . . . But the biggest threat to American soft power is the backlash against immigration. Thanks to the networks created by immigration, America is richer, more innovative and far more influential than it would otherwise be. Yet these advantages could all be frittered away if the nation were to close its borders.

As Richard Florida notes (and as we will elaborate in Chapter 20), places like California and its Silicon Valley are extremely tolerant of diversity, are liberal with regard to social policy, accept gay relationships as perfectly normal, and have the high-quality educational institutions that attract members of the Creative Class—as do several other metropolitan areas around the United States. There is no reason that other regions of the United States couldn't be like that as well. But as he wrote in *The Flight of the Creative Class: The New Global Competition for Talent* (2005), unless we continue to encourage talented immigrants to come here and stay here via more tolerance and more flexible immigration policies, our creative, innovative performance on the world stage will clearly suffer.

In a few more years, the United States will be composed entirely of minorities. And if William Donald Hamilton's theory of the "selfless gene" turns out to have any credibility at all, the survival of our collective gene pool here on planet Earth will depend on members of the species *Homo sapiens* who cooperate with one another, who care for one another, and who value limbic resonance as much as acquiring more and more stuff.

CHAPTER 19

COMPETENCE
AND SMART PLANNING:
WHEN IT WORKS, IT WORKS

Arguably, the most important economic trend in the
United States over the past couple of generations has been the
ever more distinct sorting of Americans into winners and losers,
and the slow hollowing out of the middle class.

—*Don Peck, "Can the Middle Class Be Saved?" (2011)*

If Jesus Christ had wanted us to think,
He would have spoken to us in parables.

—*John Friel, chapter title in* Rescuing Your Spirit:
When Third-Grade Morality Isn't
Enough for Christians *(1993, p. 59)*

One of the key components of genuine self-esteem is competence. Our competencies determine our ability to meet our physical survival needs, which, up to a point, profoundly affect the quality of our relationships and our ability to show grace under pressure; in turn, those characteristics play a direct role in the probability of victim-perpetrator interactions occurring within our family systems. We will be under a lot more stress if our children are starving and afflicted with serious diseases than if they are not, and the more stress we are under, the harder it is to act from our best selves—up to a point. After a certain basic income level is met, after we know that our children are not starving and that our medical needs will be taken care of, people act well or poorly for very different reasons.

No matter what you call it—ignorance, lack of education, being misinformed, lacking the ability to think critically and to sift through the tsunami of information coming at us through so many electronic channels —it adds up to serious trouble for the United States, including the weakening of its families, but not in the ways some might think.

Contrary to the opinion of some, the lowest divorce rate in the United States is in Massachusetts, a liberal "blue" state that was the first to legalize gay marriage. According to the Centers for Disease Control (cdc.gov) as of 2007, the five states that legalized same-sex marriage—Connecticut, Iowa, Maine, Massachusetts, and Vermont—all had an average divorce rate that was nearly 20 percent lower than the average of the rest of the country (divorce.com blog, 2012). In a story that appeared in *USA Today*, Johns Hopkins University sociologist Andrew Cherlin noted that divorce rates in Alabama, Arkansas, Georgia, Kentucky, Mississippi, Oklahoma, Tennessee, and Texas were high, and that in states in the Northeast, like Massachusetts, New York, and New Jersey, they were very low:

> In the South, people tend to marry earlier and often have less education, both of which increase divorce risk, [Cherlin] says. Those in the Northeast tend to have more education and marry later. "The lesson here is that *a higher level of education leads to more stable families.* Sometimes the data surprises people because regions we think of as socially conservative have higher rates of divorce, but that's largely because people have less education and marry younger." (Jayson, 2011; emphasis added)

The State of Competence in the United States
Many families are struggling to keep a roof over their heads, leaving little energy to ensure that their children are receiving a decent education so that they can survive in the modern world. And as we discussed in

more detail in Chapter 11, many who already enjoy more than adequate financial success are babying their children, leaving them unable to grow up and leave home because of the lack of emotional rather than financial resources (Doherty, 2000; Friel & Friel, 1999).

Whose children will continue to thrive? Whose will be trapped by the collapse of the American Dream? How the more powerful treat the less powerful is at the very heart of what drives victim-perpetrator dynamics in a society. The emotional and spiritual health of a society is a direct reflection of how that society treats "the least of these."

We wonder: What sorts of things are our children learning these days? Are they things that will prepare them to survive in a complex, highly competitive, challenging world, or will what they are learning prepare them to move back home, live with their parents, and work at McDonald's?

In *The Soul of Adulthood* (1995), we noted that at the time the book was being written, U.S. schoolchildren ranked themselves at the top of the heap in math and science compared with children around the world, "which means that they have very high self-appraisal and self-worth" (p. 83), but unfortunately they actually ranked somewhere between eleventh and fifteenth worldwide at that time.

In other words, when it comes to math and science, our children are pumped up with so much hot air that they could probably fly. This is a sad state of affairs, because while building the self-esteem of a child is indeed important, it isn't healthy to build it with no foundation.

Things have only worsened since the mid-1990s. The Program for International Student Assessment (PISA), first implemented in 2000 and coordinated by the Organization for Economic Cooperation and Development (OECD)—an intergovernmental organization of thirty-four member "rich" countries—measures the performance of fifteen-year-olds in reading, mathematics, and science literacy every three years. Sixty countries and five other educational systems participated as partners in PISA 2009. U.S. students ranked nineteenth in science literacy and thirty-first in math literacy.

A 2005 PBS documentary titled *1-800-India* (Cater, 2005) reported that, during their training, Indian call center staff who are there to help callers from the United States with their televisions, refrigerators, computers, or other appliances are allegedly given the following advice for handling difficult customers:

> Ten equals thirty-five . . . Remember, a thirty-five-year-old American's brain and IQ is the same as a ten-year-old Indian's brain. . . . Americans are dumb; just accept it. I don't want anyone losing their cool during the calls.

At a recent Aspen Ideas Festival, Edward Reilly, CEO of Americas of FD International, a global communications consulting firm, said that in an attempt to bring some of his call center jobs back to the United States, his company decided to open a call center in San Antonio, Texas. He offered 600 jobs paying between thirteen and fifteen dollars per hour. He had 7,000 applicants. Reilly sadly reported that over half of those applying were unqualified (Minnesota Public Radio, 2010). He commented,

> As a large business with computer and telephony technology, I can get them [employees] anywhere in the world. . . . I've got 1,500 people in Belfast, I've got 1,000 people in India, we've got the Philippines . . . and it's ugly out there. . . . We decided to put a call center in San Antonio . . . 600 jobs that paid 13 to 15 bucks an hour. . . . We could have put it anywhere in the world. . . . We decided we needed to do something for America. . . . It's only 600 jobs . . . but you get started . . . everybody gets working on it. Seven thousand people applied. I bet half of them couldn't qualify. . . . You just got to read a computer screen and talk about insurance. . . . You gotta have some training . . . but unless we fix this, the American system won't work. Gradually what happens is that businesses just adapt. I gotta service policies tomorrow, so if I can't find somebody to do it here, I hire somebody in Ireland. *And those governments and those businesses work better together on educating the workers than we do in the United States.* (Minnesota Public Radio, 2010; emphasis added)

The Confusion About American Exceptionalism

Ever since the World Trade Center tragedy on September 11, 2001, a lot of U.S. citizens have been understandably embracing expressions of patriotism. In one corner, a vocal group in the United States has dusted off the term "American exceptionalism" to use as an argument against anyone who suggests that we have lost our edge as a nation—or implying that we need to do something to fix this country. But denial of problems isn't patriotism. Blind allegiance to one's country is akin to the blind loyalty often displayed by family members toward an abusive or alcoholic family system—it "feels" right, except that it isn't—and it is often the immediate precursor to the acceleration of a nation's decline, or to the increasing pathology within a family system.

> *Denial of problems isn't patriotism. Blind allegiance to one's country is akin to the blind loyalty often displayed by family members toward an abusive or alcoholic family system—it "feels" right, except that it isn't.*

The French writer Alexis de Tocqueville was one of the first observers to discuss our national uniqueness in his 1835 work, *Democracy in America*, written after studying our young nation for nine months in 1831, along with his fellow observer, Gustave de Beaumont. Tocqueville wrote,

> The position of the Americans is therefore quite exceptional, and it may be believed that no democratic people will ever be placed in a similar one. Their strictly Puritanical origin, their exclusively commercial habits, even the country they inhabit, which seems to divert their minds from the pursuit of science, literature, and the arts, the proximity of Europe, which allows them to neglect these pursuits without relapsing into barbarism, a thousand special causes, of which I have only been able to point out the most important, have singularly concurred to *fix the mind of the American upon purely practical objects*. His passions, his wants, his education, and everything about him seem to unite in drawing the native of the United States earthward; his religion alone bids him turn, from time to time, a transient and distracted glance to heaven. *Let us cease, then, to view all democratic nations under the example of the American people*. (1863b, vol. 2, p. 42; emphasis added)

Washington Post columnist Richard Cohen (2011) notes that "The phrase [American exceptionalism] has an odd history. As Princeton history professor Sean Wilentz reminds me, American exceptionalism once applied to the hostility that the American worker—virtually alone in the industrialized world—had toward socialism." In fact, the actual term was coined in 1929 by none other than Soviet leader Joseph Stalin, when he referred to "the heresy of American exceptionalism" in confronting the American Communist Party's argument that U.S. workers were not likely to spark a Communist revolt because the nation's social and economic system was so strong and so beneficial to the U.S. worker. A few years later the term was expanded to mean that America was destined to be the world's leader among nations (Pease, 2007).

British columnist Richard Wolff supported the notion that our strong economy made life so good for the average American worker that the possibility of a massive revolt was remote, and then added more depth to the story from recent social and economic developments here in the United States:

> One aspect of "American exceptionalism" was always economic. US workers, so the story went, enjoyed a rising level of real wages that afforded their families a rising standard of living. Ever harder work paid off in rising consumption. The rich got richer faster than the middle and poor, but almost no one got poorer. Nearly all citizens felt "middle class." A profitable US capitalism kept running ahead of labour supply. So, it kept raising wages to attract waves of immigration and to retain employees, across the 19th century until the 1970s.
>
> Then everything changed. Real wages stopped rising, as US capitalists redirected their investments to produce and employ abroad, while replacing millions of workers in the US with computers. The US women's liberation moved millions of US adult women to seek paid employment. US capitalism no longer faced a shortage of labour.
>
> US employers took advantage of the changed situation: they stopped raising wages. When basic labour scarcity became labour excess, not only real

wages, but eventually benefits, too, would stop rising. Over the last 30 years, the vast majority of US workers have, in fact, gotten poorer, when you sum up flat real wages, reduced benefits (pensions, medical insurance, etc), reduced public services and raised tax burdens. *In economic terms, American "exceptionalism" began to die in the 1970s.* (Wolff, 2011; emphasis added)

The Purpose of Shame (Humility) Is to Help Us Correct Our Flaws

A few observations are in order regarding the use of the term "American exceptionalism." First, Tocqueville did not say that the United States was the greatest nation on Earth. He said that it came to be—it was formed—under a unique set of circumstances, and these circumstances were unlikely to be repeated elsewhere or in the future. He wrote, "Their strictly Puritanical origin, their exclusively commercial habits, even the country they inhabit, which seems to divert their minds from the pursuit of science, literature, and the arts . . ." and "Let us cease, then, to view all democratic nations under the example of the American people" ([1835] 1945, Chap. 9, p. 42)

Second, anyone with even a modicum of wisdom knows that as soon as people believe that they are "the best," or that their sports team is "the best," or that their racehorse is "the best," they are heading for a lesson in humility. Years ago, comedian Steven Wright said, "You can't have everything. Where would you put it?" *Time* magazine reported,

> The following rankings come from various lists, but they all tell the same story. . . . We rank 12th among developed countries in college graduation (down from No. 1 for decades). We come in 79th in elementary-school enrollment. Our infrastructure is ranked 23rd in the world, well behind that of every other major advanced economy. American health numbers are stunning for a rich country: based on studies by the OECD and the World Health Organization, we're 27th in life expectancy, 18th in diabetes and first in obesity. Only a few decades ago, the U.S. stood tall in such rankings. No more. There are some areas in which we are still clearly No. 1, but they're not

ones we usually brag about. We have the most guns. We have the most crime among rich countries. And, of course, we have by far the largest amount of debt in the world. (Zakaria, 2011)

The authors of a *Newsweek* (2010) study of the world's greatest countries looked at education, health, quality of life, economic dynamism, and political environment, and the United States ranked eleventh.

One of the measures used in the above rankings was income inequality. According to Jon Stewart, currently one of the most trusted news sources on television (Linkins, 2009), "The U.S. ranks 64th in the world in income inequality" (*Daily Show with Jon Stewart*, 2011, August 18). Interestingly, before midnight of that same day, and following Stewart's report, the CIA adjusted the GINI Index to put the U.S. at 39th. Our score of 45 remained the same, so adjustments must have been made to other countries' ratings. Writing for allgov.com, Noel Brinkerhoff (2010) reported,

> The gap between rich and poor Americans grew wider than ever last year, according to new data from the U.S. Census Bureau. Those making more than $100,000 annually (the top 20% of the population) received 49.4% of all income generated in 2009, while those living below the poverty line (the bottom 20%) earned only 3.4%. This disparity amounted to a ratio of 14.5-to-1, the greatest on record and almost double what it was in 1968 (7.69-to-1). According to figures compiled by economist Emmanuel Saez, in 2008 the richest 1% of the population gained 21% of the nation's income.

At the beginning of this book, we stated, "The only constant in the universe is *change*. The organizing principle is *balance*." The problem with income inequality is not only that the current U.S. ranking is an international embarrassment but also that at some point it becomes a question of our national stability and security. Remember that the term "American exceptionalism" was first coined by Joseph Stalin when he angrily confronted the American Communist Party for stating that a revolution was not possible in the United States because of the large middle class and the stability and prosperity of the average working person. In other words, communism was not going to establish a strong foothold in the United States because the conditions that made other countries ripe for revolution were simply not present here.

What about now? *Can we maintain our balance when our nation is so unbalanced?* If the middle class continues to disappear and the wealthiest Americans continue to get wealthier, what will happen? Poverty will escalate. Unemployment will escalate, or at the very least, the quality of employment will decline dramatically. Then fear—anxiety—will escalate, hopelessness will escalate, and anger and rage will escalate, which will lead to a dramatic increase in victim-perpetrator patterns of interaction within affected families, as well as between members of affected families and society at large, as was seen in London and other cities in the United Kingdom in the summer of 2011 and around the world in the fall of 2011.

The irony is that for all of the anxiety about the United States becoming a "socialist country," our social safety net—the *weakest* social safety net among the wealthy, industrialized nations—has prevented ideologies like communism from ever taking hold here. And yet just when the gap between rich and poor becomes the widest in recent history, a number of far-right senators and representatives in Washington are calling for the dismantling of our social safety net and, at the very extreme, most of government altogether. For example, Igor Volsky reported on August 19, 2011, that Senator Tom Coburn (R-OK) said, "You can't tell me the [health-care] system is better now than it was before Medicare." But, Volsky added,

> Here are the facts: since 1965, "the health of the elderly population has improved, as measured by both longevity and functional status," and senior poverty rates have plummeted. According to a study from Health Affairs, life expectancy at age 65 increased from 14.3 years in 1960 to 17.8 years in 1998 and the chronically disabled elderly population declined from 24.9 percent in 1982 to 21.3 percent in 1994.
>
> Prior to Medicare, "about one-half of America's seniors did not have hospital insurance," "more than one in four elderly were estimated to go without

medical care due to cost concerns," and one in three seniors were living in poverty. Today, nearly all seniors have access to affordable health care and only about 14 percent of seniors are below the poverty line. (2011)

The potential tragedy is that if U.S. residents continue to become less able to think critically and to sort fact from fiction amid the information flood on the Internet and on cable television, they will continue to vote against their own best interests, and the downward spiral will only worsen.

Larger social systems follow the same rules as do family systems. When things within a family system get far enough out of balance, there is inevitably a dramatic and often troubling attempt to restore balance. If Dad is physically and emotionally violent and Mom is quiet, fearful, and withdrawn, producing a large power imbalance in the family system, some kind of unconscious, unintentional, and often quite severe acting out typically occurs. The kids may become depressed or abuse alcohol or drugs in vain attempts to soothe the massive anxiety pervading the household. One child may become a "saint" and attend church services compulsively. Another may become over-responsible and act like the parent he wishes was there to raise the kids. One of the kids may become violent outside of the home or may sexually abuse a sibling inside of the home. As bizarre as it may seem, when looked at from a systems perspective, each of these actions becomes an attempt on the part of family members to create some kind of balance within the family (Maddock & Larson, 1995). Unless societies employ constructive balancing maneuvers before the critical mass of imbalance occurs, the same kinds of unconscious, overreactive balancing maneuvers will begin to happen in the country at large as well.

Hope for the Future

In "Can the Middle Class Be Saved?" Don Peck noted that "even in boom times, many more people than we would care to acknowledge won't have the education, skills, or abilities to prosper in a pure and globalized market, shaped by enormous labor reserves in China, India, and other developing countries" (2011, p. 71). And as quoted above, Edward Reilly, CEO of Americas of FD International said, "And those governments and those businesses work better together on educating the workers than we do in the United States."

Perhaps the tide will have turned by the time this book gets to print, but as of the time of its writing, now roughly 30 percent of the population and 30 percent of our legislators are trying to severely restrict and even paralyze federal and state governments. If that trend continues, it is questionable whether we—that is, *our* government *by the people* and *for the people*—can keep up a reliable infrastructure to support commerce, a social safety net that prevents civil unrest and poverty, and collaborative partnerships between government, business, and educational institutions to ensure that enough properly educated citizens can maintain our high-tech economy steaming along at full throttle.

In late 2011 Thomas Friedman and Michael Mandelbaum released *That Used to Be Us: How America Fell Behind in the World It Invented and How We Can Come Back*. In his critique of their book on Bloomberg.com and summarized in *The Week* magazine, Craig Seligman wrote, "It's the feebleness of their solutions that disappoint most. Higher taxes? More education spending? . . . Good luck with that" (2011). And yet, as we show in the rest of this chapter and in the next, those two solutions are actually the only way out. They just aren't new, glamorous, or sexy enough for some.

Hope *does* spring eternal. Hope is grounded in the reality of a human species that has already endured 200,000 years of the most God-awful upheavals and tragedies one could imagine. Putting one foot in front of the other is what has always saved us before. Today, the criticisms of these strategies to improve the United States that we hear from a few pundits and politicians is that putting one foot in front of the other is too hard, not fast enough, or too much work. Our response to them is the same one that we give to clients who are far enough along in the therapy process to take in what it really means: *Start putting one foot in front of the other and see what happens.*

We believe that there are many reasons to be hopeful. Despite all of the economic and educational doom and gloom, plenty of bright spots appear on the horizon for the United States. But we must also note that there is a strong current of elitism and racism under-lying the conservative mantra about the poor and underprivileged that is wrapped in a cloak of pseudo-patriotic misuse of the word "socialism" in the United States, which makes hope appear to be hopeless—except that it isn't. The United States is a very socialist nation. We subsidize oil companies to the tune of billions of dollars. Halliburton and its subsidiaries "misplaced" billions of dollars during the Iraq War. We subsidized failing financial institutions, many of which will be shown to have been guilty of criminal actions. But if we pay for Medicare or Social Security or food stamps, then we must be a "crumbling socialist nation."

> *Start putting one foot in front of the other and see what happens.*

People who think this way are the equivalent of modern-day Neanderthals who act *as if* they lack the brain structure to be able to grasp the nuances of these arguments. Over and over, the facts prove that people who are underprivileged and/or poor have the same work ethic and potential entrepreneurship of the currently wealthy; they just need to have a few of the breaks that kids from wealthy families get.

If you believe that poor people are poor because they are lazy, and that they have no motivation to improve their lot in life, just look at the stunningly successful outcomes of programs like the KIPP Schools, the work of the Bill and Melinda Gates Foundation, and of the program initiated by former NBA star Kevin Johnson, who grew up in the inner city of Sacramento, and who is the current mayor of that city. He founded St. Hope Academy, an innovative, no-nonsense, nonprofit charter school designed to help disadvantaged kids get a leg up in the competitive academic world. As reported on the *Oprah Winfrey Show* on April 12, 2006,

> Just as important as motivating the students, Kevin says, is motivating their parents. St. Hope involves them the old-fashioned way—through regu-

lar face-to-face meetings. "If a parent does not want their son or daughter to go to college and if they're not willing to do whatever it is to help their son or daughter get there, this is not the school for you," Kevin says. "This is not the choice that you should make."

And, of course, there is the recent notoriety about the Oprah Winfrey Leadership Academy for Girls in Henley on Klip, South Africa, in which 75 students started the program and 72 will graduate. All of them are headed to universities in South Africa and the United States to pursue such studies as medicine, law, engineering, and economics. Apartheid ended in South Africa in 1994. Oprah spent $40 million on her campus and said her focus was "just to change one girl, affect one person's life." But she acknowledged hers "is not a sustainable model for most people in most countries" (Bryson, 2012). But is that completely true? Do you have to be a multimillionaire in order to help the disadvantaged? Or do you simply have to have a quality college education, the limbic ability to connect with other human beings, and *a heart as big as your mind*, and vice versa? We will always come back to Erin Gruwell and her "lost kids" at Long Beach High School in Southern California, because she is the ultimate model of *one single person* who changed the lives of 150 doomed kids simply because she was smart, well-educated, and gave a damn.

Watch the movie *Freedom Writers*, which was made about them. It was good. But don't stop there. Go to the source. See the real students and the real teacher who were involved. Watch Connie Chung's original report on this remarkable teacher and her remarkable students, and you will never again believe that people who are "down-and-out" are doomed to stay there . . . ever.

The Freedom Writers of Wilson High

[*Authors' note*: This section is adapted from Friel and Friel, *The 7 Best Things (Smart) Teens Do*.]

In the fall of 1994, brand-new, preppy, twenty-three-year-old teacher Erin Gruwell walked into a tough Long Beach high school classroom wondering "what my students will think about me. Will they think I'm out of touch or too preppy? Or worse yet, that I'm too young to be taken seriously?" (Friel and Friel, 2000). The class was filled with kids who were leading tragic lives that were littered with divorce, physical and sexual abuse, drive-by shootings, gangs, and drugs. With these as permanent fixtures in their daily lives, what teacher, let alone new teacher, could expect to have any impact on the kids?

It all began like this: First, there was a classroom filled with ordinary kids, many of whom were from the toughest parts of Long Beach, which means that most of them were indeed doomed. Second, there was a teacher who had an excellent education herself, so she actually had something to teach them. Third, there was a classroom filled with ordinary teenagers, period. Ordinary teenagers, no matter what their circumstances, want to be competent. The instant that anyone assumes that this is true, the chances of the teens becoming competent increase logarithmically. Erin Gruwell assumed that they were competent. Last, all of the people in that room were passionate about what they were doing there, even from the beginning. Remember, emotions and passions are the fuel that drives everything else we do. Passion provides the energy that drives the rest of the machine. The rest, as they say, is history.

And what a history it was. Miss Gruwell, as her students affectionately called her, actually began the year before as a student teacher at Wilson High, where she snatched up a racist drawing that one student had made of another. Furious at the intolerance expressed in the picture, she yelled that it reminded her of the Holocaust. When a student timidly asked what the Holocaust was, Erin Gruwell threw away the textbooks and started teaching *to* these kids instead of *at* them. Most of the kids in her class had either been shot, shot at, or witnessed gang murders, as well as having experienced the other traumas of living in troubled families and neighborhoods, and so they could relate to the Holocaust. They went to see Steven Spielberg's movie *Schindler's List* in Newport Beach, the gated community where she lived, only to be treated incredibly rudely by the wealthy, shallow, bigoted people in the theater who were shocked that she would bring her students there. But acting with personal integrity of the highest order, the local newspaper ran a front-page story *in her defense*. One of her wealthy, supposedly sophisticated neighbors screamed at her in her driveway, "If you love black people so much, why don't you just marry a monkey?"

She pressed on and had her students read *Anne Frank: The Diary of a Young Girl*, brought in a Holocaust survivor, read the book by Zlata Filipović, a fifteen-year-old girl living in war-ravaged Sarajevo, and then raised money to fly her to visit them in Southern California. Then the writing began. She had them writing diaries to process their experiences and feelings, and they nicknamed themselves the "Freedom Writers," after the freedom riders of the civil rights movement in the 1960s. When these kids started with Miss Gruwell, they could expect not to live very long, and their lives were dead-ends, hopeless. When they were done, all 150 of them who were touched by Ms. Gruwell's teaching methods were bound for college, despite the protests of colleagues who told her that she was giving them false hopes and setting them up for huge disappointments. The book of their diary entries was published as *The Freedom Writers Diary: How a Teacher and 150 Teens Used Writing to Change Themselves and the World Around Them* (1999). The authors' proceeds from the book are now used to fund the Tolerance Education Foundation, which was set up to help pay for the Freedom Writers' college tuition.

The above are just a few of the programs at the systemic level of the student in the classroom that have had profound effects on the people who participated in them. In the last chapter in our book, we demonstrate one of the ongoing systemic interventions that is being done at the state level, and therefore societal level, that has proven year-after-year that the partnership between smart business leaders, smart government, and smart people can combine to produce a resilient, viable, caring, kind, competitive, smart, well-educated, and productive society; without much of the nastiness and hatred that seem to be driving so many ineffective attempts in the United States to supposedly "make our country better."

CHAPTER 20

FROM THE ROCK OF GIBRALTAR TO MINNESOTA AND BEYOND

Dogs don't lie, and why should I?

Strangers come, they growl and bark.

They know their loved ones in the dark.

Now let me, by night or day,

Be just as full of truth as they.

—*Garrison Keillor*, Lake Wobegon Days *(1985, p. xi)*

We began this book with the poignant story of *Homo neanderthalensis*, who survived on planet Earth for 400,000 years—twice as long as us. They were strong, fierce hunters who lived during one of the harshest periods in Earth's relatively recent history, but in the end, they simply couldn't keep up with the more flexible genetic strategy of *Homo sapiens*.

Cooperation and caring among and between human beings has been one of the central themes in this book at several systemic levels—the individual, family, community, state, nation, and world. And so to complete this book, we wanted to describe a level of cooperation and caring at the state level that we have experienced ourselves for decades, and that we believe provides a guide that can be used both at the state and national levels here in the United States. It is certainly not the only example in this country of this kind of cooperation, but we think it is an especially good one.

The Week magazine (January 20, 2012, p. 13) did a one-page analysis titled "The German Colossus," explaining why of all the EU nations, Germany was the single nation that was thriving while her neighbors were drowning. The author concluded that Germans do not work harder or longer hours than many other countries, but they save 11.3 percent of their disposable income, more than twice what Americans save. They have engaged in "relentless innovation" within older, pre-WWII companies. They had to impose austerity measures in 2005 that angered many Germans. But more than anything, the article stated that "Modern Germany is neither a socialist paradise nor a model of laissez-faire capitalism. Instead, the German economy is based on close partnerships between the public and private sectors—and between management and workers. A network of state-funded research institutes helps incubate innovation, and worker representatives have long sat on German corporate boards." And the government has agreed to supplement wages if companies reduce hours for skilled workers rather than laying them off. A Mercedes factory in 2008 was told to cut production by one-half, but not a single person was fired. "If Germany has a lesson for other nations, it's that far-sighted political and business leadership can work wonders, especially if they work together," according to Steven Rattner, the financier and former Obama administration auto-industry czar.

This chapter is about a social system and a state government that has successfully demonstrated that it can improve the lives of its citizens by good planning and thoughtful use of resources, including tax revenues. We hope that the reader will be able to see just how successful a state can be when *competence and smart planning*, and the cooperation between government, educational institutions, and the people, are the norm. Scores of ideas in this chapter could be borrowed or modified for local use by people and governments in other parts of the country to drastically improve the quality of their lives, including their health care and their incomes.

Minnesota—Lousy Weather, a Model State

The jokes around here are that the Minnesota state bird is the mosquito, and that we have two seasons: winter and road construction. Garrison Keillor, of Minnesota Public Radio's *Prairie Home Companion* and Lake Wobegon fame, describes everyone here as dour, plodding, emotionless Germans, Norwegians, Swedes, and Finns. The church in his mythical town of Lake Wobegon is called Our Lady of Perpetual Responsibility. This Land of 10,000 Lakes was also known in the 1980s and 1990s as the Land of 10,000 Treatment Centers because the Minnesota Model of alcoholism treatment started here and fanned out to the rest of the world like a firestorm.

When one of the authors (JCF) moved here in the early 1970s, there was a long stretch in January when the temperature never rose above 0 degrees Fahrenheit during the day, and it plummeted to 15 to 20 degrees Fahrenheit below zero at night—and when there was wind, it was closer to 50 to 60 degrees below zero. He quickly learned why people installed engine block heaters in their cars.

At the same time, *Places Rated Almanac* ranked the Minneapolis–St. Paul metropolitan area eighth out of 354 metropolitan areas in the United States and Canada for its variety and participation in the arts (Minnesota State Arts Board, 2012). The newly relocated home of the multiple-stage Guthrie Theater complex, now overlooking the Mississippi River and designed by French architect Jean Nouvel, won *Architecture Magazine*'s best of 2006, and *Travel + Leisure*'s Design Award 2007 for Best Cultural Space. In 2008 Jean Nouvel was named the laureate of the Pritzker Architecture Prize, the architecture world's highest honor.

The Twin Cities have numerous world-class restaurants, several of which were started by recovering drug and alcohol addicts from larger metro areas like New York and Los Angeles who came for rehab at Hazelden Treatment Center in Center City, Minnesota, and who decided that the quality and support of the recovering community here were worth more than anything, so they stayed. The same is true for a number of local artists.

The kindness, decency, and care that still mostly reside here come from those "dour" Swedes, Norwegians, Finns, and Germans. And what Minnesota has continued to demonstrate decade after decade is that the brand of kindness and care for one another that still represents the best of what it means to be a Minnesotan also means that we have relatively low unemployment, great education and jobs, pretty decent health care (although there is still a long way to go with that), and a quality of life that often lands us in the top-ten largest cities in the United States, despite the weather and mosquitoes.

According to the U.S. Census, and reported by the Minnesota Office of Higher Education (2012),

> Among 25- to 34-year-olds:
>
> 48 percent had earned an associate degree or higher, ranking Minnesota 3rd in the country.
>
> 35 percent had earned a bachelor's degree or higher, ranking Minnesota 8th in the country.
>
> Among 35- to 44-year-olds:
>
> 48 percent had earned an associate degree or higher, ranking Minnesota 2nd in the country.
>
> 39 percent had earned a bachelor's degree or higher, ranking Minnesota 6th in the country.
>
> (Minnesota Office of Higher Education, 2012)

A headline in the *St. Paul Pioneer Press* regarding the November 8, 2011, special elections throughout the state for approval of extending or raising taxes for school funding read, "Despite Tough Times, Minnesota Voters Help Schools" (Boldt & Magan, 2011). The article went on to point out that 80 percent of school levy requests were approved by Minnesota voters, 59 percent of requests for *increased* school levies were approved, 57 of 58 school districts that asked to renew a levy saw their requests approved, 114 school districts had levy measures on the ballot, and that 1997 was the last time school districts had this much success with voters, who approved 86 percent of levy requests that year. That 59 percent of requests for *increases* in levies—as opposed to simply extending current funding—were approved statewide says volumes, given the nation's economy. Minnesotans take education seriously because, as discussed below, the state would lose its economic and cultural edge without a strong educational base.

There is also more diversity in Minnesota than many Americans realize. As of 2010 there were more than 66,000 Americans of Hmong heritage (both naturalized U.S. citizens and citizens born in the United States) living in Minnesota, based on U.S. Census data from the American Community Survey.

According to figures released in October 2011 by the American Community Survey (http://www.census.gov/acs/www/), Minnesota also has the largest population of Somalis in the United States—32,000 and growing. We pay more than the average amount to keep things running smoothly. "Minnesota has the 6th worst state business tax climate in the nation according to a new comprehensive report released today from the nonpartisan Tax Foundation. The North Star State is ranked 45th in the new, national report, '2012 State Business Tax Climate Index'" (Paskach, 2012). At the same time, our unemployment rate is good and is continually getting better. According to the Bureau of Labor Statistics Current Population Survey (http://www.bls.gov), the number of unemployed in Minnesota in January 2012 was 5.6 percent versus a national average in January 2012 of 8.6 percent. In discussing these Minnesota data with friends and colleagues in other parts of the country, many of these well-educated and otherwise worldly people were surprised to discover that Minnesota is the home of many Fortune 500 companies, including 3M (Minnesota Mining and Manufacturing), responsible for everything from Post-it Notes and Scotch Brand Tape to Thinsulate and nanotechnology breakthroughs; Medtronic—a leader in pacemaker technology, brain implant stimulators to treat Parkinson's disease, nerve stimulators for the treatment of chronic pain, and insulin pumps; Best Buy Company; Dayton-Hudson Companies, which includes Target Stores, Land O' Lakes, General Mills, United Health Group, Supervalu, Ecolab, St. Jude Medical, Hormel Foods, and

the original home of Cray Supercomputers and Control Data Corporation. Minnesota has very high taxes, lots of immigrants, a thriving high-
tech business community, low unemployment, and close to 200 colleges
and universities in the state. *How can this be?*

The Creative Class and the Minnesota Itasca Project

Richard Florida was the H. John Heinz III Professor of Regional Economic Development at Carnegie-Mellon University when he wrote his
groundbreaking work, *The Rise of the Creative Class: And How It's Transforming Work, Leisure, Community, and Everyday Life* (2002), which
showed how the future vibrancy or the stagnation of U.S. cities will depend
in large part on three factors. In an interview with Christopher Dreher of
Salon.com (2002), Dr. Florida said,

> My theory uses the three Ts: *technology, talent and tolerance.* You need to
> have *a strong technology base*, such as a research university and investment
> in technology. That alone is a necessary but not in itself sufficient condition.
> Second, you need to be a place that *attracts and retains talent, that has the
> lifestyle options, the excitement, the energy, the stimulation that talented, cre-
> ative people need.* And third, you need to *be tolerant of diversity* so you can
> attract all sorts of people—foreign-born people, immigrants, women as well
> as men, gays as well as straights, people who look different and have different
> appearances. My indicators try to catch elements of those three things. We
> have two indicators of technology—the *innovation index*, which is a measure
> of patents in an area of population, and the *high-tech index*, which we just
> adapted from the Milken Institute, which is in California and invented this
> great index of high-tech company concentrations. We use our *creative-class
> index*—percent creative class and percent supercreatives—as our talent mea-
> sure. On tolerance we have the *melting-pot index*, which is immigrants, and
> the *gay index*, which takes people living in households where partners in the
> household were of the same sex.
>
> **Gays are the canaries of the creative economy.** Where gays are will be a
> community—a city or a region—that has the underlying preconditions that

attract the creative class of people. Gays tend to gravitate toward the types of places that will be attractive to many members of the creative class. That said, a high score on the gay index, for example, New Orleans or Miami, does not translate into being a creative center, unless you couple that with technology assets. *It's not that gays predict high-tech growth, it's that gays signal an environment that would attract creative-class people from a variety of backgrounds.* (emphasis added)

According to Dr. Florida's research, at the time of the writing of his book, the top ten cities for attracting the new creative class were San Francisco, Austin, Boston, San Diego, Seattle, Raleigh-Durham, Houston, Washington D.C., New York, and Minneapolis.

Dr. Florida's work suggests that you create a community that attracts and supports the kind of people who are bright and entrepreneurial, *and then the businesses will follow*—not the other way around.

Minneapolis–St. Paul and the Creative Class

Several decades ago, a *nonpartisan* group of powerful, civic-minded business leaders in Minneapolis–St. Paul formed what they called the Itasca Group. The Mississippi River starts as a trickle way "up north" (as Minnesotans say) in Itasca County, Minnesota, and their first meeting was at Itasca State Park. It included the Daytons (Dayton-Hudson Corporation, Marshall-Fields, Target Stores), the McKnights (3M), the Pillsburys, and other business leaders. Their sole purpose was to determine future directions to keep the Twin Cities on the cutting edge economically and socially—and now, environmentally.

A reinvigorated Itasca Project a few years ago included Jim Campbell, the retired chairman and CEO of Wells Fargo Bank Minnesota, as its chairman, as well as Northwest Airlines Corporation CEO Richard Anderson, 3M Company CEO James McNerney, Janet Dolan of Tennant Company, and Stanley S. Hubbard of Hubbard Broadcasting. The mayors of St. Paul and Minneapolis, along with the governor of Minnesota, were also involved.

One of the guiding spirits for continued development of the Minne-apolis–St. Paul metropolitan region is Dr. Richard Florida and his Creative Class work. The Itasca Project enlisted a study by the Brookings Institution (cleverly titled "Mind the Gap," to emphasize the gap between the haves and have-nots in the state) to study the critical issues facing Minnesota going forward economically and socially. The upshot of that extensive study was that even though the gap between rich and poor in Minnesota was among the lowest nationwide, there were glaring income disparities between subgroups within the state that were doomed to hobble the economic success of Minnesota's high-tech economy if they were not addressed.

The remainder of this chapter consists of a few examples from the Itasca Project website and is used with permission of the Project. It shows what can happen when a *bipartisan* group of concerned businesses and individuals take seriously the economic stability of a state's business community; the well-being, education, and health of its citizens; and the quality of life and the environment in that state.

Race disparities

❑ The Twin Cities region has the 12th highest college attainment rate among the 100 largest metro areas—33 percent of its residents have a bachelor's degree or higher. However, only 19 percent of African Americans, 11 percent of Mexicans, and 8 percent of Hmong do.

❑ Finally, while the region's overall poverty ranks among the lowest in the country, poverty still disproportionately plagues some segments of the population. In 2000, only 4 percent of whites were poor, but one-third of all Hmong lived below the federal poverty line.

Class disparities

❏ Low-income adults have low levels of educational attainment, and educational levels, in turn, affect incomes. In the Twin Cities region, of all adults who earn less than $17,500, only 26 percent have a college degree or higher. Meanwhile, more than half—53 percent—of middle-class adults earning between $35,000 and $79,999 are college educated.

Not content with identifying the problem of racial and economic disparities, the Itasca group went on to outline why it is of the utmost importance for the economic stability of the region to "lift up" the "the very least of these."

Reducing These Inequalities Matters to the Economic and Fiscal Future of the Region

Reducing disparities is not just the right thing to do, it is the smart thing to do [emphasis added]. "Minding the gap" is crucial to preserving the region's strong economic position. Further, doing so can generate more revenues (and reduce costs) for the region.

❏ **Reducing disparities now will build a more competitive workforce for the future.** In urgent and most prescient terms, the Twin Cities is heading straight for a workforce shortage. In six years (or by 2011), the oldest baby boomers in the region, aged 54 in 2000, will start to retire. By 2029, the youngest baby boomers reach retirement age. Forty-six percent of baby boom workers had at least a college degree in 2000. This means that in 15 years, the Twin Cities region *will lose more than 350,000 highly skilled workers to retirement* [emphasis added]. It is essential to replace this skilled labor to keep the economy churning with high-quality growth. However, economic studies forecast a diminished supply of skilled workers nationwide, so regions cannot rely heavily on attracting workers from elsewhere. Instead, there will need to be an increased dependence on existing workers, and economists predict that this means more women and minorities in the workforce.

For the Twin Cities, while only 10 percent of baby boomers in the metro area are members of minority groups, minorities comprise one-quarter of the next generation of workers. And, as evidence in this report shows, racial disparities, if left unchecked, will mean a future workforce that has little education and few skills, potentially undercutting the economic strides of the last few decades.

❑ **Reducing disparities between race and income groups brings more money into the Twin Cities metro area.** Reducing disparities among race and income groups will increase local tax bases and decrease the fiscal costs associated with poverty. Having larger numbers of people earning at least a middle-class income fuels the local economy by creating a larger number of consumers with more purchasing power.

In the following section, we share with you the current priorities embraced by Minnesota's Itasca Project, to illustrate what a systematic plan for regional growth can look like when it is not constrained by ethnic fears and prejudices, or by ideological and religious constriction, and when its underlying premise is a combination of economic and business concerns married to a more nuanced understanding that what is good for people is also good for the high-tech, complex business world. At this level of capitalism, the battles over issues like gay marriage become irrelevant, which leaves business in the interesting position of having to consider people's civil rights, quality of life, and access to health care, education, and day care as integral components of making a highly successful technological corporation function at both its moral and ethical best, and, as a byproduct of that, at its most profitable.

2010–2011 Priorities of the Itasca Project

Itasca's priorities are dynamic and evolve over time with the needs of the region and interest of its members. In 2010-2011 Itasca has focused on three priorities:

1. **Generating Quality Job Growth**

2. **Advancing a Comprehensive and Aligned Transportation System**

3. **Improving Our Region's Education System**—Closely linked to job growth, education reform is a top priority for Itasca. Recent initiatives include:

   Minnesota's Future: World-Class Schools, World-Class Jobs.

   Supporting the Strategic Re-direction of Minneapolis Public Schools.

Past Initiatives Included

1. **Building a Stronger University-Business Partnership**—Using a team of loaned executives, Itasca worked with the University of Minnesota to create a "front door" to the U that would facilitate stronger cooperation with business, improve the process to commercialize intellectual property, and strengthen the U as a talent magnet.

2. **Improving Early Childhood Education**—In 2005, Itasca provided Minnesota's Governor the pro-bono services of a consulting team from McKinsey and Company to examine the current programs, develop a common fact base, and identify

opportunities for improvement. The outcome of the study was
the basis of the Governor's legislative agenda. Itasca has also
played a brokering role among a group of the critical players in
early childhood to identify and address gaps and overlaps and
to develop a common change agenda. [Read the report here:
http://www.theitascaproject.com/ECDReport.pdf.]

Many states in America could profit and benefit from just *one* of the
many projects and goals outlined above, but to do so, they would have to
make some fundamental shifts in their beliefs about what makes a nation,
a state, and a people strong and productive. We hope that contemplation
of this chapter causes at least a few readers to go beyond contemplation
toward implementation. Competence and smart planning by government,
business, and educational institutions would appear to be a fast-track way
to overcome many of the economic and social ills that have gridlocked our
nation, and many other nations, over the last twenty years.

• • •

Like Albert Einstein, Stephen Hawking, Charles Darwin, and many
others, Gregory Bateson saw the world through the filter of a unique and
remarkable mind. He saw things we don't usually see, in ways that we don't
usually see them. Thinking about problems systemically is more challenging than thinking of them in linear, either-or, black-and-white ways.
Thinking systemically appears at first glance to be more complicated and
messy, which raises our anxiety because it leaves us feeling like we have
less control over things than we would like.

But the fact is that we have very little control over the universe. We are
human beings, not gods. And so while the systemic approach to problems
may be messier "up front," it makes understanding the universe much
simpler. Seeing life in overly simplistic ways can ultimately make life very
complicated and disturbing, while accepting, with awe and wonder, the

beauty and mystery of a universe we can't control, and that we barely understand, can make life so much simpler in the long run. It can give us a sense of peace that can be found in no other way.

And so we end by returning to Bateson's quote that we have used in several places in this book. The "strange way" of looking at the world refers to the competitive, black-and-white, adversarial, right vs. wrong stance that paralyzes so many individuals, families, communities, states, and nations on this planet—paralyzing polarities.

Our hope is that as a species, *Homo sapiens* will eventually understand, and embrace, the four-decades-old warning of this brilliant systemic visionary. . . .

It is doubtful whether a species having *both* an advanced technology *and* this strange way of looking at its world can endure. (Bateson, 1971, p. 377)

About the Authors

John C. Friel, Ph.D. and Linda D. Olund Friel, M.A. are licensed psychologists in private practice in Minneapolis, Minnesota. John also has a regular, part-time practice in Reno, Nevada. John was on the board of the Nevada Psychological Association for several years, and is also an adjunct assistant clinical professor in the Department of Psychiatry, School of Medicine, University of Nevada, Reno.

John does individual psychotherapy with adults and also specializes in intensive couples and sex therapy (two- to twelve-hour blocks of time), and in helping families with grown children do reconciliation work when painful rifts have occurred in the fabric of the family. He also has a men's therapy group in Minneapolis that has been ongoing for twenty-seven years, and two in Reno that have been ongoing for nine years.

Linda specializes in helping adults resolve trauma, facilitates women's therapy groups, and helps with women's identity and recovery issues. She designed and directed the first hospital-based codependency treatment program in the United States, and along with John, developed the first conceptual/theoretical model of codependency based on Erik Erikson's Eight Stages of Development. She was also the co-developer, with John, of the first objective paper-and-pencil test to measure codependency based on that conceptual model.

The Friels are internationally recognized for their work with adults who grew up in painful families. They draw from the areas of ecological systems, family systems, object relations, cognitive restructuring, insight-oriented therapy, group dynamics, and family-of-origin in their therapy approaches.

They have been on *The Oprah Winfrey Show*, *MSNBC*, and *ABC News 20/20*, among several others, and have also been featured in *USA Today*, *Cosmopolitan*, and *Parents*. They are *New York Times* bestselling authors of eight books that have sold more than half a million copies, including *Adult Children: The Secrets of Dysfunctional Families* and *The Seven Best Things (Happy) Couples Do.*

Over the past twenty-seven years, their three-and-a-half-day ClearLife Clinic Program has helped more than 7,000 people identify and make subtle changes in childhood patterns of behavior, beliefs, and feelings so that they can begin living a clearer, more balanced life. Go to www. clearlife.com for more information.

References

Abboud, S. K., & Kim, J. (2005). *Top of the class: How Asian parents raise high achievers—and how you can too.* New York: Berkley Trade.

Abramson, P. R., & Pinkerton, S. D. (1995). *With pleasure: Thoughts on the nature of human sexuality.* New York: Oxford University Press.

Achenbach, J. (2011, May 13). The Century of Disasters: Meltdowns. Floods. Tornadoes. Oil spills. Grid crashes. Why more and more things seem to be going wrong, and what we can do about it. *Slate. com.* Retrieved from www.slate.com/articles/ health_and_science/science/2011/05/the_century_ of_disasters_2.html

Adorno, T. W., Frenkel-Brunswik, E., Levinson, D. J., & Sanford, R. N. (1950). *The authoritarian personality.* New York: Norton.

American Psychological Association. Proceedings of the National Academy of Sciences. (2011). *Monitor on Psychology, 108*(4), 16–17.

Anda, R. (2006). The health and social impact of growing up with alcohol abuse and related adverse childhood experiences: The human and economic costs of the status quo. Report to the Board of Directors of the National Association of Children of Alcoholics. Retrieved from www.nacoa.org/ pdfs/Anda% 20NACoA%20Review_web.pdf.

Anderson, D. J., McGovern, J. P., & DuPont, R. L. (1999). Origins of the Minnesota Model of addiction treatment: A first-person account. *Journal of Addictive Diseases, 18*(1), 107–114.

Bakan, D. (1966). *The duality of human existence.* Chicago: Rand McNally.

Baltes, P. B. (1968). Longitudinal and cross-sectional sequences in the study of age and generation effects. *Human Development, 11,* 145–171.

Barbeau, T. (2004). Genital mutilation common in 28 African & Middle Eastern nations. Retrieved from http://people.fmarion.edu/tbarbeau/Genital%20Mutilation.pdf.

Bartlett, T. (2010, May 21). Want smart kids? Here's what to do. *Chronicle of Higher Education.* Retrieved from http://www.chroniclereview.info/blogAuthor/Percolator/10/6/Tom-Bartlett/15/.

Bateson, G. (1971). The cybernetics of "self": A theory of alcoholism. *Psychiatry, 34*(1), 1–18.

Bateson, G. ([1972] 2000). *Steps to an ecology of mind: Collected essays in anthropology, psychiatry, evolution, and epistemology.* Chicago: University of Chicago Press.

Bateson, N. (Director/Producer). (2010). *An ecology of mind: A daughter's portrait of Gregory Bateson* [Documentary]. Released in New York City on September 12, 2011.

Baumeister, R. F., Heatherton, T. F., & Tice, D. M. (1994). *Losing control: How and why people fail at self-regulation.* New York: Academic Press.

Baumeister, R. F., Smart, L., & Boden, J. M. (1996). Relation of threatened egotism to violence and aggression: The dark side of high self-esteem. *Psychological Review, 103*(1), 5–33.

Beaudoin, C. M., Murray, R. P., Bond, J., & Barnes, G. E. (1997). Personality characteristics of depressed or alcoholic adult children of alcoholics. *Personality and Individual Differences, 23*(4), 559–567.

Beck, A. T. (1967). *The diagnosis and management of depression*. Philadelphia: University of Pennsylvania Press.

Berry, J. W., Poortinga, Y. H., Segall, M. H., & Dasen, P. R. (2002). *Cross-cultural psychology: Research and applications*. Cambridge U.K.: Cambridge University Press.

Black, C. (1981). *It will never happen to me!* Denver, CO: M.A.C. Publishers.

Boldt, M., & Magan, C. (2011, November 10). Despite tough times, Minnesota voters help schools. *St. Paul Pioneer Press*, St. Paul, MN.

Bouchard, T. J., Jr., Lykken, D. T., McGue, M., Segal, N., & Tellegen, A. (1990, October 12). Sources of human psychological differences: The Minnesota study of twins reared apart. *Science*, 223–228.

Boyd, S. J., Plemons, B. W., Schwartz, R. P., Johnson, J. L., & Pickens, R. W. (1999). The relationship between parental history and substance use severity in drug treatment patients. *American Journal on Addictions, 8*(1), 15–23.

Briere, J., & Runtz, M. (1991). The long-term effects of sexual abuse: A review and synthesis. In Briere, J. (Ed.), *Treating victims of child sexual abuse: New directions for mental health services*. San Francisco: Jossey-Bass.

Brinkerhoff, N. (2010, September 29). Income inequality in U.S. reaches record high. Retrieved from AllGov, http://www.allgov.com/Top_Stories/ViewNews/Income_Inequality_in_US_ReachesRecord _High_100929.

Brinn, D. (2005, January 23). Israeli Researchers Discover Gene for Altruism. *Israel 21C innovation news service*. Retrieved from www.israel21c.org/people/israeli-researchers-discover-gene-for-altruism

Bronfenbrenner, U. (1977, September). *Who needs parent education?* Flint, MI: Charles Stewart Mott Foundation. Position paper for the Working Conference on Parent Education.

Bronfenbrenner, U. (1979). *The ecology of human development: Experiments by nature and design*. Cambridge, MA: Harvard University Press.

Bronfenbrenner, U. (1994). Who cares for the children? In H. Nuba, M. Searson, & D. L. Sheiman (Eds.), *Resources for early childhood: A handbook*. New York: Garland. Edited paper from an individual address to UNESCO, Paris, September 1989.

Brown, C. (2010, May 29). For seven years, monks have had no peace. *Minneapolis StarTribune*. Retrieved from http://www.startribune.com/local/95194799.html.

Bryson, D. (2012, January 13). Oprah celebrates graduates from South African school. *Huff Post Media*. Retrieved from http://www.huffingtonpost.com/2012/01/13/oprah-celebrates-graduates-south-africa_n_1204177.html.

Bushman, B. J., & Baumeister, R. F. (1998). Threatened egotism, narcissism, self-esteem, and direct and displaced aggression: Does self-love or self-hate lead to violence? *Journal of Personality and Social Psychology, 75*, 1, 219–229.

California Task Force to Promote Self-esteem and Personal and Social Responsibility. (1990). *Toward a state of self-esteem*. Sacramento: California State Department of Education.

Carlson, E., Yates, T., & Sroufe, L. A. (2009). Development of dissociation and development of the self. In P. Dell, J. O'Neil, & E. Somer (Eds.), *Dissociation and dissociative disorders*. New York: Routledge.

Cartwright, D. (1959). *Studies in social power*. Ann Arbor: University of Michigan.

Cater, A. (Producer). (2005). *1-800-India* [Documentary]. *Wide Angle*. Public Broadcasting Network.

CBS News Online. (2011, June 23). Minorities make up majority of U.S. babies. Retrieved from http://www.cbsnews.com/2100-201_162-20073650.html.

Centers for Disease Control and Prevention. Marriages and Divorces. Retrieved from http://www.cdc.gov/nchs/mardiv.htm#state_tables.

Christensen, A. J., Edwards, D. L., Wiebe, J. S., Benotsch, E. G., McKelvey, L., Andrews, M., & Lubaroff, D. M. (1996). Effect of verbal self-disclosure on natural killer cell activity: Moderating influence of cynical hostility. *Psychosomatic Medicine, 58,* 150–155.

Chua, A. (2011) *Battle Hymn of the Tiger Mother.* New York: Penguin Press.

Cirillo, S., & DiBlasio, P. (1992). *Families that abuse: Diagnosis and therapy.* J. Neugroschel (Trans.). New York: W. W. Norton.

Cohen, S., Doyle, W. J., Skoner, D. P., Rabin, B. S., Gwaltney, J. M., Jr. (1997). Social ties and susceptibility to the common cold. *Journal of the American Medical Association, 277,* 1940–1944.

Cohen, E (2008, February 11). Are your politics rooted in your genes? *CNN Health.* Retrieved from http://articles.cnn.com/2008-02-11/health/politics.genes_1_david-amodio-liberals-and-conservatives-genes?_s=PM:HEALTH

Cohen, R. (2011). The myth of American exceptionalism. *Washington Post* Writers Group. Article available at http://www.realclearpolitics.com/articles /2011/05/10/taking_exceptionalism_109795.html.

Compañ, E., Moreno, J., Ruiz, M. T., & Pascual, E. (2002). Doing things together: Adolescent health and family rituals. *Journal of Epidemiology and Community Health, 56,* 89–94.

Cone, J. D. (1977). The relevance of reliability and validity for behavioral assessment. *Behavior Therapy 8,* 3, 411–426.

Cone, J. D., & Hawkins, R. P. (Eds.). (1977). *Behavioral assessment: New directions in clinical psychology.* New York: Brunner/Mazel.

Conte, J. R. (1991). The nature of sexual offenses against children. In C. R. Hollin, & K. Howells (Eds.), *Clinical approaches to sex offenders and their victims.* Toronto: Wiley.

Corwin, M. (1995, October 29). Mother turns grief, grit to memorial for slain son. *Los Angeles Times.*

Cromwell, R. E., & Olson, D. H. (1975). *Power in families.* New York: John Wiley.

Cuijpers, P., & Smit, F. (2002). Nicotine dependence and regular nicotine use in adult children of alcoholics. *Addiction Research and Theory, 10* (1), 69–81.

Cuijpers, P., Langendoen, Y., & Bijl, R. V. (1999). Psychiatric disorders in adult children of problem drinkers: Prevalence, first onset and comparison with other risk factors. *Addiction, 94*(10), 1489–1498.

deMause, L. (1974). *The history of childhood.* New York: Psychohistory Press.

Dick, D. M., Edenberg, H. J., Xuei, X., Goaste, A., Kuperman, S., Schuckit, M., Crowe, R., Smith, T. L., Porjesz, B., Begleiter, H., & Foroud, T. (2004, January). Association of *GABRG3* with alcohol dependence. *Alcoholism: Clinical and Experimental Research, 28*(1), 4–9.

Divorce.com. CDC report shows Massachusetts has lowest divorce rate. Retrieved at http://www.divorce.com/blog/cdc-report-shows-massachusetts-has-lowest- divorce-rate.

Doherty, W. J. (2000). *Take Back Your Kids: Confident Parenting in Turbulent Times.* South Bend, IN: Sorin Books.

Donadio, R. (2011, November 21). Vatican: Cardinal who resigned amid scandal retires. *New York Times.*

Dopp, J. M., Miller, G. E., Myers, H. F., & Fahey, J. L. (2000). Increased natural killer-cell mobilization and cytotoxicity during marital conflict. *Brain, Behavior, and Immunity, 14,* 10–26. Article available online at http://www.idealibrary.com.

Dreher, C. (2002, June 6). Be creative—or die: A new study says cities must attract the new "creative class" with hip neighborhoods, an arts scene and a gay-friendly atmosphere—or they'll go the way of Detroit. Salon.com. Retrieved from www.salon.com/2002/06/06/florida_22.

Druckerman, P. (2012). *Bringing up bébé: One American mother discovers the wisdom of French parenting.* New York: Penguin Press.

Druckerman, P. (2012, February 4). Why French parents are superior. *Wall Street Journal.* Retrieved from http://online.wsj.com/article/SB10001424052970204740904577196931457473816.html.

Eagleman, D. (2011, July/August). The brain on trial. *The Atlantic.*

The Economist. (2011, July 30). Welcome stranger: The human impulse to be kind to unknown individuals is not the biological aberration it might seem.

The Economist. (2011, June 11). Who needs leaders? The aftermath of the March 11th disasters shows that Japan's strengths lie outside Tokyo, in its regions.

Eisenberger, N. I., Taylor, S. E., Gable, S. L., Hilmert, C. J., & Lieberman, M. D. (2007). Neural pathways link social support to attenuated neuroendocrine stress response. *NeuroImage, 35,* 1601–1612.

Ellis, A., and R. A. Harper. (1975). *A Guide to Rational Living.* 3rd ed. Chatsworth, CA: Wilshire Book Company.

Epstein, N. (1998). *The friendly Dickens.* New York: Penguin Books. Cited in the Program Notes from the Guthrie Theater (Minneapolis) production of *A Christmas Carol* November 19-December 30, 2011.

Erikson, E. H. (1950). *Childhood and society.* New York: W. W. Norton.

Erikson, E. H. (1959). *Identity and the life cycle.* New York: International Universities Press.

Erikson, E. H. (1968). *Identity: Youth and crisis.* New York: W. W. Norton.

Evans, M. D. R., Kelley, J., Sikora, J., & Treiman, D. J. (2010). Family scholarly culture and educational success: Books and schooling in 27 nations. *Research in Social Stratification and Mobility.* Available at http://www.rodneytrice.com/sfbb /articles/home.pdf.

Evans, P. (1992). *The verbally abusive relationship.* Avon, MA: Adams Media Corporation.

Fagan, K. (2003, August 17). Giving back: A soldier's solace; One Vietnam vet finds redemption growing coffee in Laos. Available online at http://www.sfgate.com /cgi-bin/article.cgi?f=/c/a/2003/08/17/CM303149.DTL&ao=all.

Faulkner, M. G. (2010, September 29). *A Christmas Carol*: The making of a masterpiece. Back to the Best Books blog. Retrieved from http://www.backtothebestbooks.com /2010/09/29/a-christmas-carol-the-making-of-a-masterpiece.

Feldmann, L. (2003, March 14). The impact of Bush linking 9/11 and Iraq. *Christian Science Monitor.* Available online at www.csmonitor.com/2003/0314/p02s01- woiq.html.

Ferguson, C. H. (Director), & Marrs, A. (Producer). (2010). *Inside Job.* [Motion picture]. United States: Sony Pictures Classics.

Fey, T. (2005, October 29). *Saturday Night Live: Weekend Update.*

Fischer, K. E., Kittleson, M., Ogletree, R., Welshimer, K., Woehlke, P., & Benshoff, J. (2000). The relationship of parental alcoholism and family dysfunction to stress among college students. *Journal of American College Health, 48*(4), 151–156.

Fleischman, H. L., Hopstock, P. J., Pelczar, M. P., and Shelley, B. E. (2010). Highlights from PISA 2009: Performance of U.S. 15-year-old students in reading, mathematics, and science literacy in an international context. NCES report no. 2011004. National Center for Education Statistics. U.S. Department of Education. Washington, D.C.: U.S. Government Printing Office.

Florida, R. (2002). *The rise of the creative class: And how it's transforming work, leisure, community, and everyday life.* New York: Basic Books.

Florida, R. (2005). *The flight of the creative class: The new global competition for talent.* New York: HarperBusiness.

Friedman, T., & Mandelbaum, M. (2011). *That used to be us: How America fell behind in the world it invented and how we can come back.* New York: Farrar, Straus & Giroux.

Friel, J. (1993). *Rescuing your spirit: When third-grade morality isn't enough for Christians.* Deerfield Beach, FL: Health Communications.

Friel, J. C., & Friel, L. D. (1988). *Adult children: The secrets of dysfunctional families.* Deerfield Beach, FL: Health Communications.

Friel, J. C., & Friel, L. D. (1990). *An adult child's guide to what's normal.* Deerfield Beach, FL: Health Communications.

Friel, J. C., & Friel, L. D. (1995). *The soul of adulthood.* Deerfield Beach, FL: Health Communications.

Friel, J. C., & Friel, L. D. (1999). *The 7 worst things (good) parents do.* Deerfield Beach, FL: Health Communications.

Friel, J. C., & Friel, L. D. (2002). *The 7 best things (happy) couples do.* Deerfield Beach, FL: Health Communications.

Friel, J. C., & Friel, L. D. (2000). *The 7 best things (smart) teens do.* Deerfield Beach, FL: Health Communications.

Galbraith, P. (2007). *The end of Iraq: How American incompetence created a war without end.* New York: Simon and Schuster.

Glaser, R., Kiecolt-Glaser, J. K., Bonneau, R. H., Malarkey, W., Kennedy, S., & Hughes, J. (1992). Stress-induced modulation of the immune response to recombinant hepatitis B vaccine. *Psychosomatic Medicine, 54,* 22–29.

Goldner, V. (1998). The treatment of violence and victimization in intimate relationships. *Family Process, 37,* 263–286.

Goldner, V., Penn, P., Sheinberg, M., & Walker, G. (1990). Love and violence: Gender paradoxes in volatile attachments. *Family Process, 29,* 343–364.

Goleman, D. (1995). *Emotional intelligence: Why it can matter more than IQ.* New York: Bantam.

Good Morning America. (2011, January).

Gottlieb, L. (2011, July/August). How to land your kid in therapy. *The Atlantic.* Retrieved from http://www.theatlantic.com/magazine/archive/2011/07/how-to- land-your-kid-in-therapy/8555/?single_page=true.

Gottman, J. M. (1994). *Why marriages succeed or fail.* New York: Simon and Schuster.

Graybar, S. R., & Boutier, L. R. (2002). Non-traumatic pathways to borderline personality disorder. *Psychotherapy: Theory, Research, Practice and Training, 39*(2), 152–162.

Gray-Little, B., & Burks, N. (1983). Power and satisfaction in marriage: A review and critique. *Psychological Bulletin, 93,* 513–538.

Griffin, M., & Amodeo, M. (1998). Mixed psychosocial outcomes of sisters from families with alcoholic parents. *American Journal of Drug and Alcohol Abuse, 24*(1), 153–167.

Guest, R. (2011, November 27). Why we're still no. 1. Salon.com.

Haley, J. (1976). *Problem-solving therapy.* San Francisco: Jossey-Bass.

Hamilton, W. (1964a). The genetical evolution of social behaviour. Vol. 1. *Journal of Theoretical Biology 7*(1), 1–16.

Hamilton, W. (1964b). The genetical evolution of social behaviour. Vol. 2. *Journal of Theoretical Biology* *7*(1), 17–52.

Hamilton, W. (1966). The moulding of senescence by natural selection. *Journal of Theoretical Biology* *12*(1), 12–45.

Harter, S. L. (2000). Psychosocial adjustment of adult children of alcoholics: A review of the recent empirical literature. *Clinical Psychology Review, 20*(3), 311–337.

Henderson, D. J. (1983). Is incest harmful? *Canadian Journal of Psychiatry, 28,* 34–39.

Hendrix, H. (1998). *Getting the love you want: A guide for couples.* New York: Pocket Books.

Herbert, T. B., & Cohen, S. (1993). Stress and immunity in humans: A meta-analytic review. *Psychosomatic Medicine,* 364–379.

Hirraan Online. (2011). News and Information about Somalia. Retrieved from http://www.hiiraan.com/news2/2011/oct/census_estimate_says_more_than_32_000_somalis_in_minn_still_largest_somali_population_in_us.aspx.

Hitler, A. (1925). *Mein kampf.* Project Gutenberg of Australia - Mein Kampf tr. James Murphy. Retrieved 2008-08-23.

Holmes, Oliver Wendell, Sr. ([1858] 1955). *The autocrat of the breakfast-table.* New York: Heritage Press.

Hoopes, M. M., & Harper, J. H. (1987). *Birth order roles and sibling patterns in individual and family therapy.* New York: Aspen Publishers.

Horton, A. L., & Williamson, J. A. (1988). *Abuse and religion: When praying isn't enough.* Lexington, MA: Lexington Books.

Huber, R. M. (1971). *The American idea of success.* New York: McGraw-Hill.

Hunt, M. E. (1997). A comparison of family of origin factors between children of alcoholics and children of non-alcoholics in a longitudinal panel. *American Journal of Drug and Alcohol Abuse, 23*(4), 597–613.

Itasca Project. An employer-led civic alliance focused on building a thriving economy and improved quality of life in the Minneapolis–St. Paul Metropolitan Region. Retrieved from http://www.theitascaproject.com/.

Jayson, S. (2011, August 24). Marriage, divorce rates higher in the South, lower in Northeast. *USA Today.*

Jewish Virtual Library (2012). Goebbels and the "Big Lie." *The American-Israeli Cooperative Enterprise.*

Johnson, C. (1992). *Lucky in love: The secrets of happy couples and how their marriages thrive.* New York: Viking.

Judson, O. (2007, October). The selfless gene. *Atlantic Monthly.* Article available at http://www.theatlantic.com/magazine/archive/2007/10/the-selfless-gene/6196/.

Kaplan, H. I., & Freedman, A. M. (1975). *Comprehensive textbook of psychiatry.* 2nd ed. Baltimore: Williams & Wilkins.

Kaufman, G. (1980). *Shame: The power of caring.* Cambridge, MA: Schenkman Publishing Company.

Keillor, G. (1985). *Lake Wobegon days.* New York: Viking Penguin.

Kiecolt-Glaser, J. K., Robles, T. F., & Glaser, R. (2002). Psychoneuroimmunology: Psychological influences on immune function and health. *Journal of Consulting and Clinical Psychology, 70*(3), 539.

King, K. (2011, November 11). Foreign nationals take over doctorates and tech start-ups. Yahoo! News. Retrieved from http://news.yahoo.com/foreign-nationals-over-doctorates-tech-start-ups-005000775.html.

Kingston, A. (2004). *The meaning of wife: A provocative look at women and marriage in the twenty-first century.* Toronto: HarperPerennial Canada.

Kluger, J. (2010, May 2). A dose of oxytocin increases the cuddles. *Time* online. http://www.time.com.

Koerner, B. (2010, July). Secret of AA: After 75 years, we don't know how it works. Wired. Retrieved from http://www.wired.com/magazine/2010/06/ff_alcoholics_anonymous/all/1.

Kohlberg, L. (1981). *Essays on moral development.* Vol. 1: *The philosophy of moral development.* San Francisco: Harper & Row.

Kovan, N., Levy-Chung, A., & Sroufe, L. A. (2009). The intergenerational continuity of observed early parenting: A prospective, longitudinal study. *Developmental Psychology, 45,* 1205–1213.

Kraemer, G. W. (1985). Effects of differences in early social experience on primate neurobiological-behavioral development. In M. Reite and T. Field (Eds.), *The Psychobiology of Attachment and Separation.* New York: Academic Press.

Kraemer, G. W. (1992). A psychobiological theory of attachment. *Behavioral and Brain Sciences, 15,* S141–S168.

Langer, W. C. (1973). *The mind of Adolf Hitler: The secret wartime report.* New York: New American Library. [*Authors' note*: In 1943, Langer published the report as *A psychological analysis of Adolph Hitler: His life and legend* (Washington, D.C.: Office of Strategic Services), but it had remained classified for more than twenty years.]

Larson, N. (1995, July). Victim typology. Workshop for the St. Louis County Department of Social Services, Duluth, MN.

Larson, N. (1999, November). Group treatment for victims: Different models for different patterns. Paper presented at the 12th Annual U.S. Psychiatric and Mental Health Congress, Atlanta, GA.

Larson, N. (2009, February 6). Personality disorders and trauma: Understanding the connection and treating the patterns. One-day workshop for the National Association of Social Workers, St. Paul, MN.

Larson, N. (2010a, March 27). The Lone Ranger Syndrome: Helping successful women with trauma histories. Psychotherapy Networker Symposium, Washington, D.C.

Larson, N. (2010b, March). Psychodynamic/systemic psychotherapy with victims of trauma and their families. Third four-day workshop of a two-year training program for Danish psychologists, Jutland, Denmark.

Larson, N. (2011). Personality disorders and trauma: The connection and the treatment. Two one-day workshops, Chicago, IL.

Legacies of War. The secret bombing of Laos. Retrieved from https://legacies ofwar.org/about-laos/secret-war-laos/secret-bombing-laos.

Lewis, T., Amini, F., & Lannon, R. (2000). *A general theory of love.* New York: Vintage Books.

Lightman, A. (1994). *Einstein's dreams.* New York: Warner Books.

Los Angeles Times. (2011, May 21). Report indicts '60s counterculture in Catholic abuse cases. Editorial. Retrieved from http://articles.latimes.com/2011/may/21/opinion/la-ed-abuse-20110521.

Linkins, J. (2009). Online poll: Jon Stewart is America's most trusted newsman. *Huffington Post.* Retrieved from http://www.huffingtonpost.com/2009/07/22/time-magazine-poll-jon-st_n_242933.html

Loucks, E. B., Berkman, L. F., Gruenewald, T. L., & Seeman, T. E. (2006). Relation of social integration to inflammatory marker concentrations in men and women 70–79 years. *American Journal of Cardiology, 97,* 1010–1016.

Maddock, J. W. (1993). Ecology, ethics, and responsibility in family therapy. *Family Relations, 42*, 116–123.

Maddock, J. W. (1999). Personal communication with J. C. Friel.

Maddock, J. W., & Larson, N. (1995). *Incestuous families: An ecological approach to understanding and treatment.* New York: W. W. Norton.

Maddock, J. W., & Larson, N. (2004). The ecological approach to incestuous families. In D. R. Catherall (Ed.), *Handbook of stress, trauma, and the family.* New York: Brunner-Routledge.

Maddock, J. W., Friel, J. C., & Friel, L. D. (2009). Family influences and ecological context. In W. O'Donohue & S. Graybar (Eds.), *Handbook of contemporary psychotherapy.* Thousand Oaks, CA: Sage Publications.

Marucha, P. T., Kiecolt-Glaser, J. K., & Favagehi, M. (1998). Mucosal wound healing is impaired by examination stress. *Psychosomatic Medicine, 60*, 362–365.

Masterson, J. (1998). *The search for the real self: Unmasking the personality disorders of our age.* New York: Free Press.

McIntyre, W. A. (2012). Personal communication via e-mail to John Friel.

McKinley, J. C., Jr. (2010, March 12). Texas conservatives win curriculum change. *New York Times.*

Mehren, E. (1992, June 7). Unleashed memories. *Los Angeles Times.*

Memoli, M. A. (2011, November 21). Fox News viewers less informed about current events, poll shows. *Los Angeles Times.*

Menakem, R. (2006). Personal communication with authors.

Menees, M. M., & Segrin, C. (2000). The specificity of disrupted processes in families of adult children of alcoholics. *Alcohol and Alcoholism, 35*(4), 361–367.

mgfaulkner Blog. (2010, September 29). A Christmas Carol: The Making of a Masterpiece. *Back to the best books: How the classics can change your life.* http://www.backtothebestbooks.com/2010/09/29/a-christmas-carol-the-making-of-a-masterpiece/

Miller, A. (1983). *For your own good: Hidden cruelty in child-rearing and the roots of violence.* New York: Farrar, Straus and Giroux.

Miller, A. (1997). *The drama of the gifted child: The search for the true self.* Rev. ed. New York: Basic Books.

Miller, J. (2005). *Darling Judi: A celebration of Judi Dench.* London: Orion Publishing.

Mills, N. (1997). *The triumph of meanness: America's war against its better self.* New York: Houghton Mifflin.

Minnesota Longitudinal Study of Parents and Children, College of Education and Human Development. Retrieved from http://www.cehd.umn.edu/icd/Parent-child/.

Minnesota Longitudinal Study of Risk and Adaptation. Retrieved from http://www.cehd.umn.edu/ICD/Parent-Child/default.html.

Minnesota Office of Higher Education. (2012). Educational Attainment Data. Retrieved from http://www.ohe.state.mn.us/mPg.cfm?pageID=1873&1534-D83A _1933715A=fa74cd787916d55082518bce9374e393ac102681.

Minnesota Public Radio. (2010, July 19). Midday. [Radio broadcast.]

Minnesota State Arts Board. (2012). http://www.arts.state.mn.us/.

Minnesota's State and Local Tax Burden. Tax Foundation. Retrieved from http://www.taxfoundation.org/taxdata/show/462.html.

Minuchin, S. (1974). *Families and family therapy.* Cambridge, MA: Harvard University Press.

Mischel, W. (1968). *Personality and assessment.* New York: Wiley.

Moulin, P. (2008). *A history of Fort DeRussy: U.S. Army museum of Hawaii.* Honolulu: Mutual Publishing Company.

Nelson, J. B. (1978). *Embodiment.* Minneapolis: Augsburg Publishing House.

Nesselroade, J. R. (1970). Theory of psychological states and mood action. In Raymond B. Cattell (Ed.), *Handbook of modern personality study.* Chicago: Aldine Press.

Newsweek. (2010). Interactive infographic of the world's best countries. Retrieved from http://www.thedailybeast.com/newsweek/2010/08/15/interactive-infographic-of- the-worlds-best-countries.html.

Odum, H. (1983). *Systems ecology: An introduction.* New York: John Wiley.

Oesterreich, L., & Shirer, K. (1992, April). Spouse and partner abuse; Understanding abuse and neglect; Rape, an act of aggression. Understanding Abuse series. Iowa State University, University Extension, Ames, IA.

Oesterreich. L. & Shirer, K. (1998). Sexual abuse of children. Understanding abuse series. National Network for Child Care online. Available at http://www.nncc.org/Abuse/sex.abuse.html.

Oprah Winfrey Show. (2006, April 12). American schools in crisis [Television series episode].

Ornish, D. (1998). *Love and survival: The scientific basis for the healing power of intimacy.* New York: HarperCollins.

Padesky, C. (1995). *Mind over mood.* New York: Guilford Press.

Padover. (1939). *Thomas Jefferson on democracy.* New York: Mentor.

Paskach, E. (2012, January 25). Report: Minnesota ranks in the bottom 10 in state business tax climate. *Minnesota State News.* Retrieved from http://www.mnstatenews.com/capitol-headlines/1-capitol/292-report-minnesota- ranks-in-the-bottom-10-in-state-business-tax-climate.html.

Pease, D. E. (2007). Exceptionalism. In B. Burgett and G. Hendler (Eds.), *Keywords for American cultural studies* (pp. 108–112). New York: NYU Press.

Peck, D. (2011, September). Can the middle class be saved? *The Atlantic* (p. 63).

Pence, E., & Paymar, M. (1993). *Education groups for men who batter.* New York: Springer.

Penny, T. (2008, August 14). U.S. white population will be minority by 2042, government says. Bloomberg online. Retrieved from http://www.bloomberg .com/apps/news?pid=newsarchive&sid=afLRFXgzpFoY

Perlman, D. (2011, August 26). Neanderthal genome inherited by humans, study says. *San Francisco Chronicle.* Retrieved from http://www.sfgate.com/cgi-bin/article .cgi?f=/c/a/2011/08/25/BA971KQCVQ.DTL.

Pew Research Center. (2007, April 15). Public knowledge of current affairs little changed by news and information revolutions: What Americans know; 1989–2007. Retrieved from http://www.people-press.org/2007/04/15/public-knowledge-of-current-affairs-little-changed-by-news-and-information-revolutions/.

Pew Research Center's Project for Excellence in Journalism. (2008, May 8). Journalism, satire or just laughs? *The Daily Show with Jon Stewart* examined. Journalism.org. Retrieved from http://www.journalism.org/node/10953.

Pietrini, M. (2011). Personal communication with authors.

Pinker, S. (2011). *The better angels of our nature: Why violence has declined.* New York: Viking.

Pipher, M. (2002). *In the middle of everywhere: Helping refugees enter the American community.* New York: Harcourt.

Pohl, M. (2008). *A day without pain.* Las Vegas: Central Recovery Press.

Porges, S. W., Arnold, W. R., & Forbes, E. J. (1973). Heart rate variability: An index of attentional responsivity in human newborns. *Developmental Psychology, 8,* 85– 92.

Public Broadcasting Network. (2011, August 31). *Becoming human: Last human standing* [Television series episode]. *Nova.*

Ramos, C. (2010, August 4). Al Wooten Jr. Heritage Center founder to be honored by President Obama with 2010 Citizens Medal. *Orange County Ethnic Community Examiner.*

Ramsey, R. (2010, February 17). Texans: Dinosaurs, humans walked the Earth at same time. *Texas Tribune.* Retrieved from http://www.texastribune.org/texas-education/public-education/texans-dinosaurs-humans-walked-the-earth-at-same/.

Ray, J. (2011, April 19). High wellbeing eludes the masses in most countries worldwide. Gallup wellbeing surveys in 2010. Gallup online. Retrieved from http://www .gallup.com/poll/147167/high-wellbeing-eludes-masses-countries-world wide.aspx.

Reuter, M., Frenzel, C., Walter, N. T., Markett, S. & Montag, C. (2010). Investigating the genetic basis of altruism: The role of the COMT Val158Met polymorphism. *Social Cognitive and Affective Neuroscience, 6*(5), 662–668.

Satir, V. (1972). *Peoplemaking.* Palo Alto, CA: Science and Behavior Books.

Sawyer, D. (1992, July). Secret no more. *ABC News PrimeTime Live.*

Schaie, K. W. (1965). A general model for the study of developmental problems. *Psychological Bulletin 64,* 92–107.

Schnarch, D. M. (1991). *Constructing the sexual crucible: An integration of sexual and marital therapy.* New York: W. W. Norton.

Schnarch, D. M. (1997). *Passionate marriage: Sex, love, and intimacy in emotionally committed relationships.* New York: W. W. Norton.

Schnarch, D. M. (2009). *Intimacy and desire: Awaken the passion in your relationship.* New York: Beaufort Books.

Seligman, C. (2011, September 30). Review of T. Friedman and M. Mandelbaum, *That used to be us: How America fell behind in the world it invented and how we can come back.* In *The Week.*

Seligman, M. E. P. (1991). *Learned optimism: How to change your mind and your life.* New York: Alfred A. Knopf.

Settle, J. E., Dawes, C. T., Christakis, N. A., & Fowler, J. H. (2010). Friendships moderate an association between a dopamine gene variant and political ideology. *Journal of Politics, 72*(4), 1189.

Silberman, J. (Director). (2001). *Bombies.* PBS documentary. Produced by Lumiere Productions Inc. in association with CFCF-TV, Vision TV, Knowledge Network, and the Saskatchewan Communications Network, and with the support of the John D. and Catherine T. MacArthur Foundation, the Rogers Documentary Fund, and the Government of Canada through the Canadian International Development ment Agency (CIDA).

Spitz, R. A. (1946). Hospitalism: A follow-up report on investigation described in volume 1, 1945. *The Psychoanalytic Study of the Child, 2,* 113–117.

Sroufe, L. A. (2005). Attachment and development: A prospective, longitudinal study from birth to adulthood. *Attachment and Human Development, 7,* 349–367.

Sroufe, L. A. (2007). The place of development in developmental psychopathology. In A. Masten (Ed.), *Multilevel dynamics in developmental psychopathology: Pathways to the future* (pp. 285–299). *The Minnesota Symposia on Child Psychology,* vol. 34. Mahwah, NJ: Lawrence Erlbaum Associates.

Sroufe, L. A., Egeland, B., Carlson, E., & Collins, W. A. (2005). *The development of the person: The Minnesota study of risk and adaptation from birth to adulthood.* New York: Guilford Publications.

Sroufe, L. A., & McIntosh, J. (2011, July). Divorce and attachment relationships: The longitudinal journey. *Family Court Review, 49,* 464–473.

Sroufe, L. A., & Siegel, D. (2011, March/April). The verdict is in. *Psychotherapy Networker,* 34–39, 52–53.

Steinbeck, J. (1945). *Cannery row.* 1st ed. New York: Viking Press.

Steinem, G. (1993). *Revolution from within: A book of self-esteem.* New York: Little, Brown and Company.

Stierlin, H. (1969). *Conflict and reconciliation.* New York: Science House.

Stock, W. (1985). The influence of gender on power dynamics in relationships. In D. Goldberg (Ed.), *Contemporary marriage* (pp. 62–99). Homewood, IL: Dorsey.

Sydney Morning Herald. (2011, July 26). Thousands throng Oslo flower vigil for victims of attacks. Retrieved from http://www.smh.com.au/world/thousands-throng-oslo-flower-vigil-for-victims-of-attacks-20110726-1hxjq.html.

Taibbi, M. (2011, November 17). Woman gets jail for food-stamp fraud; Wall Street fraudsters get bail-outs. Taiblog. Retrieved from http://www.rollingstone.com.

Taylor, S. (1998). The social being in social psychology. In D. T. Gilbert, S. Fiske, & G. Lindzey (Eds.), *The Handbook of Social Psychology,* 4th ed. (58–95).

Taylor, S. E. (2007). Social support. In H. S. Friedman and R. C. Silver (Eds.), *Foundations of health psychology* (pp. 145–171). New York: Oxford University Press.

Teilhard de Chardin, P. (1960). *The divine milieu.* New York: Harper & Row.

Teilhard de Chardin, P. (1967). Sketch of a personalistic universe. In *On love* (p. 15). London: William Collins.

Teilhard de Chardin, P. (1969). *Human energy.* Trans. J. M. Cohen. London: William Collins Sons & Co.

The Freedom Writers (1999). *The freedom writers diary : How a teacher and 150 teens used writing to change themselves and the world around them.* New York: Broadway Books.

The World Fact Book: What's New. (August 18, 2011). Data for many of the economy fields have been revised to reflect the latest estimates. Central Intelligence Agency, Washington, D.C.

Tocqueville, A. de (1835/1945). *Democracy in America.* New York: Vintage Books.

Tocqueville, A. de (1863a). The example of the Americans does not prove that a democratic people can have no aptitude and no taste for science, literature, or art. Chapter 11 in *Democracy in America,* vol. 2 (pp. 40–46). Henry Reeve (Trans.). Cambridge, MA: Sever and Francis.

Tocqueville, A. de (1863b). Why the Americans are so restless in the midst of their prosperity. Chapter 13 in *Democracy in America,* vol. 2 (pp. 163–167). Henry Reeve (Trans.). Cambridge, MA: Sever and Francis.

Trepper, T., & Barrett, M. J. (1989). *Systemic treatment of incest: A therapeutic handbook.* New York: Brunner/Mazel.

Turner-Cobb, J. M., Sephton, S. E., Koopman, C., Blake-Mortimer, J., & Spiegel, D. (2000). Social support and salivary cortisol in women with metastatic breast cancer. *Psychosomatic Medicine, 62,* 337–345.

Twenge, J., & Campbell, W. K. (2010). *The Narcissism Epidemic: Living in the age of entitlement.* New York: Free Press.

Uchino, B. (2009). Understanding the links between social support and physical health: A life-span perspective with emphasis on the separability of perceived and received support. *Perspectives on Psychological Science, 4,* 236–255.

Unden, A. L., Orth-Gomer, K., & Elofsson, S. (1991). Cardiovascular effects of social support in the work-place: Twenty-four-hour ECG monitoring of men and women. *Psychosomatic Medicine, 53*(1), 50–60.

UPI.com. (2012, January 19). Poll shows PBS is most trusted for TV News. Retrieved from http://www.upi.com/Top_News/US/2012/01/19/Poll-shows-PBS-is-most-trusted-for-TV-news/UPI-7773 1327007277/.

U.S. Journal Training's 1st Annual Conference on Sexuality and Intimacy: Conflict, Passion, and Power, Las Vegas, Nevada, April 17–19, 2002, and in New Orleans, Louisiana, May 8–10, 2003.

Vaiva, G., Ducrocq, F., Jezequel, K., Brunet, A., Marmar, C. R. (2003). Immediate treatment with pro-pranolol decreases post-traumatic stress disorder two months after trauma. *Biological Psychiatry, 54*, 947–949.

Vegso, P. (2007). Personal communication from the president of Health Communications, Inc., to John Friel.

Velleman, R., & Orford, J. (1999). *Risk and resilience: Adults who were the children of problem drinkers.* Amsterdam: Harwood Academic Press.

Volsky, I. (2011, August 19). Tom Coburn: America was better off before Medicare. Article available at http://thinkprogress.org/health/2011/08/19/299515/tom-coburn-america-was-better-off-before-medicare/.

Walsh, J. (2008, December 22). *Independent* (London). Retrieved from *http://www.independent.co.uk/*arts-entertainment/books/features/christmas-a-dickens-of-a-time-1207068.html#

Walsh, J., & Roberts, R. (2010, December 15). How to handle anger during low blood sugars. Diabetes net.com. Retrieved from http://www.diabetesnet.com/diabetes-control/low-blood-sugars/emotion-control.

Webb, A., Lind, P. A., Kalmijn, J., Feiler, H. S., Smith, T. L., Schuckit, M. A., Wilhelmsen, K. (2011). The Investigation into CYP2E1 in relation to the level of response to alcohol through a combination of linkage and association analysis. *Alcoholism: Clinical and Experimental Research, 35*(1), 10–18.

The Week. (2012, January 20). The German Colossus. Wegscheider-Cruse, S. (1981). *Another chance: Hope and health for the alcoholic family.* Palo Alto: Science and Behavior Books.

Wegscheider-Cruse, Sharon. *Hope and Health for the Alcoholic Family.* Deerfield Beach, FL: Health Com-munications.

Weinfield, N. S., Sroufe, L. A., Egeland, B., & Carlson, E. (2008). Individual differences in infant-caregiver attachment. In J. Cassidy & P. Shaver (Eds.), *Handbook of attachment: Theory, research and clinical applications.* 2nd ed. (pp. 78–101). New York: Guilford Press.

White House. (2010). The Presidential Citizens Medal. Retrieved from http://www.whitehouse.gov.

Williams, R., & Williams, V. (1998). *Anger kills: Seventeen strategies for controlling the hostility that can harm your health.* New York: HarperTorch.

Woititz, J. G. (1983). *Adult children of alcoholics.* Deerfield Beach, FL: Health Communications, Inc.

Wolff, R. (2011, January 18). The myth of "American exceptionalism" implodes. *The Guardian.* Retrieved from http://www.guardian.co.uk/comment isfree/cifamerica/2011/jan/17/economics-globalrecession.

Woodward, K. L., Friday, C., & Springen, K. (1992, June 1). The sins of the father. *Newsweek.*

Wynne, L. (1988). An epigenetic model of family processes. In C. Falicov (Ed.), *Family transitions: Continuity and change over the life cycle.* New York: Guilford.

Zakaria, F. (2011, March 3). Are America's best days behind us? *Time.*

Note: An italicized *t* following a page number indicates a table.